Business Ethics

Ethical aspects of business and the economy are of increasing concern in business practice, higher education, and society in general. This concern results from significant business scandals and economic crises, such as the financial crisis of 2008 and the following great recession, as well as from pressing current and future challenges for the economy, such as sustainability and globalization. As a result, there is a growing demand for normative analysis and orientation for business and the economy, where business ethics has become a crucial part of organizational management, risk management, branding, and strategic management.

Business Ethics: Methods and Application provides a new systematic approach to normative business ethics that covers the complex and various ethical challenges of modern business. It aims to train analytical thinking skills in the field of business ethics and to approach ethical issues in business in a rational and systematic way. The book develops a number of specific methods for business ethics analysis that are tailored for ethical decision-making in business and for analyzing complex ethical topics in business.

The book discusses fundamental ethical questions regarding the meaning of business and the economy for the individual person, society, the environment, and people around the world. As a result, *Business Ethics: Methods and Application* develops normative guidelines for business in the 21st century and its fundamental challenges and will be key reading for undergraduate, postgraduate, and MBA students of business ethics, business strategy, business and society, and related fields.

Christian U. Becker lives with his family in Fort Collins, Colorado, USA, and is a faculty member at the College of Business at Colorado State University. He earned his Ph.D. in economics from Heidelberg University (2003) and his Habilitation in philosophy from Kaiserslautern University (2010). His primary research and teaching interests are in theoretical and applied ethics, the history of economic thought, and sustainability studies. He has taught business ethics for more than ten years in Germany, Canada, and the United States. Becker has published on ethical and economic topics in various journals, such as *Archives for Philosophy of Law and Social Philosophy*; *Ecological Economics*; *Ethical Theory and Moral Practice*; *Ethics, Policy and Environment*; *Environmental Values*; and *European Journal for the History of Economic Thought*.

Business Ethics
Methods and Application

Christian U. Becker

Routledge
Taylor & Francis Group

NEW YORK AND LONDON

First published 2019
by Routledge
2 Park Square, Milton Park, Abingdon, Oxon OX14 4RN

and by Routledge
52 Vanderbilt Avenue, New York, NY 10017

Routledge is an imprint of the Taylor & Francis Group, an informa business

British Library Cataloguing-in-Publication Data
A catalogue record for this book is available from the British Library

Library of Congress Cataloging-in-Publication Data
Names: Becker, Christian U., author.
Title: Business ethics : methods and application / Christian U. Becker.
Description: New York : Routledge, 2019.
Identifiers: LCCN 2018038506| ISBN 9781138493681 (hardback) | ISBN
    9780367027872 (pbk.) | ISBN 9780429397707 (ebook)
Subjects: LCSH: Business ethics.
Classification: LCC HF5387 .B4243 2019 | DDC 174/.4—dc23
LC record available at https://lccn.loc.gov/2018038506

ISBN: 978-1-138-49368-1 (hbk)
ISBN: 978-0-367-02787-2 (pbk)
ISBN: 978-0-429-39770-7 (ebk)

Typeset in Sabon
by Swales & Willis Ltd, Exeter, Devon, UK

Visit the companion website: www.routledge.com/cw/becker

For
Elisa, Luca, and Luana

Contents

1 Introduction to business ethics
Approach and subject matter

This book provides a systematic approach to business ethics. Based on ethical theory and economic thought, the book develops tailored methods for analyzing and addressing ethical challenges of business practice. The book addresses ethical topics at the individual, organizational, societal, and global levels, and discusses a range of business ethics topics, such as ethical decision-making in business contexts, professional ethics, leadership ethics, organizational ethics, corporate responsibility strategies, whistleblowing, global business ethics, and sustainability ethics. The methods developed in this book are specifically designed to address ethical challenges of business in the 21st century. A particular focus is on new challenges that result from the global character and increasing complexity of modern business, as well as from issues of sustainability.

At the center of this book are core questions of business ethics:

- What is the relationship between ethics and business?
- What ethical aspects matter in business and economic contexts?
- How can one analyze and effectively address ethical issues in business?

Various aspects of these questions are discussed in detail, and answers are provided throughout the book. However, to introduce the topic, the remainder of this chapter will outline some aspects of, and fundamental perspectives to, these questions.

1.1 What is the relationship between ethics and business?

Someone may intuitively think that ethics and business do not have much in common, do not go well together, or even contradict each other. This book will argue to the contrary: ethics and business are interrelated in various ways, and it is important for the success of business and the wellbeing of society that ethics and business are properly correlated. A specific focus of the book is on the proper implementation of ethics in business so that it contributes to business success and ensures that business is a positive force in the world. We will demonstrate the crucial role of ethics for business and emphasize that a substantial lack of ethics is a serious risk for business and can result in large damage to both business and society.

Of course, there can be conflicts between business goals and ethical norms. These may be not as common as one might think, and sometimes such conflicts are only perceived conflicts and not actual dilemmas. However, the book discusses typical dilemmas in business contexts, such as whistleblowing, and develops tools to analyze and address them. On the other hand, it is also important to uncover apparent dilemmas and myths about conflicts of ethics and business. It is generally more fruitful to first identify the potential win-win between ethics and business, understand how ethics and business can support each other, and explore ways to realize this win-win potential. This approach allows one to better distinguish actual, serious areas of conflict between business and ethics, identify real dilemmas, and address them properly.

On a more fundamental level, though, the current economy has systemic ethical limitations, particularly with regard to adequate ethical consideration of future generations and the environment. The book identifies and discusses such systemic ethical shortcomings of the capitalist market economy. It argues for a reconsideration of the ethical underpinnings of the 21st century economy and suggests a broader ethical framework for future business. Some normative shifts can already be observed in today's business practice, and the capitalist market economy may be capable of an inherent ethical reorientation to meet the ethical challenges of the 21st century.

For discussing the relationship between ethics and business, we will throughout this book distinguish and apply two fundamental perspectives: the *instrumental perspective* and the *philosophical perspective*. We outline the main characteristics of both perspectives in the following.

1.1.1 The instrumental perspective of business ethics

The instrumental perspective of business ethics considers the function of ethics for business. The crucial questions here are: What is the meaning of ethics for business? Does ethics matter, and is it useful for business practice? In this perspective, one wants to know in what ways ethics is relevant for business and business success. The task of business ethics is to develop ethical tools that support business success and to provide knowledge of how to optimally implement such tools into business strategies, operations, and organizational design (see Figure 1.1).

There are many ways in which ethics matters for business success. A few examples illustrate this. On a basic level, ethical values and principles matter for everyday business activities and are an inherent part of successful business. For instance, consider small businesses that operate in one location, a smaller town or city, and serve mainly local customers. Honesty, reliability, and trustworthiness are crucial factors for the long-term success of such a business. If the business starts using unethical practices, e.g., by tricking or neglecting customers and local suppliers, it probably will not stay in business long. Generally, as the Internet today allows for reviews to quickly spread and for customers to share information about businesses, ethical business practice becomes increasingly crucial for business success.

Another example for the relevance of ethics for business is the proper organizational functioning of larger corporations. The success of corporations depends on various ethical factors, such as a sound ethical culture, ethical leadership, proper design and implementation of rules and policies, proactive prevention of internal frictions and wrongdoing, and a shared commitment of the leadership and employees to the core values of the company. Lack of organizational ethics can result in significant risks and harm for a business. For instance, an ethically corrupt culture, internal frictions, and distrust can undermine successful work. Significant instances of internal wrongdoings, such as harassment cases, stealing from the company, and bribery cases, can threaten business success and result in serious legal issues. Ethical aspects

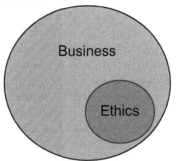

THE INSTRUMENTAL PERSPECTIVE: ETHICS AS A CRUCIAL FACTOR FOR BUSINESS SUCCESS

- Examples:
  - o Basic business ethics
  - o Organizational ethics
  - o Professional ethics

- How do we implement ethics in business so that it optimally supports business success?

- There is no systematic conflict between ethics and business, but rather a potential win-win that needs to be identified and developed

Figure 1.1 The instrumental perspective of business ethics.

are also important for managing the relationship of a corporation with its external framework; that is, its stakeholders and the societies and environments in which it operates. The downfall of Enron in 2001 or the VW emission scandal in 2015 show that lack of ethics can do significant harm to a company.

A third example of why ethics matters in business contexts is the relevance of ethics for individual careers. Ethical principles, values, and virtues matter in professional life. Two main factors are crucial for a successful career: excellent professional knowledge and display of professional ethics. Basic ethical principles, such as integrity, reliability, loyalty, and responsibility, matter for any position and career. In addition, certain positions or professions require ethical principles that are specifically relevant to them. For accountants, trustworthiness and objectivity are crucial; engineers have a specific responsibility for public safety; leaders need to be responsible and fair; and employees are expected to be reliable and trustworthy. Also, in professional life, one can encounter various ethically difficult situations and dilemmas and may have to make, communicate, and justify tough decisions. It is crucial to be able to clearly identify the rationale, values, and principles that guide such decisions.

The book discusses the various functions of ethics in business systematically and in detail and provides methods for effectively using ethical reflection and ethical instruments in business practice. For practical purposes, it is not only crucial to develop an ability to understand and identify the various functions of ethics for business, but it is also important to determine how to optimally and effectively implement ethics into business contexts and operations. A wrong or improper implementation of ethical instruments may not serve the purpose and unnecessarily waste resources. Although it is not in all cases possible to exactly determine the optimal investment, the book aims to identify the optimal design of ethical instruments and strategies as far as possible.

From an instrumental perspective, it is also crucial to understand that business ethics is a highly dynamic and increasingly complex challenge. Businesses are constantly facing new ethical challenges and need to have tools to recognize and effectively address new and shifting ethical landscapes. There are, for instance, new ethical challenges in business that result from technological progress, such as issues of security and privacy related to data storage and analysis, or ethical challenges and risks related to social media use. Another set of new ethical challenges for business results from the increasing globalization and global complexity of modern business. In global contexts, businesses need to develop the ability for reasonably interconnecting different normative requirements: adherence to their own values, principles, and rules, compliance with various legal frameworks of the countries in which they operate, and following fundamental global principles, such as human rights, and respecting cultural differences. Current and future business also faces fundamental systemic challenges, such as the challenge of sustainability. Due to systemic environmental limits on a global scale, businesses increasingly must assume responsibility for the environmental, global, and future effects of their business operations, supply chains, and product life cycles. The ability to systematically analyze these challenges is crucial for long-term business success and an important aspect of strategic management.

1.1.2 The philosophical perspective of business ethics

The philosophical perspective on the relationship between ethics and business starts from an ethical viewpoint and asks: What is the ethical meaning of business? What is the meaning of business or economic aspects within a broader ethical context? (See Figure 1.2.) These are more abstract, philosophical questions. However, a discussion of such questions is crucial for properly understanding the full scope of the relationship between ethics and business, and it is also crucial for fully grasping the meaning of ethics for business practice.

What is the philosophical perspective about? Traditional philosophical ethics asks questions, such as: What is a good life, or what is a good and just society? Economic aspects matter for these questions. We all participate in some way or the other in the economy: as consumers, entrepreneurs, investors, employees, or professionals. On an individual level, one may wonder how these economic aspects of life fit into one's overall life plans and ideas of a good life. How much does a job, or career, or being a professional in a certain field, contribute to one's overall self-identity and individual happiness? How important are professional success, money, and material wealth in comparison to other ends in life, such as family, health, friends, or hobbies? If someone asks these questions, she considers the relationship between ethics and business from a philosophical perspective. She considers the ethical meaning of economic and business aspects against the backdrop of her personal values and her conception of a good life.

The philosophical perspective also includes more general ethical questions about the economy: What is a good economy? How does (a certain design of) the economy fit to the overall values of a society and promote the flourishing of that society? How can we define and realize business as a positive force in the world? Such

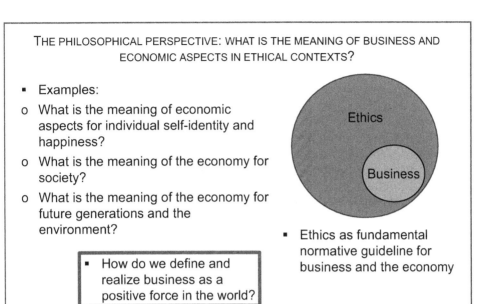

THE PHILOSOPHICAL PERSPECTIVE: WHAT IS THE MEANING OF BUSINESS AND ECONOMIC ASPECTS IN ETHICAL CONTEXTS?

- Examples:
  o What is the meaning of economic aspects for individual self-identity and happiness?
  o What is the meaning of the economy for society?
  o What is the meaning of the economy for future generations and the environment?

  - How do we define and realize business as a positive force in the world?

Ethics

Business

- Ethics as fundamental normative guideline for business and the economy

Figure 1.2 The philosophical perspective of business ethics.

questions have always been discussed. Defining and developing optimal forms of economy have been crucial philosophical and political topics throughout history. There are, for instance, (ethical) reasons for having a capitalist market economy. Proponents of capitalism have argued that this type of economy serves individuals and society best and supports fundamental ethical principles, such as individual freedom and equality. Capitalism is supposed to provide opportunities to everyone, enable everyone to choose a career and pursue goals, promote fair competition, reward performance, stimulate innovation and growth, and realize an efficient allocation of goods and services (see Chapter 3).

However, in an ever-changing world and economy we have to reassure ourselves that the economy is still 'good' with regard to traditional ethical criteria, and we also need to discuss whether these ethical criteria are still sufficient to define a good economy. In other words, we need to reflect on the question of what it means for business in the 21st century to be a positive force in the world against the backdrop of the characteristics and challenges of today's economy. We need to carefully analyze ethical aspects of the current economic system and consider whether we need to modify the economy to properly address new ethical challenges and normative requirements. For instance, new ethical challenges result from the issues of sustainability. Sustainability implies ethical requirements and expectations for the economy and business that we have not particularly emphasized so far. In the sustainability perspective, the economy needs not only be good for our current society and its individuals, but also good for future generations, nature, and contemporaries around the world. Contemporary business thus faces new ethical challenges and needs to consider new ethical requirements to be a positive force in the world. In today's business practice, one can indeed observe significant shifts of business norms and values, resulting in new business models and new legal types of business. We will analyze such shifts within the broader context of the ethical underpinnings of a capitalist market economy and a sustainable economy (see Chapters 3 and 7). Business is an important and powerful societal force, and it is imperative to make this force fruitful for addressing societal challenges and for positively contributing to the future development and flourishing of society.

Although the book focuses overall more on the instrumental perspective, the philosophical perspective outlined above is a crucial background. Ultimately, both perspectives are interconnected. A key function of business ethics is to properly relate business to its societal contexts, i.e., to the norms and values of stakeholders and society. With this, the internal function of ethics for business cannot be separated from the general ethical frameworks of societies and the overall societal expectations toward businesses and the economy in general. For an encompassing analysis of business ethics, the interrelation of both perspectives needs to be considered.

1.2 The levels of business ethics

The functions of ethics in modern business are various and complex. There are many ethical aspects of business, and one prerequisite for successfully addressing them is to properly identify the type of ethical aspect that matters in a specific situation or case. For instance, an ethical issue could be related to individual decision-making, organizational design, the structures and the rules of the industry, or societal and legal aspects, or have a global dimension. The proper identification of the specific type of ethical issue is a necessary precondition for successfully analyzing and solving the issue. This book discusses the entire range of ethical aspects in modern business and distinguishes issues on various levels. We discuss ethical aspects related to individuals in organizations and the economy, the organizational level, the level of the economic system, the societal and legal frameworks, the global and environmental context, and the sustainability context (Figure 1.3). This particularly includes new ethical challenges resulting from global complexity and systemic environmental constraints, and the ethical evaluation of impacts of modern business to people around the world, future generations, and nature.

It is important to properly identify what ethical issue belongs to which level, to analyze the interrelation of different ethical levels, and to understand what level is best suited to approach a specific ethical issue. Some ethical challenges cannot be fully addressed by individuals but require an organizational approach and a solution on the organizational level. Other challenges may even exceed the organizational level and ability, and so may require concerted actions in the industry, or societal and legal solutions. However, even in such cases, individuals or organizations sometimes need to make ethical decisions and take action by themselves, particularly in cases where the level in charge does not, or cannot, fix the issue. With regard to more complex ethical issues of business, a model of shared responsibilities might be the best answer and solution. In a complex modern business world, many ethical issues are caused by the interplay of various actors, such as companies, suppliers, customers, and regulatory agencies, each of which has some responsibility for an issue, and thus needs to join together and make concerted efforts to address the issue (see Chapter 4).

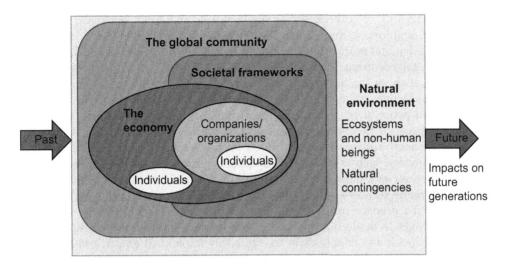

Figure 1.3 The levels of business ethics.

1.3 The relevance of business ethics – why is it important?

Ethics has become increasingly relevant for business for various reasons. First of all, the ethical challenges of business have become increasingly complex due to globalization, technological developments, and sustainability issues. Businesses need sophisticated and tailored tools to meet these challenges, manage related risks, and recognize implications for strategic management. Analyzing and addressing ethical aspects related to one's business can help identify new opportunities, markets, and competitive advantages, and also helps to identify and avoid risks and potential damage to the business. Neglect of, or insufficient dealings with, ethical aspects can result in substantial damages and costs. Examples such as the Enron scandal of 2001, the financial crisis of 2008, the Gulf of Mexico oil spill in 2010, or the VW emissions scandal in 2015 show the harm that can result from a lack of ethics for business, society, and the environment.

Ethical challenges are often at the same time business opportunities or can be turned into business opportunities. It would therefore be too narrow to see ethics as a restriction, hindrance, or unavoidable burden of business practice. Integrating ethical analysis into strategic management can reveal many new business opportunities, such as further efficiency potentials, new markets, new ways to more robust supply chains, overall improved products and product life cycles, ethical branding, and reputation gains. More and more corporations and smaller businesses are using ethics as a strategic management tool, and we will discuss several examples later in the book. There is a strong business case for perceiving ethics this way. As many ethical concerns and challenges are directly related to systemic real-world issues, particularly global environmental constraints and societal issues, it is crucial for businesses to carefully consider the implications for their own operations and products, and strategically consider solutions to these issues that make them more competitive.

There are also increasing societal and legal expectations for business. The ethical expectations of stakeholders have increased in recent years. Consumers, communities, employees, and investors increasingly make value-based economic decisions and demand more ethical responsibility from businesses. Also, there have been more legal requirements for business ethics. For instance, in the US, legal frameworks, such as the Sarbanes–Oxley Act, the Dodd–Frank Act, and the US Sentencing Guidelines, require businesses to develop, and adhere to, various ethical standards and procedures, to ensure ethical integrity, and to pay more attention to ethical aspects of their organization and operations. Against the backdrop of increasing societal and legal expectations, businesses have increasingly adopted ethical instruments, such as ethics and compliance programs and corporate responsibility strategies (see Chapter 4). The overall increased demand for business ethics has also led many business colleges to integrate business ethics into their curriculum in order to prepare future employees and business leaders for the complex ethical challenges in modern business, prepare them to understand the function of ethics for business, and enable them to effectively implement ethical tools to promote business success.

Finally, business ethics provides a fundamental level of reflection for business. Many people participate in one way or the other in the business world, and most people in business probably want to have a positive impact on the world with their professional activities. Business ethics is a tool of self-reflection and guidance: how can we ensure that business is a positive force for society and the world, and what ethical norms should guide us in shaping the future of business? This self-reassurance and guidance is not only crucial for business, but also for society and its future.

1.4 How to analyze and address ethical aspects of business: the approach of this book

Successfully analyzing and addressing ethical aspects of business requires solid knowledge of ethics and a detailed understanding of the characteristics of the contemporary economy. The approach of this book thus is grounded in fundamentals of ethics and economic thought. The traditional reference points for ethical analysis is philosophical ethics. Philosophy has developed ethical approaches for more than 2000 years and offers various methods to analyze ethical issues. This book refers to important approaches of philosophical ethics as theoretical background, such as utilitarianism, Kantian ethics, virtue ethics, ethics of care, Rawlsian ethics, and discourse ethics. With regard to these theories, the focus of the book is not so much on philosophical details but more on breaking theory down to applicable methods that can be used in business contexts. We will develop a set of basic methods for ethical analysis and ethical decision-making that can then easily be applied to business situations.

Although ethical theory is an important reference point for business ethics, its simple application is not sufficient for analyzing all aspects of today's business. We also will develop more specific methods to address specific characteristics and ethical aspects of modern business practice. This includes, for instance, the internal and external aspects of organizational ethics, the ethical aspects of specific individual roles in businesses, ethical aspects of globalization and sustainability challenges, and ethical aspects of certain business functions and professional roles. The book develops tailored methods to properly analyze and address such specific ethical aspects of business.

We will refer to various aspects of organizational ethics and develop methods for ethically analyzing stakeholder relationships, supply chains, and product life cycles. We will provide methods for evaluating corporate responsibility strategies, and we will analyze professional responsibilities and leadership ethics. The underlying methodological approach here is twofold: we consider the economic or business function of specific areas or individual roles in business to determine related specific ethical requirements and challenges, and we consider new ethical challenges and requirements resulting from the (systemic) characteristics of today's complex business world. The book specifically considers the background of economic theory and the history of economic thought, as well as ethical assumptions and implications related to the concept of the capitalist market economy.

The remainder of the book is organized as follows: Chapter 2 introduces ethics and develops a set of methods for case analysis and ethical decision-making in business contexts. The focus is on utilitarianism, Kantian ethics, and virtue ethics. The chapter (i) discusses the philosophical background of these approaches, (ii) breaks them down to basic methods for ethical decision-making, (iii) provides basic examples of application, and (iv) suggests exercises to practice them. The application to business cases is demonstrated in detail with three example cases. The chapter also introduces further ethical methods based on ethics of care, Rawlsian ethics, and discourse ethics. Overall, the chapter develops eight methods for ethical analysis and decision-making. With this, the chapter lays the theoretical background in ethics for the remainder of the book.

Chapter 3 reflects on the various normative aspects of the economy and business. It critically discusses the ethical underpinnings of modern capitalism and the new ethical challenges of the economy of the 21st century. The chapter identifies and reflects on the various norms and values attached to the capitalist market economy and presents various types of criticism of capitalism from an ethical viewpoint. A particular focus is on the question how we can define and realize business and the economy as a positive force in the 21st century. The chapter illustrates that the characteristics and new (ethical) challenges of the 21st century economy require a reconsideration of the ethical foundations of modern business. Overall, Chapters 2 and 3 are more theoretical and provide the methodological underpinnings for the following, more applied chapters.

Chapter 4 discusses ethical aspects of the organizational level. The chapter defines the concepts of *responsibility* and *business-specific responsibility* and introduces two methods for identifying and addressing the business-specific responsibilities of a given company: *Ethical Life Cycle Assessment* (ELCA) and *Ethical Stakeholder Analysis* (ESA). The chapter then defines corporate responsibility (CR) and introduces the *Pillar Model of CR*, which encompasses the various responsibilities of a modern business in the 21st century economy. The chapter also develops a method for analyzing and evaluating CR strategies. Finally, the chapter discusses various aspects of internal organizational ethics, such as ethical culture, diversity and inclusion, and ethics and compliance programs.

Chapter 5 focuses on ethical aspects of specific roles, functions, or positions that individuals can have in business contexts. The chapter demonstrates that certain roles, functions, or positions usually come with specific ethical challenges and responsibilities. The chapter discusses the ethical aspects of crucial functions in detail: ethical aspects of being an employee, ethical leadership, and professional ethics. Marketing ethics is discussed as an example for ethical aspects of a specific business field. Finally, the chapter discusses whistleblowing as a specific ethical dilemma of individuals in the business context.

Chapter 6 is about global business ethics. It discusses specific ethical challenges and responsibilities that businesses face on the global level. The chapter starts with three example cases to illustrate typical ethical issues in the global economy: child labor in the chocolate industry, outsourcing of manufacturing jobs, and e-waste. The chapter then explains the origins of certain ethical issues in the global context by the specific characteristics of the global economic system. Finally, the chapter defines ethical guidelines for global business by distinguishing two approaches: basic global business ethics that comprises minimal ethical requirements for global business activities and advanced global business ethics that promotes business as a positive force in the world.

Chapter 7 discusses sustainability from a business ethics perspective. Sustainability is introduced as a major challenge for business and the economy of the 21st century. The chapter defines the concept of sustainability, explains the ethical dimension of sustainability, and demonstrates the relevance of sustainability for contemporary business. The chapter then discusses with examples the challenges and the business opportunities resulting from sustainability, such as efficiency gains, strategic advantages, and new markets. Finally, the chapter reflects on normative changes in contemporary business and the resulting adaptions of the legal framework for business using the example of the benefit corporation. The book ends with a short overall conclusion.

2 Ethical theory and its application to business contexts

Specific ethical topics require specifically tailored methods for properly analyzing them. In this chapter, we develop a set of methods that can be applied to the analysis of ethical issues in business contexts. For this, we refer to the tradition of moral philosophy and established ethical theory and make the insights of philosophical ethics fruitful for the purpose of this book. Established ethical theory can, as we will demonstrate in this chapter, be directly used as a tool for ethical decision-making and justification of decisions in business. The application of ethical theory to business cases is limited, though, to certain types of case and certain situations. In later chapters we will further build on the ethical approaches developed in this chapter and develop more complex methods for further types of business ethics cases.

We will start by introducing the subject matter and questions of ethics in general, and then outline the main ethical approaches of *utilitarianism, Kantian ethics*, and *virtue ethics*[1]. We discuss the application of these theories for the analysis and solution of ethical issues and for ethical decision-making in business contexts. Finally, we will also refer to some additional, more recent ethical theories, such as *ethics of care, Rawlsian ethics*, and *discourse ethics*, to complete our set of business ethics methods.

2.1 The meaning of ethics

We first want to clarify the concept of ethics. What is ethics about? Ethics generally deals with norms and values, with questions of what is right and what is good, what one ought to do and ought not to do, and what is a good person or life. Norms and values have an important function for individuals and societies. They provide guidance for individual actions and societal interactions.

In societal contexts, it is crucial to have some understanding and agreement about basic rights and responsibilities, about how one should treat others and what one can expect from them. This guarantees the functioning and the flourishing of societies and its members. Some norms and values are well established in our society. For instance, freedom and equality are fundamental values; we have private property rights; and stealing and harming others are considered wrong. In other cases, society and individuals tackle more controversial and difficult normative questions: Is abortion wrong? Is the death penalty just? Is health care a right? Despite the difficulties of these questions and disagreement on the issues, people put a lot of thought into them and discuss them a great deal because we understand their importance for our lives and our society. Norms and values are also crucial for individuals and establish a fundamental layer of motivation and decision-making. We might often do things simply because they are (economically) beneficial to us, and this can be quite alright. However, we also make decisions and plan our lives based on norms and values. For instance, we may reject an economically attractive action, deal, or job offer because it is not in line with our values, looks shady, conflicts with fundamental norms, contradicts what we stand for, potentially tarnishes our reputation and integrity, and so on. Personal values are a crucial part of our self-identity. We strive for a good life and wonder about doing right to others, specifically regarding difficult situations and decisions. As these examples demonstrate, norms and values are crucial for society as well as individual lives, and it is important that we properly establish them.

In many everyday situations, norms and values are actually not difficult, and we do not even actively reflect on them. We know rather well what is right, what we are supposed to do, and intuitively follow given norms and values. For instance, we know that it is wrong to steal and that it is wrong to lie to our partner or parents about serious issues; we know that we are supposed to keep commitments; we know what is appropriate and inappropriate when interacting with others; we know that we are not supposed to cut the line, or queue jump; we know that insider trading, bribery, and certain types of price discrimination are wrong; and so on. There already exist a large amount of written and unwritten norms, rules, principles, and values that guide one's actions.

Where do these norms and values come from, and how do we come to know them? In modern, diverse, and dynamic societies like the US, there are various sources that provide such knowledge, and their influence on individual persons differ to some extent depending on personal and societal circumstances. An individual learns many norms and values by socialization: from parents, friends, and school. Through socialization, we learn what is right and wrong, and apply it automatically without explicit reflection. For instance, we do not need to reflect on the question: is it right or wrong to cut the line? We automatically do not cut the line – it is common knowledge in our society. Another important source is the law. Many things we will or won't do because we know that there is a rule or a law that tells us what is right or wrong. For instance, we do not need to make our own decision about the appropriate speed on a specific road – a sign tells us the speed limit. In many cases, authorities are crucial. Parents, teachers, and various other authorities provide us with norms and values, either by formulating explicit rules or by being role models. Traditionally, religion also plays a crucial role in establishing norms and values for individuals, groups, or even entire societies.

2.1.1 Sources of everyday values and norms, and the function of ethics

There is an important difference between having values, knowing norms, getting them from some of the sources discussed above, and acting according to them on the one hand, and *explicitly thinking* about values and norms by oneself, or explicitly discussing them with others, on the other. One can receive norms and values from authorities, rules, religion, or custom, and accept them as guidance for what is right and wrong, or one can reflect on what is right and wrong, and ask for reasons and justification for norms and values. The latter, the explicit reflection on norms and values, is traditionally called *ethics*. The former, having values and norms, is sometimes called *morality*, to distinguish it from ethics.

Ethics, thus, refers to another source from which every person can get norms and values: human reason. In contrast to all other sources above, reason is an *internal* reference point everyone can refer to, not an external one. Ethics assumes that humans are beings endowed with reason that can ask themselves what is right and wrong and make judgments about right and wrong actions. In other words, ethics assumes that one does not need to be religious to be ethical, and one does not need any authority telling one what to do in order to act ethically, but everyone has the potential to be an ethical person just in virtue of one's rational potential to reflect on the question of right and wrong and to exchange rational arguments with others.

Why do we need ethics? Why is reflecting on, and rational argumentation about, norms and values important? What is the relevance and function of ethics, if we already have established external sources that tell us what is right and wrong, such as parents, school, authorities, laws, rules, or religion? Against the background of the various external sources of norms and values, ethics has a crucial function for every individual person and for society. Ethics is the ultimate reference point and justification for right and wrong actions as well as for institutions that establish and oversee societal norms and values. Ethics is important because the sources mentioned above cannot give us complete and secure normative guidance for every situation. Ethics is the basic tool for normative guidance that we have as human beings. In the following, I give some examples to support this claim.

First, all external sources of norms and values discussed above are substantially underspecified. They do not always provide complete, reliable ethical guidance. It is possible that an authority issues unethical orders. Think, for instance, about evil dictators. Additionally, no one can and should expect that authorities provide guidance for every single decision and action. For instance, asking a supervisor for advice for every small action would probably not be very well received. We expect in most jobs, and particularly from well-trained professionals, that individuals have the ability to make their own judgments and decisions, at least to some extent. The law also does not provide complete ethical guidance. Law and ethics are not equivalent. Not all ethical aspects of life are ruled by laws, and not all laws are automatically ethical. There is, for instance, no law that forbids lying to one's partner or parents (except contractual and similar contexts) about a serious matter. However, in most cases, one would consider private lies as unethical, although they are technically legal. It is also possible that a law is unethical. In extreme cases, it can even be the ethical right thing to act against the law. For instance, in Nazi Germany there were laws that discriminated against Jews and led to their persecution and, ultimately, to the Holocaust. No one would seriously claim that it was ethical to follow these laws, but rather that it was ethical to resist them. Another example is actions during the civil rights movement against some laws in the US; for instance, when Rosa Parks broke the law and freely chose a seat on the bus. The intention here was to protest against an unethical law. Modern businesses increasingly operate globally and may connect to areas in the world that show substantial lack of law or law enforcement. In such cases, businesses need to decide for themselves what is the right thing to do and what actions they should refrain from. Lack of law or loopholes in legal frameworks do not imply that actions are ethically permissible. For instance, lacking laws against child labor or forced labor in some area in the world would not automatically imply that it is ethically OK for a business to employ children or use forced labor in this area.

Custom and etiquette are also not sufficient guidance for what is ethically right and wrong. Generally, custom and etiquette are not so much about fundamental ethical guidance, but rather about politeness and smooth societal interactions. In some cases, customs and etiquette can become ethically relevant, though. Violation of custom and etiquette could be ethical in certain situations. This would be the case if the etiquette expresses and reinforces questionable norms. Think about, for instance, gender patterns reinforced by fashion etiquette in the 19th and early 20th centuries. Acting against such etiquette can be a form of ethically legitimate public protest against gender patterns. Other serious ethical reasons may also override custom and etiquette, even if we generally approve them. For instance, cutting the line is considered to be wrong. Like many customs, the custom of lining up has an underlying reason which supports and justifies it: lining up makes societal interaction smooth and avoids chaotic and potentially dangerous situations. However, there may be circumstances that justify cutting the line as an ethically right action. Imagine a physician, who needs to get to an urgent surgery and is facing an unexpectedly long line at the rental car desk after arriving at the airport. It may be justifiable in this case for him to cut the line, and one may expect others to agree that this is the ethically right action. On the other hand, however, it can be unethical to ignore customs, e.g., if someone visits another culture and deliberately ignores customs and, by doing so, offends people unnecessarily. This could be considered as disrespectful.

A second reason why reflection on, and rational argumentation about, norms and values is crucial is the occurrence of conflicts and dilemmas. The various sources that provide us with norms and values can sometimes contradict each other. For instance, someone may have religious values that are in conflict with laws, in cases such as abortion or same sex marriage. In such a conflicted situation, a person needs to ethically reflect and make a personal decision about what the right thing to do is. Other common types of conflict arise from conflicting values or norms themselves. It is not always the case that all our personal norms and values are in accordance with each other and give clear advice about the right thing to do in each situation. It can happen that we have, for instance, duties, obligations, or responsibilities to various persons, which we cannot all satisfy at the same time. We may have professional duties, duties to friends, family members, our community, and so on. We can come into situations in which we face a serious conflict between those. For instance, if you work in a human resources department and have confidential knowledge that a very good friend is going to get fired, and you also know that he is just about to make a long-term investment buying a new home, should you tell that friend or not? Should you override your professional duty of confidentiality by the virtue of friendship? In such cases, we need to ethically reflect on our entire set of values, norms and principles – on our various duties, obligations, and responsibilities – and make a decision about their hierarchical order: What norm or value has priority and overrides others in such a conflict?

A third reason for the importance of ethical considerations is novelty and change. We live in a highly dynamic world that is changing quickly and producing new situations and ethical challenges that no rules, laws, or etiquette have thus far anticipated. For instance, new technologies in medicine and information technology, and the emergence of social media, have all resulted in new types or options for action and in new ethical challenges and questions of what is right and wrong. Increasing dynamics and change is one reason why ethical reflection today is more important and more challenging than in previous times.

Overall, ethical reflection is crucial to guide our actions, and it is becoming increasingly important for all the reasons discussed above, and particularly for modern businesses. Ethical challenges in business have become more complex due to the increasing dynamic, global complexity, and sustainability challenges of today's business world, and the ability to address ethical challenges is crucial for successfully managing modern businesses. Ethics is crucial for ensuring the normative foundation of organizations and institutions; ethics is crucial for making decisions in cases of conflicts and dilemmas; and ethics is crucial for making decisions when facing new situations or situations that lack ethical guidance. In all these cases, one needs to have the ability to reflect on the question of what would be the right thing to do.

It is also important to develop the ability to properly judge whether ethical reflection is necessary in a situation. It may not be fruitful to start a fundamental ethical discussion about each small issue. This can unnecessarily undermine efficiency and effective action. On the other hand, it can be dangerous to not recognize the need for ethical reflection in serious situations. For instance, it would be dangerous if the traveling physician, whose patient's life is at stake, lacks the ability of ethical decision-making and just lines up at the rental car desk as usual, instead of cutting the line claiming an emergency. It is an important ability and exercise to ask from time to time, particularly in crucial situations: Is what I do (still) in line with who I want to be? Is the action in line with my personal values and fundamental ethical principles? Pressures can be high in business contexts, and forces can pull people in various directions. It is important to have and maintain an inner moral compass to guide one's actions. Ideally, businesses and organizations offer positive challenges and ethical guidance themselves, e.g., by organizational shared values and ethical leadership. Such positive forces can support individual members' professional, personal, and moral development. However, one has to be aware that this is not always the case, and be prepared to recognize, and potentially resist, negative and ethically unacceptable pressures in one's professional career.

2.1.2 A definition of ethics

To review the discussion so far, ethics is not having values and norms, receiving them from other sources, and intuitively acting according to them. Rather, ethics is the explicit systematic reflection on values and norms.

> Definition 2.1: **Ethics** is the systematic reflection on values and norms: their content and changes, and their meaning, justification, and determination.

Generally, there are different ways of reflecting on values and norms. First, one can identify, analyze, and explain norms or values in a given society or group. I call this *empirical ethics*. Questions of interest in empirical ethics are: What values and norms exist in a specific group? What function do they have for the interaction within the group? Where do the norms and values come from and how are they established? How do the norms and values change over time? Such questions concern empirical subject matter and are studied in the (social) sciences, such as psychology, sociology, and anthropology. Empirical studies of norms and values have been of increasing interest in the business context. It is of interest to understand which norms and values have what functions in what areas of business. For instance, which types of behavior, strategic action, or bluffing are typically accepted in business negotiations, and which are not? What is respected as toughness in negotiations, and what would be considered rough, aggressive, and inappropriate? Somewhat differently, what ethical qualities do employees expect from leaders? Would certain ethical qualities make employees more trusting and apt to follow? The analysis of such questions is of direct practical relevance for business, and it can help to optimize the functions of ethical elements in business contexts.

However, such analyses are not at the core of traditional philosophical ethics, as they do not actually deal with and answer normative questions like: What is the right thing to do? What is right in action and life? What is good character or a good person? What kind of person should I become? These are all classical questions in moral philosophy. Traditional philosophical ethics aims to analyze and answer such questions, and we will call this way of reflecting on norms and values *normative ethics*.

The following example illustrates the difference between empirical and normative ethics. A mafia organization may be quite successful in achieving its goals. One might want to study what role values and norms have in the operations and success of this organization. One may figure out that specific, strictly enforced norms, such as confidentiality and absolute obedience, are crucial for the mafia organization's success, and some character traits, such as brutality and recklessness, are highly evaluated and admired among its members. One can also study how these norms are implemented and enforced in the organization: possibly by pressure, intimidation, and force. Through empirical ethical studies, one can get a pretty good understanding of what norms and values exist in this organization, what function they have, and how they are implemented. However, what is not addressed is the simple but important question of whether the mafia is a good organization at all, or whether the mafia's values and norms are good and its actions are right. These are normative questions which cannot be analyzed by the methods of social sciences but require specific methods from normative ethics. We will explore these in detail in the remainder of this chapter.

A third field of ethical analysis is *analytical ethics*, which has been a larger field of study in 20th century philosophy, particularly in the US. Analytical ethics is engaged in the systematic reasoning about the use and meaning of evaluative and normative concepts. It engages in questions such as: What is the meaning of the concept *good*? How is this concept used, and how is it related to other concepts? There is no well-established field of analytical business ethics, but questions of analytical ethics certainly matter for business ethics. Many concepts in business, and specifically economic concepts, are value-laden or have some normative or evaluative connotation. Identifying the normative dimension of concepts and statements is a prerequisite for proper ethical analysis. In practical contexts, normative and factual statements are often mixed, which can mislead decision-making and discussions. For clarity of ethical reflection of business issues, it is crucial to properly identify and analyze normative connotations and statements.

This book has a focus on normative questions in business contexts; that is, on normative business ethics. However, empirical insights are an important reference point for any normative business ethics. One needs to know what specific norms and values matter in business contexts, and what specific ethical aspects and challenges are of relevance, in order to discuss the normative ethical questions that really matter for modern business. We also will do some analytical business ethics; that is, analysis of fundamental economic and business concepts. We will particularly discuss the ethical underpinning of the capitalist market economy, the norms and values that are (implicitly) related to this type of economy, such as individual freedom or efficiency, and the normative connotation of economic concepts such as markets, economic rationality, and profit maximization. We also discuss the ethical dimension of business and of various conceptions of business, such as stakeholder vs shareholder orientation, purpose- or value-driven businesses, and new legal forms of business, like the benefit corporation.

2.1.3 (How) is normative ethics possible?

The remainder of this chapter is devoted to traditional philosophical ethics; that is, to the analysis of normative questions, such as: What is right and wrong in action and life? What kind of person should one become? What is a good character? What are virtues? What is a good life? We will study different approaches to such normative questions and develop methods to analyze normative aspects in business cases.

It is important to discuss what type of questions these normative questions are and how one can analyze and answer them. To clarify this, it is helpful to compare the subject of normative ethics with other areas in which we distinguish right and wrong and search for answers about what is right and wrong. Crucially, we continuously ask whether there is one objective answer, and by what method do we figure out what is right and what is wrong?

In some areas of investigation, right and wrong are pretty well defined, and there exist methods for rationally and objectively deciding what is right or wrong. For instance, mathematics is such an area. Regarding questions or claims in mathematics, we usually expect that there is one right answer and that we can find it by rational procedures and reflection. For instance, one can prove that the famous Pythagorean theorem is right. It states that, for any given triangle with one right angle, $a^2 + b^2 = c^2$ (whereby c is the length of the side opposing the right angle, and a and b are the lengths of the other two sides). Or, if one wants to know the length of the diagonal x in a square with the side length of 1, one can easily find the right answer by applying the above theorem: $1^2 + 1^2 = x^2$. That is, $2 = x^2$. It follows that the length of the diagonal x equals the square root of 2. In other areas, in contrast, there is not one, well-defined right answer, and it makes no sense to try to apply rationality in search of the right answer. There simply is no method and no objectively right answer. For instance, this generally holds for matters of taste. Is it right to eat vanilla ice cream or to eat strawberry ice cream? This question is not rationally and objectively decidable. It would not make sense to start a rational inquiry. The decision is completely subjective.

Compared to both types of areas discussed above, ethics is a rather difficult field because it falls into neither of the above categories. In ethics, unlike mathematics, there is not one right answer that can be absolutely objectively determined. However, ethics is also not like taste: completely subjective and rationally unapproachable. Rather, ethics is in between – although I tend to put it closer to mathematics than to taste (see Figure 2.1). What does this mean? Normative ethical questions are rationally approachable, and there are methods for systematically analyzing normative questions. There is not one right answer, though, as in mathematics. However, some answers can be better supported by reasons than others. Also, there is not a single method, as in mathematics, but several methods of ethical analysis. In contrast to

COMPARE: RIGHT AND WRONG – METHODS OF DECISION/PROOF

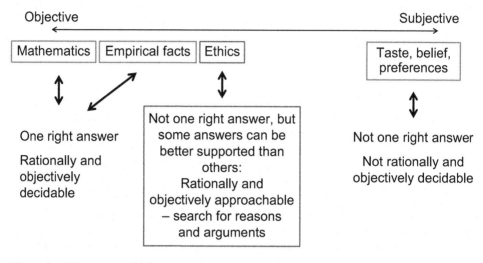

Figure 2.1 The status of right and wrong in normative ethics.

matters of taste, however, it makes sense to rationally analyze and discuss normative matters. We can come to some conclusion, and at least distinguish some ethically better (more feasible) actions/decisions from worse ones. Some actions and decisions can be better ethically justified and supported by reasonable argumentation than others.

For instance, in matters of taste we do not think that rational discussion is possible, and thus we would also not look for any rational justification. It would seem ridiculous if I approach a person who is eating vanilla ice cream and demand a justification: 'Why are you eating vanilla ice cream and not strawberry ice cream? Please justify your action!' Any reasonable person would probably consider my interference in this case as inappropriate and recommend I mind my own business. Taste in this case is a matter of subjective preference, and I have no right, and no substantial reason, to interfere and ask for a justification. However, if we consider the same scenario with regard to an ethical matter, the difference becomes obvious. Imagine you see a person on a public street beating another, obviously much weaker person (e.g., a child) without any obvious reason. If you were to approach this person and ask him to justify his action, your intervention would make sense to every rational person, and would even be considered something you should do. It makes sense to approach that person and ask: 'Why are you beating this other person?' One can (and should) demand a justification. We consider the action here to be wrong and assume that others would also agree that it is wrong. If that person were to answer that he likes to beat other weaker persons, that this is his personal preference or 'taste,' and that we should mind our own business, we would not accept this as a sufficient answer or reason. We would believe that this action can be the subject of rational argumentation, and that there are strong ethical arguments against beating others without any reason. However, how can one develop such ethical arguments and reasons and support an ethical position? This question will be discussed in detail in the following section.

2.2 Moral philosophy and methods for ethical decision-making

Moral philosophy offers several approaches for making decisions about the ethically right action and for analyzing normative and evaluative issues in a systematic and rational way. This section outlines the three traditional ethical theories of *utilitarianism*, *Kantian ethics*, and *virtue ethics*. We will keep the philosophical aspects short, though, and aim at breaking ethical theory down to applicable methods for ethical decision-making that can be used to analyze and solve business ethics cases. These methods will enable us to systematically analyze normative issues and provide rational frameworks for ethical decision-making and ethical justification of decisions in business contexts. We will practice the application of these methods with some sample cases in the following, Section 2.3. Later on, in Section 2.4, we will provide further ethical methods based on ethics of care, Rawlsian ethics, and discourse ethics.

Ethical theories explicitly spell out modes of ethical thinking and decision-making which people already use intuitively to approach everyday ethical issues. However, it is useful to develop more explicit and formal approaches to better define and understand different types of ethical argumentation, and to transfer intuitive approaches to explicit formal approaches that allow more systematic and precise analyses of ethical issues. Basic modes of ethical argumentation refer to consequences of actions, principles, and the character of persons. These three modes are reflected in the ethical theories of utilitarianism, Kantian ethics, and virtue ethics.

2.2.1 Utilitarianism

Philosophical background

Utilitarianism is a theory of normative ethics that ethically evaluates actions by their consequences and their impact on overall happiness of all affected by an action. The action which maximizes overall happiness is considered to be the ethically best action. In other words, utilitarianism claims that 'it is the greatest happiness of the greatest number that is the measure of right and wrong' (Bentham, 1988a, p. vii). Utilitarianism is one of the main ethical theories today. Important original contributions to the development of modern utilitarianism were made by Jeremy Bentham (1748–1832), John Stuart Mill (1806–1873), and Henry Sidgwick (1838–1900). Bentham's *Principles of Morals and Legislation* (1988) and Mill's *Utilitarianism* (1998) have been influential to the discussion of utilitarianism through today.

Utilitarianism has become a diverse field with several variations. For the purpose of the book, we refer to four basic characteristics of the original approach, as follows.

First, utilitarianism refers to *consequences of actions* as crucial base for ethical evaluation and justification of actions. This comes with some difficulties in the application of utilitarianism. First of all, we do not always foresee and know all consequences of our actions. There is a substantial amount of uncertainty and ignorance regarding future consequences of actions. However, a reasonable way to deal with this difficulty is to consider only the consequences that are reasonably foreseeable at the time the decision is made.

Second, utilitarianism considers all persons (beings) who are affected by an action. This means that what matters with regard to the consequences of actions is the effect of those actions on the person (entity) acting and on others. Again, it may be difficult to determine the exact group of people (beings) affected by an action, and so the best approach is to consider those persons that we can reasonably foresee will be affected.

Third, utilitarianism evaluates the effect an action has on the actor and others by the *harm or benefit* it inflicts on them. Originally, Bentham considered the amount of 'pain' and 'pleasure' an action inflicts on others. This does not just refer to physical pain and pleasure, but to all kinds of pain and pleasure, including psychological and economic ones. Pain and pleasure are subjective feelings. Utilitarianism assumes, though, that we can to some degree objectively evaluate the pain and pleasure that comes to others. We will see in later examples that this proves difficult for the application of utilitarianism in some cases. However, there usually is a reasonable range of agreement about the magnitude of pain and pleasure that results from certain actions. Further, it is also noteworthy that utilitarianism is an ethical theory that naturally expands beyond human beings: if pain and pleasure matter for ethical evaluations, then not only human beings matter, but also all other beings that are capable of feeling pain and pleasure, e.g., higher mammals (Bentham, 1988b; Singer, 1975).

Finally, utilitarianism considers *the overall happiness of all affected* by an action. That means we need to consider how each individual is affected by the action in terms of pain and pleasure, and then come up with an evaluation of the overall effect. We need to sum up all pains and pleasures to evaluate the effect of the action on the overall happiness of all affected. The difficulty here is that we need to properly compare and quantify pain and pleasure (economics, for instance, would shy away from such interpersonal comparison of utility and consider this not possible). In the following, we will explain how utilitarianism can be applied to concrete cases of ethical decision-making.

Method

We want to break down utilitarianism and transform it into an applicable method for ethical decision-making and case analysis. For this, we use a basic consideration, which refers to the essence of utilitarianism, that the action that maximizes the overall happiness of all affected is the ethically right action.

> **Utilitarian method:** Which action (of the alternatives at hand) maximizes the overall happiness of all affected?

To properly apply this method and answer this question for a given case, we need to apply the following four steps of analysis (see also Figure 2.2):

1   We need to determine what the possible alternative actions are in the given case; that is, we need to identify all feasible options to act.
2   We need to determine who is affected by the consequences of those actions; that is, identify (the reasonable range of) all persons affected.
3   We need to consider in what way those persons are affected by each alternative action; that is, what amount of pain or pleasure (harm or benefit) is inflicted on them. A basic way to do this is to introduce a numeric scale that allows us to measure the amount of pain or pleasure inflicted on a person on a scale of +10 to

−10. +10 represents the maximum pleasure possible (think about the best things that could happen to a person in life, such as marriage or winning in the lottery). −10 represents the worst, most painful things one could imagine happening to someone in life. Using this scale, in a given case, we need to judge the pain or pleasure inflicted on each person and assign a certain value for the pain or pleasure involved.

4   We need to sum up all harms and benefits resulting from each alternative action to calculate the impact of each alternative on the overall happiness of all affected. We now can easily determine which alternative maximizes overall happiness. This action would then be the ethically right one.

Example of application

CASE: HELPING OR NOT IN THE CASE OF AN ACCIDENT

Jack is driving through a very remote area on his way to a regional airport that is about four hours away. He wants to catch a flight to visit two friends. Jack is taking a short cut, a remote dirt road, which is rarely used. Unexpectedly, Jack comes across an accident. A car seemingly came off the road and fell downhill several feet into thick bushes. Jack is checking the situation and learns that two people are injured in the car; their injuries are not life threatening, but serious enough that they cannot help themselves and need some assistance. One has a broken leg; the other is bleeding. Cell phones won't work because there is no service.

Jack is (for simplification) faced with two alternatives: He either can assist the two people, get them out of the bushes and up to the road, and then drive them back the other direction to a small hospital one hour away, or he can just drive on to make sure he catches his flight, knowing that another car might not come before several hours. Both alternatives are mutually exclusive. If he assists, he will definitely miss his flight, be out of pocket $500, and need to buy another ticket to fly the next day.

Question: What is the ethically right action according to the utilitarian method?

Intuitively most people may already think that helping is the right thing to do here, and they may have different justifications for that. However, we want to apply the utilitarian method and see what action can be supported as ethically right based on utilitarianism. We will come back to the example later in the chapter and apply other modes of ethical reasoning and discuss further alternatives of action.

For applying the utilitarian method, we need to consider the four steps of analysis defined above (see Figure 2.2). First, we need to identify all possible alternative actions. For the sake of simplification, we have already determined that there are only two alternatives for Jack: (1) help and miss the flight or (2) not help and catch the flight. Second, we need to figure out who is affected in this case. Obviously, the two injured persons are affected, Jack is affected, and his two friends are affected. There might be others who could be affected and considered in the analysis, such as the airline, people at the hospital, or the next drivers coming along the same road. However, the story does not provide more detailed information. For simplification, we will thus restrict out consideration just to the few persons identified above.

1. Consider all possible alternative actions (A_1,....,A_n)
2. Consider who is affected by those actions (P_1,...,P_m)
3. Consider how everyone is affected in terms of benefit and harm (quantitative evaluation/numeric scale)
4. Sum up benefit and harm for each possible action – the action that maximizes overall happiness is the ethically right one

⇩

	A_1	A_2	...	A_n	Definition of numeric scale:
P_1	+4	+3		0	
P_2	–7	–1		+3	max. benefit: +10
...					
P_m	+2	+1		–2	
Σ	–1	(+3)		+1	max. harm: -10

Figure 2.2 Applying the utilitarian method.

The third step now is the most difficult step of the analysis. We need to evaluate in what ways the persons are affected by the consequences of both alternative actions and quantify the effects in terms of pain and pleasure (harm and benefit). We need to discuss each alternative separately.

Alternative 1: Jack helps   This alternative results in some harm/pain for Jack and also for his friends because he will miss his flight, lose money, and his friends will have to wait for him. On the other hand, this action is positive for the two injured persons who get help with their physical pain and their desperate situation. To quantify this, we need to put these different effects into perspective. On a scale of –10 to +10, how serious a pain would we consider is the missing of the flight? This may depend on some further circumstances. For instance, the pain of losing $500 may vary with Jack's income. If he works for minimum wage and has little savings, the loss might matter more to him than if he has a decent income and sufficient savings. Regardless, missing the flight and losing money is something negative, and so we need to choose a value between –10 and 0. Most people would probably consider the resulting pain to still be minor, if –10 defines a maximum pain; that is, some of the worst things that can happen to someone in life. So, it seems reasonable to choose a number in between –5 and –1. Let's choose –3 for now. For the friends, we may consider waiting one or two more days for Jack as a minor nuisance (assuming they, like Jack, are looking forward to meeting up). So, let's choose –1 for their pain. The two injured persons definitely will be much better off if they get help. Now, physically they are still in pain until they get to the hospital, but we need to consider the effect Jack's action will have on their situation. It will certainly be a huge relief for them if they get help and know that they will be at the hospital soon. We should therefore go into the positive part of the scale. Getting help after an accident may not be among the greatest things in life, but certainly something positive. It makes sense to choose some value between 0 and +5, say +3 for now.

Alternative 2: Jack does not help   If Jack does not help and just drives on to the airport, he personally does not lose or gain anything, neither do his friends. Everything goes as planned for him and his friends. One may think that he feels guilty and has some pain because of that, but let's exclude this effect for now, as we did not include any pleasure Jack possibly could feel in the instance in which he helps. For the two injured persons, however, this alternative is a worst-case scenario. They have physical pain, are in a desperate situation, cannot help themselves, and see the only person that might be able to help within the next several hours driving away. This may not qualify as the worst thing that can happen to someone in life, but it may come close. To the physical pain adds the psychological pain, the desperation and disappointment, and the knowledge that they probably will have to wait hours until another person shows up on that road. So, it seems reasonable to choose a number on the higher negative scale, in between −5 to −9. It is also useful in the entire evaluation to compare the numbers one chooses for different types of pain. So, if we chose a −3 for evaluating the pain of missing a flight and losing $500, we need to put the pain of the two injured persons getting no help into perspective, and it seems reasonable to evaluate that as a higher pain. Let's choose −7 for now.

We have evaluated and quantified all effects to all persons for the two alternative actions. In the fourth step, we can now calculate the overall happiness for each alternative action and determine which alternative maximizes overall happiness. We will do this in the chart in Table 2.1 by putting in and adding up the numbers we have determined in step three above. It is important in this step to consider each person as one; that is, to multiply the effects with the number of persons actually impacted.

   We have calculated in Table 2.1 how each alternative action impacts the overall happiness of all persons affected. The ethically right action is the action that maximizes overall happiness. So, we need to choose the action with the highest number in the bottom row. Here, this is +1. So, the ethically right action for Jack according to the utilitarian method is to help the two injured persons.

   You might think that the result is obvious anyway and that it is a waste of time to apply the utilitarian method. However, by applying such a method, we transform an intuitive decision into a decision that is based on a transparent process of ethical reasoning. With this, the ethical decision can be justified, supported by reasons, and discussed with others. This is what normative ethics can provide: methods of systematic reasoning about what is ethically right and wrong, in order that we are not stuck

Table 2.1 Utilitarian analysis of the example case: helping or not in case of an accident

Alternative actions Persons affected	Jack helps	Jack does not help
Jack	−3	0
Jack's two friends	−1 × 2 = −2	0
Two injured persons	+3 × 2 = +6	−7 × 2 = −14
Overall sum (Σ)	+1	−14

in different opinions or subjective values, but instead enter a reasonable, more objective discussion about ethical issues, and thereby distinguish the ethically better from the ethically worse.

SOME REMARKS ON THE UTILITARIAN ANALYSIS OF THE CASE

Evaluating the degree of pain and pleasure with numbers might seem somehow vague and arbitrary. It is hard to determine, and agree on, an exact number. However, the case we analyzed shows that there is some range of numbers that almost everyone would exclude and some range which is more reasonable. For instance, everyone would understand that the injured people, if they get no help, suffer pain, and thus no one would choose a positive value. Also, most people would consider the pain of the two injured as a more severe pain, as it is a combination of physical pain with psychological pain. So, most would probably consider a higher negative number between −3 and −8 as an appropriate evaluation, and if we would administer a poll among 1000 persons, we may expect some statistical distribution within this range. We can then call this range the *reasonable range*. Within this range, there is certainly room for interpretation, but we are not stuck with completely arbitrary, subjective opinions. By evaluating the effects using a numeric scale, we make possible a reasonable discourse about them. Persons who choose different numbers can enter into a discussion and explain their evaluations. That way the ethical judgment becomes a more transparent process of ethical reasoning. Furthermore, we could easily add to the method a test of robustness of the result: we could check whether it actually matters for the overall outcome which number within the reasonable range we are choosing. In other words, if we would all agree that some number between −3 and −8 is reasonable, we could check whether the overall result depends at all on the specific number we choose in that range. If the result stays the same no matter what number between −3 and −8 is chosen, we have a robust result and would not need to spend any time further discussing the exact number. With regard to the case discussed above, one can easily test that our result is pretty robust and will not change within the range of numbers we considered as reasonable.

In the above case, one may also wonder if we excluded other alternatives, other feasible ways of action, that are more reasonable, and even ethically better. What about, for instance, if Jack would ask the two injured persons to compensate him for his loss – that is, $500 – for him driving them to the hospital? Would not most people consider this a reasonable course of action and as fair? The utilitarian method cannot address the aspect of fairness, and this third alternative would probably not turn out to be ethically better in comparison to the action of helping without compensation. The reason is that in a utilitarian perspective any compensation would probably be considered a zero-sum game: if the injured persons pay $500 to Jack, they lose the same which Jack gains, so overall there is no increase in overall happiness. Still, one may think helping with compensation is a fair solution and the right way to act. However, to support this position, one needs to have criteria for fairness, i.e., criteria for deciding what is fair and what is not. Famously, John Rawls provided such criteria, and we will discuss later how a Rawlsian argument can support the position that compensation of $500 is the fair solution in this case (see Section 2.4.2).

We will also consider later a certain type of economic reasoning and why it is misleading in this specific case: What would the economic actor (the self-interested rational utility-maximizer as defined in neoclassical economic theory) do in this case, and why is a classical bargaining solution (market solution) problematic here? As an economic actor, Jack could, for instance, ask a price for helping the others, and try figure out how much they are willing to pay. In this situation, Jack could probably ask a pretty high sum, say $2000, and the other two might agree. If all deliberately agree in this deal, it looks technically like a *Pareto improvement*; that is, a deal by which all parties are better off. As we will discuss in Chapter 3, the quality of free bargaining resulting in Pareto improvements, and of free markets being *Pareto-efficient*, is a strong argument for the capitalist market economy. However, this case shows that economic solutions are not always good, and usually only work in situations where people have roughly equal power, abilities, and information, in order that they actually can choose deliberately. This is not the case in our example, and pure economic reasoning and action would easily qualify as exploitation. The situation is one of asymmetric power and abilities, and the willingness to pay would increase with the misery and pain of the injured. The bargaining solution and the concepts of Pareto improvement and Pareto-efficiency do not consider this, but most ethical theories would. This is one reason why additional ethical underpinnings of markets is crucial in certain contexts and situations.

ON THE FRUITFULNESS OF THE UTILITARIAN METHOD

Utilitarianism has some obvious difficulties, and it is easy to criticize the approach, e.g., regarding the predictability of consequences, the measurement and comparability of pain and pleasure, and the reference to consequences and happiness as criteria for ethical judgment. However, utilitarianism is a fruitful tool for analyzing and better understanding complex issues. First of all, it is always useful to consider what alternative and feasible actions are in a given situation. This may also help to identify new/further options and overcome false alternatives. Second, it is important to gain some clarity about the consequences of actions and of the parties affected by them. In modern, complex, and global business, the consequences of business activities are not obvious at all, and some reflection may reveal crucial effects or stakeholders that had not been considered so far. It is neither ethical nor in a business's interest to inflict substantial negative effects and harm to stakeholders just by ignorance or neglect. In many cases, there might be feasible, or even economically better, alternatives available. So overall, despite some philosophical shortcomings, utilitarianism is a fruitful tool for analyzing complex issues and for ethical decision-making in business contexts.

Exercises

1   Case: Speeding in a case of emergency
     You are hiking with a friend when he gets bitten by a snake. You have no phone, and the only way to get help is to drive the friend to the hospital. Every minute counts, and so you decide to drive significantly faster than the speed limit, as there is barely any traffic.
     Is it ethically right for you to break the law and speed in this situation, or would the ethically right action be to obey the speed limit? Analyze this case by applying the utilitarian method to determine the ethically right action.

2.2.2 Kantian ethics

Utilitarianism provides a straightforward method for distinguishing the ethically better action from the ethically worse, based on the consequences of the actions to all people affected. The utilitarian approach seems reasonable, as it correlates with an intuitive mode of thought. It is reasonable to consider the consequences of one's actions for oneself and for others, and it makes sense to ethically condemn actions that do more overall harm than good. However, utilitarianism does not capture certain further criteria for ethical decision-making and ethical judgment that we intuitively refer to.

Utilitarianism is more focused on the outcome of actions and does not seem to consider the motivation of actions enough. However, intuitively, motivation seems to matter for our ethical judgments. For instance, if a two-year-old child brings a cup of coffee to her mother and drops and breaks the cup because it is too difficult for the young child to carry securely, the mother would probably not judge the child and its action based on the consequence alone. She would not think that the child is behaving unethically or being evil, but instead probably value the good intention of the child to do something nice for her.

Another aspect of utilitarianism that may be perceived as unsatisfactory or even counterintuitive is the fact that the same action can be right in one situation but wrong in another in virtue of the consequences and the context of each situation. It could be right to lie in one case, if overall happiness is maximized by lying, and wrong in another. In extreme scenarios, utilitarianism might even consider cheating, stealing, or killing as right, as long as these actions happen to maximize overall happiness. This is counterintuitive to many people who consider ethics as something that should provide clear guidelines of right and wrong, and definitely distinguish good and evil.

Many people have and follow ethical principles. In other words, they have absolute binding norms of action that they consider ethically right, no matter what, and certainly they are not contingent on consequences. For instance, most people think that stealing or cheating are always wrong. Many may think that what is right is right, independent of consequences, and even independent of individual or overall happiness. For instance, if my children do not behave well, I may decide to punish them by cancelling the planned trip to the zoo. This probably decreases overall happiness of all involved: my children are not happy; I am not happy; and my spouse isn't happy either. We all were excited about the trip. Nevertheless, I may think that this is the right thing to do, in principle, to establish clear guidelines and expectations.

Since motivation and strict moral principles seem to matter intuitively in our ethical judgments, some philosophical theories have focused specifically on those aspects. Ethical approaches that focus on the idea of absolute binding ethical norms, ethical principles, and moral duties are labeled *deontology*. A key and very influential example of deontological ethics is the ethical theory of Immanuel Kant (1724–1804). In contrast to utilitarianism, Kant claims that neither consequences nor happiness are relevant for ethical decisions, but rather that the right motivation and fundamental binding principles that rational beings understand as ethically right are relevant. Before we go into Kant's rather complex philosophical approach, we will look at some basic examples for the general role of principles in moral guidance, and particularly in business contexts.

Ethical principles

Well-defined principles are very useful for personal and professional action. Principles provide simple guidance and are more efficient to apply than, for instance, utilitarian calculations. In everyday contexts, various types of principle are relevant and guide our actions. On the individual level, most people have some personal principles. Principles help to define what one would and would not do, what someone stands for, and what is fundamental to someone. For instance, personal principles could be: I am always loyal to my friends; I only make promises that I can keep; I always respect others. Such principles, if taken seriously and expressed in all actions, can build someone a reputation as being a person of integrity. In other terms, principles can define one's personal brand. In business contexts and professional careers, clear ethical principles can be a very important factor for being successful and well respected.

That principles are crucial to business success has been recognized and demonstrated in many ways. For instance, the Daniels Fund Ethics Initiative promotes eight business ethics principles: integrity, trust, accountability, transparency, fairness, respect, rule of law, and viability. The Initiative claims that those principles were at the core of the success of the businessman Bill Daniels (DFEI, 2016). Many professions have their own professional ethical codes and principles; for instance, the accounting profession has defined specific professional principles of being truthful, objective, competent, and considerate of the public interest (AICPA, 2018; see Section 5.3). Professional principles are not as subjective as personal principles but are shared among, and expected from, all professionals working in the field. Mission statements and core values of companies can also be interpreted as normative principles because, for many companies, mission statements and core values constitute important normative guidelines for their interactions with stakeholders, strategic management decisions, and everyday business activities.

There are also more fundamental ethical principles that are broadly shared in a society and guide overall societal and political actions and decisions. For instance, the US constitution provides fundamental principles regarding individual freedom, equality, and rights, which are broadly shared across the political spectrum and across the diversity of personal values and life-styles. Constitutional principles matter for business in the US because business, as any other societal actor, is expected to uphold them in their activities. There even exist global ethical principles, such as human rights. Throughout different cultures, legal systems, and religions, the fundamental ethical principles defined in the *Universal Declaration of Human Rights* (UN, 1948) are broadly shared and agreed upon. Generally, global business activities are expected to follow commonly shared global principles and respect human rights.

Principles are crucial for practical contexts and provide important normative guidelines for business action. However, they do not ultimately answer the question of what is ethically right and wrong. Any person or organization could come up with any set of principles, and there may be ethically better and worse principles. For instance, even a mafia boss probably has principles, but we would usually not consider them as ethically good. Even if principles are shared by a majority of people, this does not automatically make them ethically right. For instance, in Nazi Germany it is likely that a majority were willing to accept the norms and values of the Nazi regime at the time, but this would still not make those norms and values right. So, how can we distinguish ethical from unethical principles, or ethically better from ethically worse principles? We need criteria, a method that allows us to approach this subject and provide reasons for judging principles. Kant's ethics provides such a method for analyzing principles and their ethical quality.

Kantian ethics: philosophical background

The German philosopher Immanuel Kant (1724–1804) certainly is one of the most powerful and influential thinkers of the last 500 years. It is fair to say that no philosopher after Kant could ignore him, and most are directly or indirectly, in one way or another, influenced by him. Kant's thought has also extended beyond philosophy to other fields such as humanities and science.

Kant's philosophy essentially focuses on the power and limits of human reason. He generally argues that human reason is a powerful source for cognition and deliberation. In the field of ethics, Kant argues that all ethical insight comes from reason. What is ethically right does not depend on consequences, feelings, happiness, pain, and pleasure, or any other empirical criteria, but is solely determined by reason-based deliberation. For Kant, the right motivation matters for the ethically right action, and the right motivation is motivation by the good will, that is, the will guided by reason. Only because reason establishes by itself what is ethical, can there be such things as ethical necessities, moral duties, and moral obligations, which Kant thinks are in line with our intuition: we understand and experience the idea of moral duties, we often think that what is right is right no matter what. If ethical judgments depended on empirical criteria, such as consequences or pain and pleasure, we never could establish moral necessity or absolute moral duty. Empirical criteria are uncertain and, to some extent, arbitrary. Therefore, Kant argues that only reason by itself, without any reference to empirical criteria, can be a reliable source of ethical guidance. In the following, we will break down Kant's rather complex ethical theory into two basic methods, which we can apply to ethical decision-making and case analysis in business contexts.

Method

CI METHOD A

Because Kant rejects any empirical criteria for ethical guidance, reason must just refer to itself and the very idea of a necessarily binding and, therefore, general principle of action. Kant calls this general principle the *categorical imperative* (CI), which is an unconditional (logically necessary) command of action: 'act only in accordance with that maxim through which you can at the same time will that it become a universal law' (Kant, 1998, p. 31). This formula is also called the *basic formula* of the CI, as Kant provides several other formulations. Some explanation of the wording here helps to simplify that formula: a 'maxim' simply is a personal rule of action, or a personal principle. 'Universal law' here means a universal principle of action. The categorical imperative thus states that one should only act by such personal principles one could reasonably want everyone to adopt and act by. In other words, every person should check whether her own personal way of acting could (hypothetically) be universalized: Could I reasonably want everyone in the world to adopt the principle and act the same way as I? We can thus transform the categorical imperative into the following method:

> **CI method A (universalizability):** Which way of action (of a given set of alternatives) can reasonably be universalized? That is, which way of action (personal principle) could one reasonably want everyone to adopt?

For analyzing what the ethically right way to act is in a certain situation, one need to check for each alternative whether one can reasonably want that way of acting to become a universal guiding principle for everyone. Actions that can be universalized qualify as ethical. Actions that cannot be universalized are not ethical. This method does not necessarily determine one single right way of action. There may be more than one ethical way of action in a given case. However, the method provides a criterion to distinguish ethically feasible ways of action from unethical ways of action and excludes certain alternatives of action in a given case.

It is important to understand that this is a *hypothetical* thought experiment regarding the questions: What if everyone *were* to act the same way? Can one reasonably want everyone acting the same way? The question is not if in reality everyone acts the same way. The fact that everyone acts a certain way has no ethical relevance. Even if everyone in the world acts a certain way, that does not say anything about whether that way of action is ethical.

Let's discuss a basic example for applying the CI method A before we go on to introduce another version of the CI method that is also derived from Kant's ethics and reflects a very important criterion that is relevant for business ethics.

EXAMPLE FOR APPLYING THE CI METHOD A

Consider the following rather simple example that Kant discusses himself: someone wonders whether it is OK to make a 'false promise' in an extraordinary situation; that means, a promise that he does not intend to keep. The person desperately needs some money and wants to ask a friend for it. He knows that the friend will only lend him the money if he promises to pay it back within two weeks. However, he will not be able to pay the money back in time. Thus, the only way to get the money from the friend is to make the false promise to pay it back within two weeks. The person decides to make the false promise, thinking that the desperate situation he is in justifies it. The question is: Would this be ethically right? Note, that the utilitarian method could find this permissive under certain circumstances, specifically if the overall happiness is maximized by the action. However, the CI method A is not considering specific consequences and circumstances, but rather reflecting on the question of whether this action is right or wrong in principle.

To apply the CI method A, we need to identify the underlying way of action or the underlying personal principle in this case and then discuss whether this way of action could be universalized. The personal principle here seems to be the following: in desperate situations, it is OK to make false promises. Now, can we reasonably want this personal principle to become a universal principle of action? Can we reasonably want everyone in the world to act that way? If everyone in the world starts making false promises in whatever situation that might qualify as desperate to him or her, the very meaning of the concept promise would be destroyed. A promise means a binding commitment. If everyone in the world uses the concept 'promise' in a contingent way, this would plainly contradict the original meaning of the concept. Universalizing this personal way of action is obviously self-defeating. If making false promises would become a universal principle of action, the concept of the promise would actually make no sense anymore, and no one would use the concept or trust it anymore. Therefore, one cannot reasonably want everyone in the world to adopt that way of acting, and thus the CI method A shows that making false promises is unethical.

Kant emphasizes that one should recognize the logical contradiction here: the very fact that this principle of action is self-defeating. Rational beings will understand this and recognize that false promises are unethical. Kant would not refer to consequences, such as no one being able to trust others and their promises, but just emphasize the logical contradiction to the very meaning of the concept 'promise' and the self-defeating character of the principle underlying the false promise. However, we sometimes may use the CI method A in a loose way in the context of this book and also allow the argument that one cannot reasonably want everybody to act in a certain way because the universalization of the action would result in a world in which rational persons would not want to live.

Norman Bowie (1999, p. 13) discusses a business example that is analogous to the example of the false promise. Visiting a small college town, Bowie recognized that many businesses did not accept checks from the students. The reason, he figured out, was the high number of uncovered checks that the businesses had received (Bowie, 1999). Writing a false check, that is, a check that is not backed up by money in an account, is a form of false promise. A check is meant to be a binding commitment to someone that she will receive money from the person writing the check. Writing a check to someone does not mean that maybe she will get the money, but rather that the writer is committing to pay the money for sure. Applying the CI method A reveals the contradiction: if writing false checks becomes a universal principle, the very concept of the check is destroyed – it has no meaning anymore. Someone might think she can justify writing a false check in a desperate situation, but universalizing this way of action reveals that it is ethically wrong.

CI METHOD B

Kant's philosophy is rather complex and far reaching. Related to his ethical thought, Kant also establishes the concepts of each individual's free will and dignity as a being endowed with reason (a reasonable/rational being). Ethical principles are a necessity that reasonable beings understand and act upon. However, we can, at the same time, understand that it is reasonable beings that constitute this necessity. As such, we are an origin of necessities, of moral laws, in the world. We do not just depend on and follow some necessities, as nature does, but we are the starting points of necessities. Ethics is in the world because we as reasonable beings bring it into the world. The hungry lion has to eat the young animal. The lion is by instinct driven to do so. It has no ability to deliberate and cannot discuss with fellow lions whether it is right to eat the young animal or if it would be more ethical to only eat older animals. As such, the lion is unfree – it is fully determined by its instincts. In contrast, humans can separate themselves from their inclinations; they can deliberate about whether it is good to eat now or later, whether it is right to eat meat or not, and so on. Humans are free because they are beings endowed with reason and thus can establish ethical principles and follow them (or not). Humans are ends in themselves and not just mere objects driven by inclinations and other external forces. For Kant, this constitutes the dignity of the human being. Respecting the dignity of each person for Kant means respecting individuals as ends in themselves; as beings endowed with reason and capable of ethical deliberation. Thus, Kant provides another formulation of his categorical imperative, sometimes called the *respect-for-persons formula*: 'So act that you [treat] humanity, whether in your own person or in the person of any other, always at the same time as an end, never merely as a means' (Kant, 1998, p. 38). In other words, one should never treat others as mere objects but always consider them as ends in themselves.

We can break this thought by Kant down to another method that we can use for ethical decision-making situations:

> **CI method B (respect-for-persons formula):** Which action respects the dignity of all persons (as reasonable beings) involved in or affected by it?

For the purpose of the book we may also reframe this question for the business context, and ask: Does a business respect the dignity of all persons involved in or affected by its operations?

The CI method B is relevant for many business aspects. Generally, there is some risk within the context of business that people are treated as mere objects, and thus businesses and economic actors need to pay particular attention to this ethical risk and respect the dignity of all actors involved in, or affected by, the business activities. Of course, to some extent, people are means of business activities and objectives: employees are hired as a means to do something for the business and help to achieve some business goals. This is not an issue from a Kantian perspective, as long as employees are not *merely* treated as means, as long as they are at the same time respected as ends in themselves, as beings endowed with reason.

This has many implications for business, some of which we will discuss later in the book in more detail: this includes moral rights of employees, such as respectful treatment (see Section 5.1), respecting and not exploiting vulnerable groups in business contexts, for instance, in marketing (see Section 5.4), or respecting human rights and not exploiting people in global business contexts (see Chapter 6).

Example for application

We already provided a basic example for applying the CI method A. Let's also discuss the example we introduced in Section 2.2.1 for illustrating the utilitarian method, helping or not in case of an accident, by using both CI methods A and B.

What would be ethically right in that case when applying the CI method A? First, we need to identify the ways of action or the underlying personal principles in this case. Jack considers whether he should help the two injured and helpless people who had an accident. How could we formulate Jack's way of action; that is, the underlying personal principle that drives his actions? For the case of helping, one could, for instance, say the underlying principle is: 'I always help others that are in a desperate situation and need help, insofar as I am capable' (P1). For the case of not helping, the underlying principle could be: 'I always act in all situations to my personal advantage' (P2a); or 'I only help others if I am not disadvantaged by doing so' (P2b). Which of these principles can be universalized, and which cannot? What principle can one reasonably want everyone in the world to adopt and act upon? P1 can easily be established by the CI method A: one can reasonably want everyone in the world to help others in desperate situations insofar as they are capable. P2a and P2b cannot reasonably be universalized, though. As rational persons we do not want a world in which P2a or P2b become universal principles of action.

However, in this case, the Kantian argument can only be fully developed by additionally referring to the CI method B. A reasonable person cannot want P2a or P2b to become universal principles of action because P2a and P2b contradict the very concept of reasonable beings as ends in themselves; that is, they contradict the CI method B. Not helping because one is securing one's advantage (or the end of getting on the flight) based on P2b reduces the injured persons to mere objects, as does the bargaining solution of asking money in exchange for help, which would be the natural action from P2a. The latter is, in addition, clearly a case of exploitation. Exploiting the desperate situation of injured persons for making some extra money clearly disrespects their dignity and reduces them to mere means.

REMARKS ON THE CI METHOD AND KANTIAN ETHICS

1   The CI is not the golden rule, although it is similar. The *golden rule* states that one should treat others as one would like to be treated. This is a reciprocal mode of reflection that asks one to switch perspectives and consider a situation the other way around: what if the other person was doing to me what I am doing to him? Would I want that? The CI provides a more general mode of reflecting on one's actions. With the CI method A, I ask whether I could reasonably want everyone in the world to act in the same way that I do. In other words, I can check my own action by reflecting on the question of whether I could reasonably want everyone to act like me and to treat others (and me) like I treat them. This way, the CI method A can be interpreted as a mode of reflection that includes the golden rule as a special case. If I reflect on whether I can reasonably want everyone in the world acting as I do, this would include me becoming subject to such actions myself. If everyone acts like I do, this includes the possibility that I am confronted with such action, that someone acts that way toward me. Both the CI and the golden rule provide abstract modes of ethical reflection, or meta-principles. They have no specific moral content or advice, but rather enable one to check, for any given action or principle, whether it would be ethical or not.

2   Kant does not claim that there is one well-defined set of right ethical principles. He is not advocating a narrow idea of universal ethics. He merely claims that for a principle to qualify as an ethical principle, it has to pass the CI. Many principles could pass the CI, though, and there is no given limit to the number and contents of ethical principles (as long as there is no internal contradiction between them). In this sense, Kant's ethics is open to diversity and cultural considerations. The only universal element in Kant's ethics is the assumption that all people apply the same reasonable deliberation. That is, Kant assumes that all people would exclude certain principles as unethical and approve others as ethical.

3   Kant does not think that 'the natural' is the good but rather that 'the reasonable' is the good. In civilized societies, we are indeed committed to not act as nature

does, for instance, letting the physically stronger subdue the physically weaker, but we establish ethical principles as guidance for our societal interactions.

4   By focusing on the motivation that drives an action, Kantian ethics considers an aspect of ethics that matters in practice and particularly in many legal systems. In many legal systems the intention or motivation that drives an action matters for court decisions and punishment of crimes. For instance, many legal systems distinguish different degrees of murder, depending on the underlying intention. Intentionally killing another person is considered to be more nefarious, and will be punished more severely, than killing someone by affect (crimes of passion), accidentally, or through negligence. The consequence of the act is the same in all cases – a person has been killed by another – but is evaluated ethically and legally differently, depending on the underling motivation that drove the action.

The analytical challenge with the CI method A is to (i) interpret the personal way of action – that is, the personal principle that underlies a specific situation and single action – and then (ii) to properly universalize the action. We will practice this method in Section 2.3 with some business cases and see that there can sometimes be various possibilities to interpret and universalize a specific action. However, the investigation of these different possibilities is a useful analytical practice to gain a broader perspective on a specific action and its ethical implications.

Exercises

1   a)   Formulate five personal principles of action that you consider as most important to you. In other words, what do you stand for?
     b)   Verify with the CI method A that the principles you formulated are ethically feasible.
2   Use the CI method A to demonstrate that cheating on one's partner is unethical.

2.2.3 Virtue ethics

The third ethical theory we discuss in this section is *virtue ethics*. Virtue ethics is a normative ethical theory about the definition and realization of virtues and human excellence. In contrast to utilitarianism and Kantian ethics, virtue ethics is not focusing so much on the single ethically right action, but more on questions such as: What is a good person? What is a good character? What is human excellence? What is a good life? These are fundamental ethical questions of everyday life. We do not only ethically evaluate actions as right or wrong, but also judge persons as good or evil, and many people implicitly or explicitly reflect on the notion of a good life and how it could be achieved. By switching the perspective from the right action to the good character and good life, virtue ethics adds important ethical aspects to other theories, such as utilitarianism and Kantian ethics.

Philosophical background

Modern virtue ethics often refers to Aristotle (384/3–322/1 bc) and his *Nicomachean Ethics*. Important contributions to contemporary virtue ethics have been made by

Anscombe (1958), MacIntyre (1981), and Hursthouse (1999). To introduce the basics of virtue ethics, in the following we will discuss the concept of virtue, the relevance of virtues for business, and the relationship between virtues and human excellence.

THE CONCEPT OF VIRTUE

> Definition 2.2: A **virtue** is an excellent, durable character trait that a person develops over time by (inter)action, reflection, and experience, and enables a person to act and get along with other people in an exemplary way (Solomon, 1992, p. 192; Becker, 2016, p. 9).

There is no well-defined definite list of virtues. What counts as virtues may change to some extent with the underlying concepts of the human being, society, and human excellence. However, some character traits have been considered as virtues throughout different contexts and times. For instance, some of the virtues that Aristotle discussed may still qualify as virtues today, such as courage, benevolence, generosity, and temperance (Aristotle, 2000).

More important than the single specific virtue is the general idea of virtue as an excellent character trait that a person develops over time in a societal context. A person is not born with virtues but needs to develop them. Individuals are born with specific character traits, and everyone is different. For instance, some are rather shy whereas others are more outgoing; some are rather anxious and others are risk-takers. However, virtue ethics assumes that everyone can work on his or her given disposition and develop certain virtues. Crucial factors for developing virtues are self-reflection, societal feedback on one's behavior and actions, practice and experience, and practical wisdom.

For instance, let's imagine someone who by nature is rather hot-tempered. That means he is quick to anger if something or someone bothers him. He tends to over-react in situations and recognizes this as an issue. He feels sorry after such situations and is unhappy about his behavior. Also, some friends may indicate to him that he overreacts and that he should show more self-control. However, despite his awareness of this issue, he cannot just change his hot-tempered disposition by theoretical insight from one day to the next. This requires practicing judgment and self-control in many different situations. Virtue ethics assumes that over time this person can develop the virtue of being even-tempered, the proper way of reacting to various situations and persons, by paying attention to his disposition and working on it continuously. Generally, virtue ethics assumes that through reflection and practice, everyone is able to transform into the person she wants to be.

Virtues are, therefore, crucial for the identity of a person. Virtues define the person, the person's actions, and the way the person is recognized by others. Virtues also constitute the motivational basis for ethical action. The way in which a virtuous person acts is determined by his virtues: an honest person just acts honestly in all situations, a courageous person acts courageously, a trustworthy person acts trustworthy, and so on. Virtue ethics does not discuss the ethical aspects of single actions but assumes that the virtuous person acts ethically. In other words, in virtue ethics, the right action is the action which is, or would be, done by the virtuous person.

Virtues are to some extent contextual, but even so, they are not completely relative to contexts. For a character trait to be considered a virtue, it must be generally admirable by reasonable persons and be part of a reasonable concept of human excellence. For instance, in specific societal contexts, such as sport, military, or business, specific character traits are internally defined to enable people to act excellently and be successful in the context. In the military, courage traditionally is considered a crucial character trait of an excellent soldier. Although courage is specific to the military context, courage is also generally admirable and relevant to other societal contexts, and courage can be an integral part of a broader concept of human excellence (not just the excellence of a soldier). In contrast, brutality might be an excellent character trait for a member of the mafia, which enables that member to become successful in the mafia context. However, one would not reasonably consider brutality as a generally admirable character trait or an integral part of any reasonable concept of human excellence. Thus, we will consider only such excellent character traits as virtues, which refer to reasonable concepts of excellence, and are generally admirable.

BUSINESS VIRTUES

Do virtues matter for business? Are there excellent character traits that are crucial in business contexts? Do certain virtues matter for acting in an exemplary way and being successful in business or a career? Indeed, there are many such *business virtues*. Just consider the following examples.

Integrity, honesty, and fairness can be considered general business virtues. These virtues matter for many business activities: they help individuals get along with customers, co-workers, suppliers, and other stakeholders in an exemplary way, and, by this, support business and professional success. Some virtues specifically matter for certain functions in businesses. Loyalty is important for employees. It is expected from them to some degree and the display of loyalty is a crucial component of succeeding in a company. Successful and excellent leadership also requires virtues such as courage, responsibility, fairness, or care. Further, there are virtues that are specific to a profession or a certain job. An exemplary accountant displays objectivity, trustworthiness, and loyalty to the clients; an excellent lawyer has virtues that express fiduciary duties, such as confidentiality and trustworthiness; an excellent service person has developed the virtue of attentiveness and responsiveness; an excellent negotiator possesses the right amount of toughness (Solomon, 1992, pp. 207ff); and so on (Becker, 2017).

VIRTUES AND HUMAN FLOURISHING

An important aspect of Aristotelian virtue ethics is the claim that the virtuous life is the good life. According to Aristotle, developing virtues and acting according to them is not only key to becoming a good person but also key to a good life, happiness, and human flourishing. This is backed up by Aristotle's conception of the human being but can also be framed in more general and modern terms: if someone strives to become the person she ideally wants to be, this is more satisfactory than most other things in life, such as material wealth or money. Developing virtues means developing excellence, developing one's full potential as a human being. Having virtues means being excellent in an authentic way and acting in accordance with one's self-identity. Virtues define one's personality and one's way of acting and interacting with others. Others will experience a person's honesty, reliability, generosity, or trustworthiness. Such a virtuous person will be recognized and admired in society, by friends, and by colleagues.

From a virtue ethics perspective, a positive societal context matters for an individual's flourishing and development of virtues and excellence. As business is an important societal context, in which many people spend a substantial part of their time and life, how business contexts contribute to the development of personal virtues and, with this, to individual flourishing and happiness is crucial. Business certainly has the potential to be a positive force and to provide a positive context of interaction and opportunity for individual and professional development and excellence. Ideally, organizational design and leadership promote and support flourishing of all members of a business or organization. However, business can also fail to do so, and even become destructive to individual and professional development and flourishing. Thus, system design, organizational ethics, and organizational culture are crucial topics of business ethics, and we will discuss them in detail in Chapter 4.

Method

We can break down virtue ethics to applicable methods for ethical decision-making in business. One way to do this is to refer to the concept of virtue and the idea that the right action is the action a virtuous person would perform or the action that is in line with the identity of a virtuous person. Regarding specific actions or decisions in business contexts, we can then simply ask:

> **Virtue method A:** Which action/decision is consistent with who someone is, and wants to be, referring to reasonable concepts of excellence?

Alternatively, one can ask: Which action/decision is consistent with the action/decision of a virtuous person or professional? What would a virtuous person or professional do? What virtues matter?

In this method, we need to consider certain desired or expected virtues of the person or organization at stake. On the individual level, this could be personal virtues that someone emphasizes for herself. For instance, someone might ask oneself when making a difficult decision: Is this decision in line with who I am and who I want to be as a virtuous person or professional? In many situations, the ability to reflect on actions and decisions this way and to follow one's moral compass in the midst of external pressures and demands is crucial. However, as long as such personal virtues are not communicated explicitly, they remain on the subjective level, and external observers would not be able to consider them when judging, for instance, a person's decisions and actions.

In business contexts, there are often objective aspects that characterize who a person or organization is and more well-defined objective expectations and virtues. There are, for instance, generally admired business virtues, such as reliability, honesty, and trustworthiness; specific virtues that are related to who someone is as a professional; and virtues related to the specific function someone has in an organization. We can also apply the virtue method A to an entire business or organization instead of a single person; that is, we can refer to what an organization is and wants to be. What an organization is or wants to be is often expressed in its mission statement or core values. When ethically evaluating a management decision, we might then simply ask: Is this decision in line with the mission or core values of the company?

Another way to frame a decision method based on virtue ethics is by referring to the link between virtues and human flourishing. Virtue ethics aims at the good life, at the flourishing of individuals through development and actualization of virtues. In this regard, one can also ask how an action/decision impacts the ability of individuals to flourish: Is the action – or its consequences – increasing the potential for flourishing of all affected, or is it decreasing this potential?

> **Virtue method B:** Which action/decision best supports the development of personal or professional potential and ensures thriving of all affected?

Individuals can only develop and actualize virtues within proper societal contexts that are supportive. Thus, ultimately, virtue ethics also asks for the right design of societal contexts, in order that they optimally support the development of virtues and human flourishing. Virtue ethics, therefore, is also a crucial ethical backdrop for aspects of organizational ethics and leadership ethics.

Examples for application

1   An attorney is asked by her husband to reveal details about her latest client, whom she is defending in a murder case. What would be ethically right from the perspective of virtue method A: To tell the details or not tell them?

Providing the information would not be in line with the professional virtues of integrity, trustworthiness, and confidentiality. Although, as a spouse, the attorney ideally should also have the virtue of care and fidelity with her husband, in this case it seems that expressing professional virtues and upholding confidentiality to the client does not actually contradict her personal relational virtues. Not revealing information about the client usually cannot be interpreted as being dishonest to or not caring about her spouse. It does not undermine the specific trust between them.

2   A company produces high-quality outdoor clothing, and its mission statement emphasizes a strong commitment to environmental sustainability. The company recently learned that its suppliers of cotton cause serious environmental damage. What would be an ethically good reaction to this situation from the perspective of virtue method A?

What action would be in line with who the company is and wants to be? Taking no action would not be in line with the company as defined by its mission statement. To uphold the mission statement and identity of the business thereby, the company would need to address the issue and aim at reducing the environmental impacts of their supply chain. One option would be to work with the suppliers and farmers to improve the situation.

3   Global supply chain decisions from the perspective of virtue method B: How can people in the supply chain thrive?

In global supply chains, we often find situations in which people contribute to the product and business of a company, but yet do not benefit in the sense that they or their communities do not develop themselves and flourish in kind. In extreme cases, there is exploitation such as child labor, unhealthy or dangerous working conditions, human rights violations, and even slavery. Such situations clearly hinder an individual's or community's ability to thrive. However, even in less extreme situations, people may have a job but no real opportunity for personal or professional development, and there is no actual contribution to the development of local communities.

In many cases, businesses could improve the situation, empower employees in the supply chain, and enable them to flourish and actually benefit from their participation in the supply chain. The investment of time and money may be quite reasonable for a given business and may result in long-term business benefits, such as reduced risks in the supply chain, stable supply chains, better commitment and quality, and securing or improving reputation (see Chapter 6 for a more detailed discussion of this topic).

Exercises

1   Formulate three character traits that you consider as being important virtues.
2   Formulate three character traits that you consider important business virtues, and explain how these virtues matter for being successful in a business context or career.
3   What virtues would you expect from an ideal friend?
4   What virtues would you expect from an ideal leader or supervisor?

2.3 Applying ethical theory to case analysis and ethical decision-making in business

In this section, we want to apply the methods for ethical decision-making, which we have developed in the previous section, to some basic business cases. We will analyze each case from two perspectives. First, by applying ethical methods, we will analyze what is the ethically right decision. Second, we will discuss what is the best business decision by using some economic criteria for business success, such as profit, competitiveness, market share, and growth. It is of particular interest to see whether the ethically right decision is also the best business decision.

We will discuss in this section more basic cases which represent classical decision-making scenarios. In later chapters, we will consider more complex business ethics situations, which involve organizational and systemic ethical aspects and require more elaborate methods and additional considerations for analysis.

2.3.1 Case 1: the underperforming friend

Jim, an engineer, works for ABC Engineering, Inc., which provides engineering and safety consulting to construction businesses. ABC Engineering has an excellent reputation for the quality and accuracy of its service, and many general contractors depend on the company's calculations to ensure the safety of their construction projects, such as buildings, bridges, and roads. ABC Engineering recently hired Allen, whom Jim knows quite well from his golf club. Naturally, Jim was quite happy when he learned that his friend Allen joined the company. However, when working with Allen on some projects, Jim recognized that Allen was not able to perform his tasks according to professional standards. Allen made several mistakes in calculations and Jim had to correct Allen's work to ensure proper results. After observing the issue continuing for a couple of weeks, Jim is wondering whether or not he should inform his supervisor that Allen cannot properly perform his tasks.

Questions

1 What is the ethically right decision? Apply the utilitarian method, CI method A, and virtue method A to analyze the case and argue for a decision.
2 What is the better business decision with regard to the business success of ABC Engineering?

Analysis

1 What is the ethically right decision?

UTILITARIAN METHOD

The alternative actions in this case are (i) Jim informs the supervisor or (ii) Jim does not inform the supervisor regarding Allen's lack of performance. So, we need to analyze which of these two actions maximizes overall happiness of all persons affected. Who is affected by these actions? Obviously, Jim and Allen, but also the company; that is, all people working for and invested in it. Ultimately, all stakeholders may be affected in some way, but for the sake of keeping the analysis simple, we will here just consider the customers of ABC Engineering. How are all these persons/parties affected in terms of harm or benefit (pain or pleasure)? By informing the supervisor, Jim may feel sorry for Allen, but on the other hand he benefits from showing his loyalty and responsibility to the company. I assume these two aspects together still result in a negative effect for Jim. Not informing, however, may also harm Jim in several ways: he would keep a co-worker who underperforms and potentially makes serious mistakes, and if it turns out that he did not warn the company about Allen, it could backfire on him. So, this option is harmful overall to him. What are the effects to Allen? If Jim informs the supervisor, this is certainly very negative for Allen, as he will probably lose his job. Conversely, Allen would benefit if Jim does not inform the supervisor. However, his benefit from keeping the job might be reduced by him being overwhelmed with, and not fit for, the job.

Crucial in this case, however, are the further effects to the company and the customers. If Jim does not inform the supervisor, the company continues to employ an underperforming person who makes mistakes in calculations that will likely jeopardize the safety of the customers and, thus, harm them. As the company consults about safety in construction, Allen's mistakes, and the resulting flawed service to the customers, could have serious consequences. Therefore, both the company and the customers would be better off if Jim informs the supervisor. Importantly, the company and its customers represent many individuals who are involved and affected. In utilitarianism, the potential harm or benefits need to be considered for each individual involved. I assume here that N persons are involved in the company (employees, investors) and M persons are involved with the customers (construction companies with employees and investors). N and M are probably rather high numbers, and the individual harm needs to be multiplied by N and M. If we sum up the quantitative effects of harm and benefits for each alternative of action, it is easy to see that M and N matter and dominate the outcome. Given the example of my quantitative evaluations in Table 2.2, for any numbers $N, M \geq 1$, the sum for informing is greater than the sum for not informing. That means informing maximizes overall happiness and is, therefore, the ethically right decision according to the utilitarian method.

Table 2.2 Utilitarian analysis of case 1: the underperforming friend

	Informing	*Not informing*
Jim	−2	−2
Allen	−8	0
Company	+1 × N	−4 × N
Customers	+1 × M	−4 × M
Overall sum (Σ)	$N + M - 10$	$-4N - 4M - 2$

The specific numbers of evaluating harm or benefits here do not actually matter, as long as we assume rather high numbers of N and M, and further assume that some harm is done to the company and the customers by not informing. The number of individuals comprising the company and the customers who are negatively affected will determine the result of not informing being worse in terms of overall happiness than informing.

CI METHOD A

We need to interpret the personal way of actions or the underlying personal principles in this case, and then discuss whether they can be universalized. The action of Jim not informing the supervisor could be interpreted as putting personal relationships before professional responsibilities or safety issues, or could be interpreted as weighing friendship more than qualification in the context of employment decisions. We cannot reasonably want such types of actions to be done universally. If these would become universal principles of action, professional responsibilities would be substantially undermined, safety in all areas would be jeopardized, and employment decisions would systematically be influenced by personal relationships instead of qualifications. This would be in conflict with fundamental principles, such as the best qualified person being employed rather than the person who is less qualified but has better contacts or relationships. On the other hand, Jim informing the supervisor can be interpreted as an act of putting professional responsibilities in serious matters of safety before personal relationships, which qualifies as a universal rule of action. We can reasonably want everyone in the world to apply this as a universal principle of action.

One may wonder, though, if Jim informing the supervisor is not simply an act of telling on a friend, and we cannot reasonably want everyone in the world telling on their friends. This would substantially undermine the very concept of friendship. However, Jim's action is specifically contingent: he is telling on a friend due to serious concerns about the safety and wellbeing of others. Interpreting his action as a general telling on a friend would be too broad an interpretation and miss crucial circumstances of the case.

In conclusion, not informing the supervisor is wrong according to the CI method A, and informing the supervisor would be ethically right.

VIRTUE METHOD A

We don't know Jim as a person. However, we know that Jim is an employee, a professional, and a friend of Allen. What virtues would one expect from an ideal employee, professional, and friend? An ideal employee is supposed to be responsible and loyal to his company. As such, if Jim informs the supervisor, that would be in line with Jim being an ideal employee. In addition, this is an engineering company, and one might also argue that Jim needs to uphold basic ethical principles of engineering, such as the responsibility for public safety. Again, informing the supervisor would be in line with this specific responsibility.

On the other hand, we would also expect loyalty from an ideal friend. So, the question is, does loyalty toward the organization in this case trump loyalty toward a friend? One can argue that it does in this specific case. Jim's professional responsibility and loyalty seems to be more crucial than his loyalty to a person he basically knows from his membership in the same golf club. However, generally friendship and loyalty between friends are important virtues, and there may be other cases in which friendship could be considered more fundamental than loyalty to an employer. This depends on the specific situation and circumstances. In conclusion, in this specific case, I have argued that, based on the virtue method A, the ethically right action is to inform the supervisor.

Altogether, in this case, the three ethical methods that we have applied result in the same evaluation: informing the supervisor would be the ethically right decision, and not informing would be wrong.

2   What is the better business decision?

From a business perspective, all parties seem to be better off when Jim informs the supervisor. Employing an underperforming person is a burden for any business and at a minimum is inefficient. Allen cannot perform properly and does not produce desired results. So, at a minimum, the business is wasting some money and will experience frictions if other team members need to do the work and correct results. In the worst case, mistakes made by Allen could frustrate and harm customers (the construction companies that got consultation) and even result in liability issues. Overall, by informing the supervisor, Jim will prevent the company from significant risks and potential costs that might otherwise result from Allen's lack of performance. In addition, with regard to Jim's professional career, Jim probably will also be better off by informing the supervisor. The company will certainly appreciate that Jim is a responsible employee who cares about the wellbeing of the company. Finally, Jim informing the supervisor might even be better for Allen's career in the long term. It is probably better for Allen's career to leave the company now than to get fired at some later point due to serious mistakes.

2.3.2 Case 2: XYZ Shoes, Inc.

XYZ Shoes, Inc. has specialized in shoes for children and is a leading brand in the market. The company is located in a mid-size US town, has been committed to its community for many years, and sponsors local educational and health programs for children. As is common in this industry, most of the company's shoes are produced outside the US by various suppliers. XYZ Shoes has recently learned that one of its suppliers is employing a number of children under the age of 14. In a team meeting, consequences are discussed. Some team members suggest stopping cooperation with the supplier immediately, as the employment of children is violating XYZ Shoes' code for suppliers as well as international labor standards. Other team members have concerns about this suggestion. The supplier is the only employer in a very poor area, and the children and local communities would suffer from the termination of the contract. They suggest that XYZ Shoes should work with the supplier to fix the issue as follows: XYZ Shoes should ask the supplier to remove the children from the workforce, sponsor an educational program for the children, and support them financially while they go to school. Further, the supplier should agree to rehire the children after they turn 16 and have finished school. This action would require that XYZ Shoes devotes some funds to oversee and ensure the proper implementation of the program for the children. The team needs to decide what action to pursue: Stop cooperating with the supplier immediately (option 1) or work with the supplier to fix the issue as suggested (option 2)?

Questions

1   What would be the ethically better way to act? Apply the utilitarian method, CI methods A and B, and virtue methods A and B to analyze the case and provide a recommendation.
2   What is the better business decision?

Analysis

1   What is the better ethical decision?

UTILITARIAN METHOD

We will compare the two alternatives given in the case: immediately stop cooperating with the supplier (option 1); or work with the supplier to fix the issue (option 2). From a utilitarian perspective, we need to find out which option produces more overall happiness for all parties affected.

We first need to identify the parties affected by XYZ's decision. The decision will obviously have effects on XYZ itself and on the supplier. Further, we should consider the effects on the child workers and the poor area in which the supplier is located. These are the parties directly mentioned in the case. We could further consider other stakeholders of XYZ, such as customers, investors, and employees. However, for the sake of simplification, we will restrict the analysis to the parties identified above.

If XYZ chooses option 1, and immediately stops working with the supplier, XYZ seems to benefit. XYZ upholds its policy and avoids any backlash from customers or legal implications resulting from the supplier's child labor issue. However, XYZ would need to find another supplier to replace the old one, which can result in significant transaction costs. One may assume that both effects, the benefits and the costs, balance out. For the supplier, option 1 would be negative. The supplier loses business with XYZ, which is the leading brand in the market, and the supplier's reputation is tarnished, which may impact its future ability to attract business from other companies. For the children, the overall effect would also be negative. Option 1 most certainly will result in them losing their jobs at the supplier's factory, and they may even be worse off than before. Likewise, if XYZ leaves the area, the economic situation of the local community would worsen.

We need to compare the effects of option 1 with the effects of the alternative option 2: XYZ working with the supplier to fix the issue as suggested in the case. For XYZ option 2 would involve some costs. The company would need to invest some money to work with the supplier and ensure that the program for the children is properly implemented. On the other hand, the company avoids the transaction costs for finding a new supplier. Let us assume, again, that these effects cancel out and the net effect to XYZ is 0. For the supplier, option 2 seems to be negative. They have to pay for the program supporting the children, for their education, and foregone wages. In addition, some further costs occur by replacing the child workers with potentially more expensive adults and by the commitment to rehire the children when they turn 16, potentially at higher wages. However, option 2 would enable the supplier to keep its contract with XYZ, which probably is financially more beneficial to the supplier than the resulting costs of option 2. The benefits from keeping the contract are the incentives that would make the supplier agree to option 2 at all. Overall, we may assume that option 2 is actually beneficial for the supplier. The children would certainly benefit most from option 2. They get an education, financial support, and a guarantee for future employment. The region in which the supplier is located also significantly benefits from this solution.

Considering all effects discussed above, option 2 seems to produce more happiness overall than option 1. Option 2 is neutral to XYZ, slightly positive to the supplier, and very beneficial to the child workers and the region. In contrast, option 1 is neutral to XYZ, negative for the supplier and negative for the children and the region. Therefore, from a utilitarian point of view, option 2, working with the supplier to fix the issue, is the ethically better action.

CI METHOD A

To apply the CI method A, we need to discuss the universalizability of the two options. For this, we first need to further interpret the options at stake to figure out what principle of action each represents. Option 1, immediately stopping the cooperation with the supplier, could be seen as strict enforcement of the rules against child labor. Can this way of action be universalized? I think one could reasonably want every company in the world to act that way and strictly enforce rules against child labor. If every company would adopt this principle of action without exception, the issue of child labor would not exist. This would make the world a better place and be consistent with supporting fundamental human rights. However, we could interpret option 1 differently. If we take a closer look at the situation, we may conclude that option 1 is more motivated by the desire to find an easy way out and actually does not help but rather harms the children involved. This way of acting may be hard to universalize. One might argue that if every company chooses the easy way out by refusing to engage with child workers, that this type of action would actually contradict the original idea of protecting children under child labor laws. In contrast, option 2 seems to be easier to universalize. Option 2 can be interpreted as the principle of ending child labor by actually taking care of, and protecting, the most vulnerable group in the situation, the children. One can reasonably want this to become a universal principle of action: that every company in the world fixes child labor issues and other human rights issues in the supply chain by actively protecting the wellbeing of child workers and other vulnerable groups. As a universal principle, option 2 would also result in a strict enforcement of child labor laws. The potential financial consequences of child labor imposed by this option would deter suppliers from using child labor in the first place. Overall, on the basis of the CI method A, one can argue for both options, depending on the interpretation of option 1. I think, though, the somewhat stronger argument can be made for option 2.

CI METHOD B

Which action respects the dignity of all people affected by, or involved, in the situation? Child labor is exploitation, and as such disrespects the dignity of the child laborers as reasonable beings. Child labor prevents children from attending school and receiving proper education. It significantly compromises the possibilities of children for developing their rational faculties and individual potential. Child workers are not considered as ends in themselves but used as mere means for minimizing production costs. Child labor can also be perceived as a form of manipulation because children lack the full potential for deliberate autonomous decision-making. Children might easily be lured into dangerous and underpaid jobs. They lack the full capacity to critically judge the consequences of such jobs, specifically the long-term consequences of foregone education. So, overall, the question is which of XYZ's actions would better protect the dignity of the children as reasonable beings and better counteract exploitation and manipulation? One can argue that option 1, stopping cooperation with the supplier, would actually not fully counteract the situation, but also treat the children as mere objects, the main goal being to get out of the situation and uphold rules and reputation. Option 1 would not care about the wellbeing of the child workers. It is instead an easy way out that disregards the children so that XYZ is able to report 100% compliance. In contrast, option 2, getting involved and working with the supplier to fix the situation, would directly stop the exploitation, restore the dignity of and respect the children by providing them an education, and empower them to make a fully informed choice about entering a contract with the supplier when they are old enough to do so. Thus, option 2 is the better ethical action according to the CI method B.

VIRTUE METHOD A

Which action is more in line with who the company is or wants to be (referring to reasonable concepts of excellence)? The only information given in the case is that the company abides by child labor rules and sponsors local programs to support children. The philanthropic focus on education and health programs for children relates to their core business: marketing shoes for children. One can argue that option 2 is more in line with the branding and identity of XYZ. Caring about the wellbeing and education of the children in the supply chain certainly is in line with their local philanthropic activities and care for children. In contrast, option 1, terminating the contract with the supplier and walking away from the situation, seems to contradict XYZ's commitment to child welfare. So, the ethically better action according to the virtue method A is option 2.

VIRTUE METHOD B

Which action better supports the thriving of all involved or affected? Option 2, working with the supplier to fix the issue, would certainly support the potential of the children and the region to thrive. The children would get an education, which is a crucial precondition for more opportunities in life, and the entire region benefits from such investment in education and jobs. In the long run, investment in education helps to break the vicious cycle of poverty, in which children have to work to support their families instead of getting an education, and consequently they have no opportunities for better jobs and a better future for their children. The financial burden for the supplier would not significantly impact its potential to thrive as a business. XYZ and its employees may benefit from supporting children in the supply chain. On the other hand, option 1, terminating the contract with the supplier, would negatively affect the potential of the child laborers and the region's ability to thrive and develop due to the negative economic impacts resulting from XYZ's exit. Overall, option 2 is the ethically better way to go according to the virtue method B.

In conclusion to the first question, considering the arguments developed above by using various ethical methods, we can recommend option 2 to XYZ as the ethically better action.

2   What is the better business decision?

What is the better action from a purely economic point of view? What option would benefit XYZ more economically? As we have very little data about XYZ, the answer depends on some assumptions and interpretation. Both options would involve costs. Option 1 requires finding a new supplier and both finding and training a new supplier involves transaction costs. Option 2 requires funding for some supervision mechanism to ensure that the supplier properly implements the program for the children. Assuming that both options involve roughly equal costs, there would be no specific financial argument to favor one for the other. However, one could argue that option 1 only involves a one-time investment, whereas option 2 requires more long-term funding. There might be a small financial benefit from option 1, then. However, option 2 might benefit XYZ with regard to further business criteria. First, it is beneficial in the long run to invest in the supply chain and build better relationships with suppliers and the regions in which they operate. This gives more stability and reliability to the supply chain and avoids running into similar or other issues with new suppliers. Second, option 2 can be linked well to XYZ's branding and core business. Option 2 could be used for marketing purposes. The involvement in the supply chain and care for children may resonate well with customers, strengthen the brand, and build reputation. Option 2 could become part of a strategic move toward more social responsibility as well as more stability and a lower risk in the supply chain, which would resonate well with investors.

In conclusion, option 2 is not only the better ethical decision in this case but also the better business decision overall.

2.3.3 Case 3: free chocolate cake

Jamie, a professor at a distinguished university, got a research grant from a major public foundation. The grant includes the possibility to invite colleagues from other universities for research workshops. After one of these workshops, Jamie invites her colleagues to a restaurant, and pays using grant money, which is in line with the rules of the grant and university policies. At dinner, Jamie orders two chocolate cakes with the intention to take one cake home and give it to her husband. She argues that there are no rules against this practice.

Questions

1   Is Jamie's action ethical? Apply the utilitarian method, CI method A, and virtue method A to analyze the case and support your judgment.
2   What are potential economic implications of this action?

Analysis

1   Is Jamie's action ethical?

UTILITARIAN METHOD

We need to compare the action of taking a cake home for her husband with the alternative of not doing it. We then need to analyze whether taking a cake for her husband increases or decreases overall happiness compared to the alternative and consider harm and benefits to all parties affected. Bringing the cake home may benefit Jamie and her spouse, as he probably will enjoy the cake, and she will be happy that he is pleased with the cake (assuming that he is not bothered by her taking grant money to pay for it). Are there others affected by this action? This is difficult to evaluate: there are many consequences and parties affected in some way, but the effects are rather small and hard to determine: the restaurant benefits, but the research project, the foundation, and the university may be harmed. The quantitative effects are hard to determine, though, and the number of people affected here is also unknown. These effects may or may not override the benefits to Jamie and her husband. Consequently, we cannot appropriately assess and argue whether Jamie's action to take the cake increases or decreases overall happiness compared to the alternative of not taking the cake. The utilitarian method is therefore inconclusive here.

CI METHOD A

What type of action do we observe here? What personal rule of action is Jamie establishing? Jamie is buying a cake for her husband using grant money, which means she uses funds for her private interest that were earmarked and given to her for a certain purpose. More specifically, the grant money is public money devoted to research that can be considered a public good. Therefore, Jamie uses funds devoted to a public good for a private good. Can we reasonably want this to become a universal principle of action? Can we reasonably want everyone who is trusted with, and responsible for, funds that are devoted to a specific purpose to use those funds for private purposes and interests? Probably not, as this would establish a general principle of misappropriation of funds. It would establish permissibility around misuse of funds for any private use. This is a slippery slope: what a cake is to one person, is a flight ticket to another, and a car to the next. People in all kinds of positions would misuse all kinds of funds for all kinds of private purposes. This would contradict and undermine the very idea of dedicating funds for specific purposes, lead to serious misallocation of funds, and destroy any trust in the persons who are responsible for such funds. Probably, people and institutions would stop giving money for specific purposes, particularly for public goods. One therefore cannot reasonably want Jamie's action to become a universal rule of action. Thus, the CI method A supports the judgment that Jamie's action is unethical.

VIRTUE METHOD A

The case provides some basic information about Jamie: she is an employee, professor, grant holder, and spouse. What ideals do we expect from these roles? From an employee, we generally expect some degree of loyalty and responsibility. From a professor of a public research university, we may expect professional responsibilities such as upholding the relevance and value of research. From a grant holder, we expect responsible use of grant money, as well as trustworthiness and accountability. The action of buying the cake to take home, as small as it might be, contradicts all these professional virtues. One might argue, though, that Jamie is also a spouse, and buying the cake for her husband displays virtues of a good spouse, virtues like care and attentiveness. However, in this case, it is questionable that this would justify neglecting professional virtues. Jamie could easily be a good and caring spouse without violating her professional virtues; for instance, by buying the cake for her husband with her own money.

Overall, in this case, utilitarianism does not give us a clear result, but the CI method A and virtue method A both lead to the same conclusion: Jamie's action to use grant money to purchase a second cake is ethically wrong.

2   What are potential economic implications of the action?

The action of buying the cake using grant money seems to be an insignificant issue. However, the action constitutes a misuse of funds, which generally, and at a larger scale, can result in serious consequences. Donors and investors who give money for well-defined purposes may withdraw their support if they learn that their money is not being used properly. The success of many non-profit organizations, such as universities, depends on donations and public support, and may be negatively impacted when their reputation is tarnished by misappropriation and waste of funds.

On a larger scale, improper use of research funds can have significant economic implications if it becomes a more widespread issue. Research can be considered a public good. Research is supposed to produce new knowledge that benefits society and contributes to the future flourishing of society. As a public good, research cannot be optimally funded by the market: investors and businesses will only fund research that is likely to turn profits for them within a reasonable timeframe. However, some of the most significant research has had delayed benefits to society and humankind, and these were unforeseeable at the time. For instance, theoretical research in mathematics at the beginning of the 20th century established the foundations of informatics, which eventually led to the development of computer technology. Many advanced societies therefore finance the public good of research through public funds and mechanisms like public research foundations. If Jamie uses money from her research grant for the cake, this actually is not a zero-sum game in which the restaurant gains what other businesses that sell materials for the research lose. Economically, Jamie shifts funding of public goods to consumption of private goods. If this were to happen on a large scale, it would have significant economic consequences. It would result in underfunding and suboptimal provision of public goods, in an inefficient allocation of means in the economy, and significant consequences for the overall wellbeing of society.

Exercises

1   Find an ethically superior solution to the two alternatives that were given in Case 1 (the underperforming friend). Use the utilitarian method, CI method A, and virtue method A to prove that your solution is indeed ethically better than the given alternatives. In other words: What would you do in this situation? Is there a better way to address the situation than the two alternatives we discussed?

2   Case: the corporate card

Joe has a new job as assistant manager at a large publicly held corporation. He is very happy with the position. The work is great, well paid, and he gets along very well with his co-workers and his boss. After less than one year, he is already being considered for promotion. However, in the last few weeks, Joe had recognized on several occasions that his boss is using her corporate card for private expenses, which is strictly against the rules. He considered raising the issue with her but is shying away from the direct confrontation. Joe is now wondering whether he should report the issue anonymously to upper management?

   a)   What is the ethically better decision? Consider all three options (talk with the boss, inform upper management anonymously, take no action) and apply the utilitarian method, CI method A, and virtue method A to analyze the case and provide a recommendation.
   b)   What is the better decision with regard to Joe's career?

3   Case: outsourcing at AAAA Cooling, Inc.

AAAA Cooling Inc. is a publicly held company with headquarters in the US that produces cooling systems for industrial and private applications. One of their divisions is producing air conditioners in a smaller town in the US. The plant employs 800 workers. Average payment is about $24 per hour, which is well above minimum wage. Most workers have been with AAAA Cooling for many years, and turnover is very low. Due to competitive pressure, AAAA Cooling has lost sales over the last three years and is having a hard time keeping up their market share. Customers increasingly prefer the lower-cost units from competitors. As a result, revenue and profit have declined over the last few years. Due to increasing complaints and pressure from investors, management is considering outsourcing production to a country in East Asia. The plan is to pay the workers at that location $4 per hour, which would be above the local minimum wage of $2. Outsourcing production would mean that the plant in the US will be closed, and all its 800 workers will lose their jobs. At a key executive meeting, the leadership must make a decision, whether or not to outsource production.

   a)   What is the ethically better decision? Apply the utilitarian method, CI method A and B, and virtue method A and B to analyze the case and provide a recommendation.
   b)   What is the better business decision?

2.4 More ethical theories: ethics of care, Rawlsian ethics, discourse ethics

We have discussed so far three main ethical theories that are without a doubt the most influential in today's ethics and applied ethics, and we will use these theories throughout the book. This section introduces three additional ethical approaches that have been developed more recently, and each highlights some aspects of ethical analysis which traditional theories do not fully consider: *ethics of care, Rawlsian ethics*, and *discourse ethics*. These theories are also fruitful for business ethics and allow us to recognize and analyze specific ethical aspects of business and its context.

2.4.1 Ethics of care

To introduce crucial aspects of ethics of care, we discuss the following well-known case.

Case: *the sinking boat*

You are on a boat with three others: your mother, your spouse, and your five-year-old child. The boat is sinking. None of them can swim, and you can only save one.

QUESTIONS

1   Whom would you save in this situation? Your mother, your spouse, or your child?
2   How would you justify your decision? Is there an ethical argument for it?

ANALYSIS

The majority of my students usually answer that they would save the child. A few would save their mother or their spouse instead.

The interesting ethical aspects here are the potential reasons or justifications for the decision. In this case, traditional ethical arguments do not seem to be that relevant. Rather, further ethical considerations seem to matter. Traditional ethical arguments could be, for instance, utilitarian in nature: the child has the longest life to live and most expected happiness, and therefore rescuing the child is best in terms of overall happiness. Another consequence-based argument would be that one can have more kids with the spouse, and thus rescuing the spouse actually will be best in terms of long-term consequences and overall happiness. On the other hand, following this logic, one could easily argue that one could replace the spouse and have more children with another person.

However, all these arguments seem somewhat awkward and missing crucial ethical aspects of this case. What actually matters in this case is the fact that you have very special relationships with the others in this boat, and that these relationships seem to imply specific ethical obligations or responsibilities. For instance, your mother is unique to you, and it is arguable that you owe your mother because she gave birth to you and raised you. You and your spouse are committed to each other, and this constitutes a very special relationship of fidelity and trust. Finally, your child depends on you and trusts you, and as a parent you have a specific responsibility for your child.

The strongest argument in this case can probably be made for the child. The mother and the spouse are responsible for themselves. They are reasonable adults. That they cannot swim is to some extent their own decision and responsibility. In addition, it is their own responsibility and decision to enter a boat knowing that they cannot swim (and not even bring a life jacket). However, that the child cannot swim is your responsibility as a parent. Moreover, you are responsible for bringing the child on the boat knowing that it cannot swim. This makes the case for you having a primary responsibility and moral obligation to rescue the child that depends on you and your decisions.

However, no matter whom you argue to rescue, the case provides an interesting ethical insight beyond traditional ethical theories: specific relationships and relational roles seem to have ethical relevance. Relationships can imply specific ethical responsibilities and obligations. You have some specific moral responsibilities to your parents that you do not have to strangers. The same holds for your spouse and your children.

The insight that the specifics of relationships matter ethically has in particular been promoted and analyzed by the field of ethics of care (see, e.g., Held, 2006). Ethics of care emphasizes that relational context and relational roles have ethical relevance. Specifically, asymmetries in power, capabilities, or knowledge in relationships matter ethically. Many areas of life and action are within the context of specific relationships and relational asymmetries rather than in a context of independent, autonomous rational agents, such as those that are assumed by utilitarianism or Kantian ethics. This extends way beyond family relationships explored in the case above. For instance, the relationship between physician and patient is also characterized by dependence, vulnerability, and asymmetry in knowledge. As a result, one can argue that the physician has specific moral responsibilities and obligations toward the patient due to the specifics of the relationship. For instance, the physician is not supposed to abuse the vulnerability of the patient, or to use her expertise to trick the patient by selling him useless drugs and thereby make money from the patient's ignorance.

The insights of ethics of care are relevant for many business contexts. Some roles in business come with specific responsibilities. For instance, a CEO of a company has other responsibilities than an intern. The CEO has been granted extensive powers and access to information to oversee the operations of the entire company. If something goes wrong with the company it is the responsibility of the CEO and not the intern (as long as the intern was not directly involved). Another example is global business contexts. Within global business contexts we often find extreme differences in capabilities and power. One can argue that businesses have specific responsibilities in such contexts and need to act responsibly with regard to the people involved in, or affected by, its global operations (see Chapters 4 and 6).

With regard to ethics of care, we can formulate the following method:

> **Care method:** Is the action/decision taking place within a specific relational context? If so, which action/decision is in line with the moral specifics of the relationship(s) involved?

2.4.2 Rawlsian ethics

John Rawls (1921–2002) published his influential book *A Theory of Justice* in 1971. Here, I will only refer to one basic mode of thought that Rawls introduced as the 'veil of ignorance' to show a further way to rationally analyze ethical aspects of decision-making situations. The ethical focus here is more specific, though. Rather than asking, what is the ethically right decision? We ask, what is the *just* decision? Following Rawls, one can formulate a basic method to decide what decision or action is just as follows:

> **Rawlsian method:** Which action/decision would rational (self-interested) persons agree to behind a 'veil of ignorance'?

The *veil of ignorance* is a hypothetical thought experiment. In this thought experiment, we assume that the persons involved, although they are rational and able to consider their own advantage, do not know who they are in the situation under consideration. The decision/action to which all the rational persons would agree behind the veil of ignorance is considered to be the just decision/action.

To illustrate this method, we reconsider helping or not in the case of an accident. We discussed this earlier as an example for the utilitarian method (see Section 2.2.1). We considered two alternatives for Jack when we discussed that case: to help or not to help the injured persons. However, there is another interesting option: the two injured persons could agree to reimburse Jack the $500 he loses when he misses his flight by helping them. Intuitively, one may surmise this is a fair solution. With the Rawlsian method, we can support this intuition by a systematical analysis and rational argument: Would the persons involved in the situation agree to this solution behind a veil of ignorance; that is, if they do not know who they are (whether they are helping or being rescued) in the situation? If the three are rational agents that consider their own interests, they would all like to be as well off as possible. They want to pay as little as possible if it should turn out that they are one of the injured persons. They also want to get paid as much as possible if it should turn out that they are the person rescuing the others. If they are one of the injured, they risk being worse off if they go above $500. If they are the rescuer and go below $500, they risk being worse off, as well. So, the equilibrium, in which they would secure their interests best, no matter who they are in the situation, is a payment of $500. As rational persons in this thought experiment, being put behind a veil of ignorance, all would all agree to this solution, which proves the solution is the fair solution.

2.4.3 Discourse ethics

Discourse ethics has its origin in the philosophy of the contemporary German philosopher Jürgen Habermas (b. 1929). Discourse ethics is to some extent based on aspects of Kantian thought. If we are all rational persons, we must be able to discuss and evaluate different alternatives of actions and be able to recognize what alternative can be supported by the strongest arguments or reasons. The alternative for which there are the strongest arguments, would then be the right way to act. In other words, if all persons involved would enter an open, deliberate discourse in which only the best argument matters, the argument that wins would determine the right way of action. Thus, in order to determine the ethically right action, we just need to ask which action could be best supported by reasons in an open, deliberate discourse (Habermas, 1991). This idea can be used to formulate the following method:

> **Discourse method:** Which decision would win by rational argument in an open, deliberate discourse?

One could also interpret the discourse method as a meta-level method, which considers ethical arguments based on the different methods we have discussed so far. The discourse method would then consider and compare various ethical perspectives and arguments (similar to the cases we analyzed in Section 2.3) and discuss which is the strongest argument (in case of disagreement or conflicting conclusions). The discourse method, thus, could integrate arguments based on principle, virtue, consequences, care, and so forth. Although there is not one specific criterion for deciding which argument is the strongest, one may consider some arguments a better fit for specific cases, or some being more reasonable given a concrete context and situation.

2.4.4 Overview: methods for ethical analysis and decision-making

UTILITARIAN METHOD:	Which action/decision maximizes the overall happiness of all affected?
CI METHOD A:	Which action/decision can reasonably be universalized?
CI METHOD B:	Which action/decision respects the dignity of all persons involved/affected?
VIRTUE METHOD A:	Which action is consistent with who someone is and wants to be, referring to reasonable concepts of excellence?
VIRTUE METHOD B:	Which action/decision best supports the development of personal or professional potential and ensures thriving of all affected?
CARE METHOD:	Is the action/decision taking place within a specific relational context? If so, which action/decision is in line with the moral specifics of the relationship(s) involved?
RAWLSIAN METHOD:	Which action/decision would rational persons agree to behind a 'veil of ignorance'?
DISCOURSE METHOD:	Which decision would win by rational argument in an open, deliberate discourse?

Figure 2.3 Overview: methods for ethical decision-making.

Note

1 These three ethical approaches are chosen because (i) they can be considered the main approaches in modern moral philosophy, (ii) they are commonly referred to in contemporary applied ethics and business ethics, and (iii) they represent three basic types of ethical argumentation: argument by consequence, by principle, and by character.

References

AICPA [American Institute for Certified Public Accountants]. (2018). *Code of Professional Conduct*. AICPA. Retrieved from http://pub.aicpa.org/codeofconduct/Ethics.aspx#.

Anscombe, G. E. M. (1958). Modern moral philosophy. *Philosophy*, 33, 1–19.

Aristotle. (2000). *Nicomachean Ethics* (R. Crisp, Trans.). Cambridge: Cambridge University Press.

Becker, C. (2016). Aristotelian virtue ethics and economic rationality. In M. White & J. Baker (Eds.), *Economics and the Virtues: Building a New Moral Foundation* (pp. 9–36). Oxford: Oxford University Press.

Becker, C. (2017). Virtue ethics enabling sustainability ethics for business. In A. J. Sison, G. R. Beabout, & I. Ferrero (Eds.), *Handbook of Virtue Ethics in Business and Management* (pp. 1383–1394). New York: Springer.

Bentham, J. (1988a). *A Fragment on Government*. Cambridge: Cambridge University Press. (Original work published 1776.)

Bentham, J. (1988b). *The Principles of Morals and Legislation*. Amherst, MA: Prometheus Books. (Original work published 1781.)

Bowie, N. E. (1999). *Business Ethics: A Kantian Perspective*. Malden, MA: Blackwell.

DFEI [Daniels Fund Ethics Initiative]. (2016). *Daniels Fund Ethics Initiative Principles*. DFEI. Retrieved from www.danielsfund.org

Habermas, J. (1991). *Erlaeuterungen zur Diskursethik*. Frankfurt: Suhrkamp.

Held, V. (2006). *The Ethics of Care: Personal, Political, and Global*. Oxford: Oxford University Press.

Hursthouse, R. (1999). *On Virtue Ethics*. Oxford: Oxford University Press.

Kant, I. (1998). *Groundwork of the Metaphysics of Morals* (M. Gregor, Trans.). Cambridge: Cambridge University Press. (Original work published 1785.)

MacIntyre, A. (1981). *After Virtue: A Study in Moral Theory*. Notre Dame, IN: University of Notre Dame Press.

Mill, J. S. (1998). *Utilitarianism* (R. Crisp, Ed.). Oxford: Oxford University Press. (Original work published 1871.)

Rawls, J. (1971). *A Theory of Justice*. Cambridge, MA: Harvard University Press.

Singer, P. (1975). *Animal Liberation*. New York: Random House.

Solomon, R. (1992). *Ethics and Excellence: Cooperation and Integrity in Business*. Oxford: Oxford University Press.

UN [United Nations]. (1948). *Universal Declaration of Human Rights*. New York: United Nations. Retrieved from www.un.org/en/documents/udhr

3 Conceptions of the economy and business
Ethical aspects

For analyzing ethical issues of business, it is crucial to have some understanding of the economic system and economic conceptions, as these are fundamental to business activities. In this chapter, we examine modern conceptions of the economy and business, the theoretical foundation of these conceptions in economic theory, and various norms and values attached to them. Theoretical conceptions do not exhibit every detail of business practice, as we will see in later chapters. However, the theoretical underpinnings of the modern economy come with some important ethical assumptions and implications that matter for business practice and are relevant to business ethics.

The aim of this chapter is to develop a basic understanding of the economy and business and the ethical dimensions of both. The modern economy and business are not ethically neutral fields but already contain, or relate to, various values and norms. It is crucial to recognize the ethics inherent to the economy and business to properly understand the subject matter of business ethics. Moreover, the economy is usually not considered to be an end in itself, as it serves further purposes, such as the wellbeing of individuals or the progress of society. As with any societal institution or human action, one can reasonably ask whether the existing economy is a good system and under what criteria an economy or business qualifies as being good. In other words, a crucial question business ethics must ask is: *How can business be understood and realized as a positive force in the world?* We will see in this chapter that there are traditional and new answers to this question, and that the normative criteria for business to qualify as a positive force are changing. Particularly, the economy of the 21st century faces new ethical challenges and, as a result, for business to be a positive force in the world, additional ethical requirements must be considered.

3.1 Basic definitions and ethical questions

We start by developing definitions for the economy and business. Some may think that the economy and business are basically about money. However, this is not a sufficiently distinctive criterion for a definition. First of all, there are many other activities that are also about money, such as robbery or the mafia, which we (hopefully) do not want to include in a definition of business or the economy. Second, money is, in the first instance, a means for the economy and business, a means to simplify economic transactions. Yet, money is neither the sole means nor the main purpose of the economy. When defining the economy, which is something rather general and abstract, one must consider its main purpose and mechanisms, and how the concept of the economy has been used and defined throughout the history and various systems of economic thought. The following definition is in accordance with most influential conceptions of the economy:

> Definition 3.1: The **economy** is the sum of all actors, actions, institutions, and organizations dealing with the production, distribution, consumption, and disposal of goods and services to satisfy human needs and desires in a rational way.

This definition includes various entities as parts of the economy: different actors, such as consumers, entrepreneurs, investors, and regulatory agencies; the various actions of those actors; institutions, such as markets, private property, and competition laws; and organizations, such as banks, companies, and corporations. The main purpose of the economy is the production, distribution, and consumption of goods and services to satisfy human wants and needs. Typically, the economy is about rational ways to do so. Most conceptions of the economy include conceptions of economic rationality, and modern economics emphasizes a specific conception of economic rationality, which is at the core of its theoretical framework. One may even say that modern economic theory primarily considers rational decision-making as its subject matter. Also, the central institution of the modern economy is the market, a sophisticated rational system that coordinates the interaction of various activities and actors in the economy.

Business has a central role in the economy as the main actor that provides goods and services. However, business clearly is a subset of the entire economy, as it is distinguished from other entities, such as consumers or regulatory agencies. The latter we usually do not call a business. Some may want to include profit motive in the definition of business: a business provides goods and services with the intent to make profits (although this may not be the only or even main intent or purpose). This is a possible definition, but it would exclude all types of non-profit organization. Whether to include or exclude the profit aspect in the definition depends on whether one prefers to call non-profit organizations 'businesses' and wants to have them included into the definition of business. The following definition of business reflects these considerations and provides both options:

> Definition 3.2: **Business** is an activity, actor, or organization that intentionally participates in the provision of goods and services in an economy to satisfy human needs and wants (with the purpose of making profits).

The economy is not an isolated system but operates in, and contributes to, a broader context. Determining what the economy or business is means understanding the economy in its broader context. Traditionally, its context encompasses a well-defined society and the individuals within it. Therefore, we need to understand what the function of the economy is in a society and for its individual members, and answer these questions: What is the meaning of the economy for the society? What is the meaning of the economy for individual life?

The function of the economy in its context has particularly been discussed with regard to normative and evaluative criteria. The basic ethical question is: *What is a good economy?* Traditionally, this question referred to individuals and society. In other words, it asks: How should the economy be organized and designed to serve individuals and society in an optimal way?

The above questions have been discussed throughout the history of economic thought and political philosophy, and different philosophical and political approaches give different answers to them. The answers to these questions depend on the understanding of the individual and society, and particularly on the criteria of 'good,' i.e., what is considered as being good for individuals and how a good society is defined. This has differed substantially among various approaches in history. Today, the dominant conception of the economy is the *capitalist market economy*. The capitalist market economy is a specific type of economy, and a modern answer to the question of what a good economy would be. The capitalist market economy is defined by specific characteristics:

> Definition 3.3: A **market economy** is an economy in which the production, distribution, consumption, and disposal of goods and services results from the interplay of supply and demand that meets on a market and defines the prices of goods and services. A market economy is called a **capitalist market economy** if the means for production are owned privately.

Proponents of the capitalist market economy have given strong ethical reasons for this type of economy and have argued that the capitalist market economy is good for individuals and for the entire society. For instance, the capitalist market economy is considered to support individual freedom by offering choices and opportunities, while at the same time contributing to the overall wellbeing of the society by promoting efficiency, innovation, and growth. In the remainder of this chapter, we will first explore in more detail some main arguments for the capitalist market economy starting with Adam Smith and neoclassical economics, before later discussing critical aspects and (ethical) limits of the capitalist market economy.

A critical aspect of the capitalist market economy, which we will discuss in more detail, is that the context it refers to – that is, individuals and society – has become too narrow for today's situation. We need to discuss a new and broader context and the function of the economy within the global community, nature, and future generations. In this broader context, new ethical questions arise: Is the capitalist market economy also good for nature, all people around the world, and future generations? What would a good economy be in this broader context? How can one define 'good' in this context? Can we expand traditional ethical criteria and requirements to this broader context or do we even need new criteria? We will discuss these questions in Sections 3.5 and 3.6.

3.2 Adam Smith: the economy as a system of natural freedom

We want to explore the main ethical arguments for the capitalist market economy. As a start, we go back to the beginnings of the modern concept of the market economy and some basic arguments supporting this type of economy. The work of Adam Smith (1723–1790) is often considered the beginning of modern economic thought and is a crucial foundation for the modern conception of the economy. Adam Smith was a moral philosopher, and his first major work was actually about ethics: *The Theory of Moral Sentiments* (2000a). However, his later book, *The Wealth of Nations* (Smith, 2000b), has become an important contribution to modern economic thought and has influenced the understanding of the economy up to today.

This section highlights some aspects of Adam Smith's economic thought. We focus on his conception of the economy, including some normative criteria for understanding the economy as a positive force for society. In particular, we review Smith's famous *invisible hand* argument for the free market economy being good for individuals and society. Although Smith did not really emphasize it or make it a main focus of his work, later on his concept of the *invisible hand* became fundamental to modern economic thought. The following two quotes illustrate Smith's concept of the economy, its underlying assumptions, and the function of the *invisible hand*.

The first quote shows Smith's view of how the economy actually works and what the main underlying mechanism and motivations of the individual actors in the economy are:

> *Give me that which I want, and you shall have this which you want is the meaning of every [bargain . . .]. It is not from the benevolence of the butcher, the brewer, or the baker, that we expect our dinner, but from their regard to their own interest. We address ourselves, not to their humanity but to their self-love, and never talk to them of our own necessities but of their advantages.*
>
> (Smith, 2000b, p. 15)

According to Smith, humans are dependent, rational beings. Humans need many things that they cannot all produce and provide by themselves, so they have to refer to others in order to satisfy their needs. As rational beings, humans refer to others in a specific way: they appeal to the self-interest (self-love) of others, knowing that this is the only way to make someone act and exchange things in the economy. In other words, in order to get something from someone else, one needs to offer something in exchange that the other person wants. One must address the other person's self-interest to agree to the deal. Generally, in the economy, one cannot expect that people will give one the things needed by mere benevolence (good will). Rather, the economy is driven by *self-interest* and everyone involved in the economy will only provide goods and services to others if it is in his or her self-interest to do so. The economy is not based on a simplistic form of self-interest, such as a mere self-centered egoism, but rather on a more enlightened form of self-interest; that is, self-interest that is able to consider and reflect on the self-interests of others. This description of the economy, as basically driven by the self-love of the actors, is a factual description by Smith of how the economy naturally works.

Even if we follow Smith in his factual analysis of the basic drivers of economic action, we still may wonder whether it is *good* that the economy works that way. Smith famously answered yes to this ethical question. His answer brings us to the core of the fascinating idea of the *invisible hand* and, subsequently, to the conception of systemic rationality in modern economic thought:

> *Every individual necessarily labors to render the annual revenue of the society as great as he can. He generally, indeed, neither intends to promote the public interest, nor knows how much he is promoting it. By [. . . engaging in economic activities], he intends only his own gain, and he is in this, as in many other cases, led by an invisible hand to promote an end which was no part of his intention. Nor is it always the worse for the society that it was no part of it. By pursuing his own interest, he frequently promotes that of the society more effectually than when he really intends to promote it.*
>
> (Smith, 2000b, p. 485)

Basically, Smith claims here that – in the context of a free market – self-love is a positive force, which ultimately benefits society as a whole. This is a crucial ethical re-evaluation of self-love. Traditionally, most philosophers had been rather skeptical about self-love as motivational force and considered self-love as dangerous for a community. Hobbes (2008) famously argued that the human being is mainly driven by self-love but concluded that this is very dangerous for societal interactions and inter-relations. Self-love, Hobbes thought, leads to a war of everyone against everyone else. He concluded that a society of individuals needs a strong government that regulates and controls the various self-interests, and that the individuals understand this and agree to such government (Hobbes, 2008). Smith, in contrast, argues that, at least in the context of a market economy, self-love is not a destructive but rather a positive force. The market coordinates all self-interests in a way so that everyone, and the society as a whole, is better off.

The fascinating aspect here is that no one in the economy actually is actively considering or intending to promote the public interest – everyone just focuses on her own self-interest. However, by doing so, everyone automatically serves the public welfare. Smith calls the mechanism that makes this happen the invisible hand. The invisible hand originally refers to the hand of God. Smith simply wants to state that there is a natural order in societal interactions the same way there is an order in nature, such as the laws of physics. Smith, as did many in his times, thought that there are laws of nature because God made nature in an orderly way (and endowed humans with reason, so that they can understand and manage nature). Smith assumed then that societal interactions, particularly economic actions, follow similar systematic laws which we can recognize and study.

Why is everyone better off in a system of interactions based on mere self-interests? In the simple case of a trade between two persons, it seems to be obvious: if two people meet to negotiate a deal, for instance, about exchanging things they own, and deliberately agree to a deal, both seem to be better off (or at least not worse off). Otherwise, they would not have both agreed but walked away from the deal. They both win or, in modern economic terms, there is some *Pareto-improvement* (see Section 3.3). In other words, in deliberate economic transactions within a free market economy, there are not winners and losers, as one may think, but rather only winners – at least in theory. We can consider self-interested interactions also from another perspective. If everyone, in order to satisfy her own interests, produces and provides goods or services for others, to be able to offer something so that she gets in exchange what she wants, others, and ultimately the entire society, benefit. All kinds of goods and services are offered, and all needs and wants will be addressed. In addition, Smith argues that everyone has an incentive to specialize and become better and more efficient at producing and offering something, because the more one can offer, the more one can get. As a result, there will be an increasing division of labor and specialization, and the entire economy and society will benefit from efficiency gains.

3.3 Modern economics: rational choice and systemic interaction

Modern economics provides theories and methods that help systematically analyze and explain the economy. Economics basically understands economic actions as results of rational decision-making of individual actors and analyzes rational choices and the results of interactions of rational agents.

In this section, we highlight a fundamental result of economic theory, more specifically, of *General Equilibrium Theory*, which is a main theoretical foundation of modern economics. This result is formulated in the *First Theorem of Welfare Economics*. The theorem states that, if all individuals maximize their own utility functions and all firms their own profits, a market equilibrium is Pareto-efficient, given a number of assumptions (Mas-Colell et al., 1995, p. 359; Arrow, 1951; Debreu, 1959). To some extent this simply means that, if all actors in the market focus on their own self-interest, the outcome is optimal for society. Optimal is here specifically defined as *Pareto-efficient*. An allocation is Pareto-efficient if it is not possible to make anyone better off without making someone else worse off. This implies nothing is wasted and all resources have been used efficiently.

The First Theorem of Welfare Economics can be interpreted as a variation of Adam Smith's invisible-hand explanation formulated within the more precise mathematical framework of General Equilibrium Theory. Similar to Smith, the theorem says that it is good overall for society if everyone acts self-interested in the economy. It just specifies 'good' by 'Pareto-efficient'. The main economic argument for a market economy, thus, is an efficiency argument: a market economy is good because it is efficient. However, one may doubt that efficiency is the only relevant criterion to define a good economy. There might be other criteria, such as justice, contribution to human welfare and development, respect to non-human nature, impact to future generations, and so on (see Sections 3.4–3.6).

Even if we only consider the efficiency argument of modern economics, there are several issues and limitations. The concept of the market in modern economics is a theoretical concept, which is based on several rather strict assumptions about human behavior and market properties. Any practical implementation of the idea of efficient markets requires well-defined rules and regulations; for instance, rules against cartels and monopolies (competition laws), and also the correction of various market failures. Letting self-interested economic actors interact without any rules and regulations would never be efficient.

Economics has been well aware of the fact that there can be many situations in which the market does not work properly and has studied various market failures in detail. *Market failures* are situations that show some or all characteristics of economic interactions (of a market), but do not produce the result of perfect markets; that is, Pareto-efficiency (see, e.g., Mas-Colell et al., 1995, pp. 350–382). These situations usually require some regulation or intervention which cures the market failure and re-establishes a perfect market that is efficient. To illustrate the concept of market failures, I will give two typical examples below: *public goods* and *external effects*.

3.3.1 Public goods

Not all goods can be provided by the market mechanism at the optimal level. Public goods are a prominent example. Public goods are goods which have two specific characteristics: (i) it is difficult or impossible to exclude people from using them, and (ii) one person using them does not reduce their availability to other persons; that is, several persons can use the public good and benefit from it. Typical examples are national defense, societal benefits from research, national highway systems, and environmental goods, such as the atmosphere or oceans. For instance, it is difficult to exclude anyone from the benefits of national defense. If the country is defended, every member of society is defended. Similarly, it would be rather difficult to exclude some individuals from using the public road system, and my use of the public road system does not significantly reduce the ability of others to use the roads. The two characteristics discussed above obviously distinguish public goods from typical (private) goods which we usually deal with in the economy. Consider for instance a cake. The cake is not a public good, but a private one. If I own the cake, I can control and decide who eats it, and I can easily exclude others from eating it. Also, if I eat the cake no one else will be able to eat it.

One problem with public goods is that, although many people have preferences for them, most would not contribute to them in a market context. Rather they would hope that others will pay for them, and that they still can use the public good as a free-rider. For instance, if we would try to establish funding for national defense based on individual preferences and willingness to pay, most people would probably deny or hide their preference for defense and would not want to pay, although they benefit from national defense. Everyone would just hope that others pay for that good and that one can benefit for free. Because of this free-rider effect, the market, based on individual self-interests and motivations to maximize one's own utility and profits, provides fewer public goods than the overall amount that is desired in a society. The market would also be inefficient in providing a national road system. Private companies would build some toll roads and some people would pay for them, but this would typically only work for a very limited set of connections between larger cities, where there is enough traffic for it to be profitable. No private company would build smaller roads connecting rural areas due to lack of return of investment, and we would never get the sophisticated network of roads that we use and want to have.

In summary, in the case of public goods, the market results in a sub-optimal allocation due to wrong price-signals that don't reflect actual preferences, and we get an underinvestment in those goods and have fewer of them than people actually prefer. Optimal allocation of public goods cannot be achieved by the market but requires some intervention, for instance by imposing taxes to finance public goods. In the case of public goods, there is, thus, an economic argument for taxation: to cure a market failure and ensure optimal allocation.

3.3.2 External effects

An external effect is an effect on the utility or profit of an economic actor that is not internal to the market mechanism. There is no price or market that would reflect that effect. External effects are typically caused by undefined property rights. A classic example is the external effect a company A, which is located upstream on a river, causes to another company B, which is located downstream. Assume both companies use the water of the river for their business operations, the water of the river is not owned by anyone, and there are no laws or regulations for the use or pollution of the water. The upstream company A uses the river simply to dump pollutants (the river is a free dump for the company, and so they can get rid of their waste at no cost). However, the downstream company B uses the water as an input for its business, as it is a fish farm or fishery. If company A pollutes the water, this results in an external effect to company B. Company A impacts the profits of company B, and the market mechanism does not reflect that impact because there is no price for using the water as a dump. The more company A pollutes the river, the less fish company B may be able to produce. In an extreme scenario, company B could completely go out of business if company A's pollution kills all fish in the river.

Why is this situation economically inefficient? Basically, the situation is inefficient because the overall value produced by both companies is sub-optimal. This is easy to see if we imagine that the two companies have the same owner. In this case, the owner would of course maximize the overall profits of both companies together. She would invest in the reduction of pollution in factory A, for instance, in a filter system, as long as this makes business sense; that is, as long as $1 of additional investment in the filter system would result in more than $1 of additional gain from company A and B together. The optimal investment in pollution reduction is exactly the amount that maximizes the overall profits from both firms together. Can a similar overall, economically better result also be achieved if the companies are owned by different persons? One way to ensure this is by government intervention, for instance, by introducing regulation or a price (a tax) for using the water as a dump.

In more general terms, it is obvious that the unregulated use of a river (the environment) as a dump causes external effects to numerous businesses or persons that also want to use the river (the environment) and is sub-optimal because it reduces the overall economic output. In an extreme case, one single company with small revenue could ruin large businesses all the way downstream by poisoning the river and, with this, significantly harm the economic development of the society. This is why environmental regulation actually can be economically important and support efficiency and economic growth.

The example of external effects also demonstrates that the business perspective and the economic perspective are different. The business perspective focuses on the operations and profit maximization of a given company, whereas the economic perspective focuses on the overall output and efficiency of an entire economy. As discussed above, both can go well together in an ideal market economy, but may also not go well together, as in the case of market failures.

3.4 The ethical underpinning of capitalism

The capitalist market economy is not a given fact but a purposely human-made system. We have a capitalist market economy because historically there have been good reasons for it. Following Adam Smith and others, the capitalist market economy has been perceived as a good economic system. There are underlying evaluations that support the capitalist market economy, some of which are linked to fundamental ethical values and arguments. We have already identified some traditional arguments in the context of economic thought in Sections 3.2 and 3.3. The following list adds some further arguments and provides an encompassing set of classical reasons supporting capitalism. Many of these reasons refer to ethical values and arguments, and thus the list can be understood as encompassing the *ethical underpinning of capitalism.*

3.4.1 Efficiency

As already discussed in Section 3.3, the main theoretical economic argument for markets is an efficiency argument. Markets are good because they are efficient – they result in an efficient allocation. Economists usually argue for market solutions based on efficiency reasons. In the case of market failures, economists would argue for (re-)establishing perfect markets, e.g., by proper government intervention. However, efficiency arguments tacitly assume that efficiency is something good and, often, that efficiency is a major or even ultimate good. It is also frequently assumed that efficiency is a good that is neutral to other ethical goods and values. In this case, striving for efficiency would not impact the establishment of ethical values, and one could consider ethical aspects separately from efficiency aspects. However, it is not self-evident that efficiency is in all cases and situations something good and that there aren't other values which are more important and may conflict with efficiency. For instance, the US and many other countries have minimum wage laws. These laws infringe on a free determination of market prices for labor and generally result in inefficiency. However, in the case of minimum wage laws, ethical reasons, such as protecting vulnerable groups and the ability to maintain oneself by one's work, are considered more important than efficiency.

3.4.2 Competition

A typical element of a capitalist market economy is competition. Competition can be inspiring and motivating but also be hard, stressful, and burdensome. So, is competition good? There is a basic economic argument for competition: it supports efficiency, and if we think efficiency is good, we should also support the idea of competition. A lack of competition can result in inefficiency. For instance, a monopoly typically results in fewer goods for a higher price compared to a competitive situation. However, competition also resonates with an ethical value that many people share: the idea that the best should win. Ideally, in a competitive market economy the person that works hardest or has the smartest ideas is supposed to win. That person will get rewarded and make the most money.

There are good economic and value-based arguments for competition. It is important to notice, however, that the competitive element has to be established and preserved in a market economy by laws and regulations. For rational economic actors, it would in some situations be more profitable to circumvent competition, for instance, by creating monopolies or by fixing prices. To have a competitive capitalist market economy, one needs laws that prohibit the undermining of competition and instead force all economic actors to engage in fair competition. Capitalist countries typically have such laws in place. In the US, a fundamental law regulating competition is the Sherman Antitrust Act. Many people may believe that a free market economy would naturally exist and that any government regulation contradicts a free market economy. However, this is not the case. Without any rules and regulations, we would never have a free market economy as understood by modern economic thought, but rather an anarchic economy, which would be anything else but efficient. A competitive capitalist market economy is a human-made construct that has to be carefully designed and maintained by a framework of well-calibrated rules and regulations, such as anti-trust laws, patent laws, and so on.

3.4.3 Optimal balance and satisfaction of individual self-interests

Another economic argument for the capitalist market economy refers to the idea that the market is a perfect mechanism for indicating scarcities and coordinating production and distribution in an optimal way. A market economy has the potential to coordinate and satisfy manifold needs, wants, and abilities within diverse and complex societies. Everyone can bring their individual interests, preferences, and skills, and negotiate those things with the interests, preferences, and skills of others. The result is many deliberate exchanges among all those individuals in a market economy. A fascinating aspect of such market interaction is that, theoretically, there are no losers in the process. Rather, everybody wins, as already discussed following Adam Smith (see Section 3.2): if two people negotiate a trade and both are fully informed and deliberately agree to a deal, one can reasonably assume that they are both better off by that deal. Otherwise, one of them would have just walked away. For instance, if you apply for a job – that is, you offer your skills to an employer – a contract would only be signed by both you and the employer if you feel the job is good for you, and the employer thinks she benefits from hiring you. So, you both feel that you are better off by signing the contract. Theoretically, this is the case for every deal in the entire market economy. Thus, by the process of balancing interests and preferences, everyone benefits in a market economy.

3.4.4 Support of individual freedom and equal opportunities

The ideal of the capitalist market economy has been closely linked to the ethical principles of freedom and equality, which are fundamental values for the US as well as other societies. The basic argument here is that the market economy supports individual freedom and equal opportunities. The market economy is considered to be a sphere of individual freedom in so far as it provides the freedom to choose what business or profession one wants to pursue, what goods and services one wants to purchase, and so on. The link between the capitalist market economy and individual freedom has particularly been emphasized by crucial modern proponents of capitalism, such as F. A. Hayek (1899–1992) and Milton Friedman (1912–2006). Whereas government intervention and ruling can be perceived as coercive, because everyone must follow them, the market allows for deliberate individual decisions and choices and is, by this, providing a larger degree of individual freedom (Hayek, 2007; Friedman, 2002). The market economy is also thought to support equality in the sense of equal opportunities. In theory, everyone is equal in having the same right and opportunity to start any business she wants and to pursue any career she wants to pursue. Together with the idea of fair competition, this has formed the famous American Dream: everyone can make it if she works hard enough and has smart ideas.

In reality, though, it is not the case that everyone has equal opportunities. In the US, and many other capitalist societies, there are many forms of discrimination and hidden barriers that significantly disadvantage various groups; for instance, minorities, women, or people with disabilities (see also Section 4.5.1).

3.4.5 Promotion of overall societal welfare

One important feature of a capitalist market economy is its contribution to the overall wellbeing of society. As already stated by Adam Smith with his invisible hand concept, in a capitalist market economy, everyone can enjoy the freedom to pursue and optimally satisfy their own interests and, by this, the society as a whole will automatically benefit as well. In addition to the efficiency of markets discussed above, proponents of the capitalist market economy expect some further benefits for the society: economic growth, innovation, and efficiency gains. The main drivers for these results are unlimited self-interests (preferences) and competition. Self-interest, the strive for satisfying as many preferences as possible and making as much profit as possible, will lead people to produce more, specialize more, and find innovative ways to produce more. Competition will push people to work harder and endeavor to provide better and more innovative products and services, or to provide the same good or service more efficiently and for a better price. All of this ideally will result in economic growth, efficiency gains, and innovations.

Again, the underlying assumption here is that all of these results (and their drivers) are actually good for society. This is not self-evident, though. For instance, in recent decades, it has been increasingly questioned that economic growth is good in itself, and new concepts such as *sustainability* or the *triple bottom line* (that is, economic, social, and environmental performance) imply that there is more to defining a good business, a good economy, or a good society than profit maximization and economic growth. Also, the traditional concept of the capitalist market economy has focused on the wellbeing of individuals and societies, but has never explicitly considered the wellbeing of nature, future generations, and vulnerable groups around the world, all of which have become crucial issues today. We will discuss such criticism and the resulting changes in normative expectations toward modern business and the economy in more detail in Sections 3.5 and 3.6.

3.5 Criticism of capitalism

The capitalist market economy has been criticized since it emerged, particularly from various ethical perspectives. In this section, we will discuss different types of criticism of modern capitalism. It is crucial for business ethics to understand both the ethical underpinnings of the capitalist market economy and its limits and ethically critical aspects. An encompassing understanding will allow for a more detailed discussion about how business can be understood and practiced as a positive force in the world, particularly in the context of the 21st century economy. We will distinguish between the following three types of ethical criticism: (i) traditional criticism, (ii) fundamental criticism, and (iii) new criticism.

3.5.1 Traditional criticism

Traditional criticism questions the claims about the benefits of the capitalist market economy that have been made by proponents of this type of economy (see Section 3.4). In other words, traditional criticism doubts that the very promises of the benefits of a free capitalist market economy are true, can be realized, or are based on reasonable assumptions. This type of criticism is as old as the idea of capitalism. In the following, I provide a few examples of prominent critics and critique which addresses ethical aspects and has been relevant up to today.

Henry David Thoreau: the market is not a sphere of individual freedom

Henry David Thoreau (1817–1862) is a prominent figure in the history of American thought and a strong advocate for individual freedom and autonomy. However, in contrast to many proponents of individual freedom, Thoreau is an explicit critic of the market economy (Becker, 2008). He disagrees with the idea that the market economy is a sphere of individual freedom. For Thoreau, the economy is instead a sphere of dependency, which substantially undermines individual freedom and autonomy. In the market economy, we tend to focus more and more on the demands and values of others (e.g., employers or customers) in order to get a job or produce something we can sell. Consequently, the values and wishes of others matter more for what we will do and who we will become than our own values and goals. In other words, the result of a market economy is that we are not truly self-reliant and independent, and do not focus on what we think is good, but rather we listen mostly to others and their wishes. Thoreau thinks that this makes us fundamentally unfree, as we are not truly ourselves anymore. For instance, we may follow the expectations employers have regarding our resumé, and volunteer, serve in leadership roles, learn languages, and so on, not because it is what we really want and consider as good, but because we want to please a potential employer. Or, we may study and learn certain fields because we think they are in demand on the job market, but not because we like them and think they are important (Thoreau, 2008; Becker, 2008).

Thoreau's criticism might still resonate today: does the economy really constitute a sphere of freedom? Many people might experience the economy as a necessity and a sphere of coercion, where they have to do a job and other things to make a living. Some may even think that we have all become slaves of the economic system and of the requirements that this system poses on us.

Karl Marx: the market is a sphere of asymmetry in power and wealth

Karl Marx (1818–1883) is another very prominent critic of the capitalist market economy. He questions, among many other aspects, three positive claims about the capitalist market economy: (i) that it is a sphere of freedom where everyone can actually make fully deliberate decisions, (ii) that everyone has the same opportunities to bring and realize their self-interest, and (iii) that the entire society benefits as a whole. Marx claims that there is a significant power asymmetry between workers and capitalists that hinders the large class of workers from bringing and realizing their interests in the same way that the capitalists can do. Marx considers the workers as being fundamentally dependent, unfree, and subject to the power of the capitalists. Because of this, the workers actually cannot make fully deliberate decisions and cannot choose deals that really would make them better off. Further, Marx claims that it is not the entire society that benefits from the capitalist market economy, but rather just one small group: the class of capitalists (Marx, 1990; Marx & Engels, 1998).

Increasing inequality of wealth and income distribution

Equal opportunity does not mean and usually does not result in equal distribution of income and wealth. In a capitalist market economy, we expect, to some extent, an unequal distribution of wealth and income: those who work harder or have the smarter ideas are supposed to outcompete others, earn more, and accumulate more wealth. As discussed in Section 3.4.2, this can be considered as fair. If everyone would get the same income, no matter how much one worked or regardless of the quality of work, this would not only raise questions about fairness but also implement problematic incentives in the economy: harder or better work, smarter ideas, and higher creativity would not pay, and consequently people might not see any reasons to challenge themselves. This would take away an important driver of innovation and economic growth. One could, however, argue against this position that the strongest driver of success and achievement is internal motivation and not external drivers like money. Many of the greatest achievements in human history have not been a result of expected gains or wealth but were driven by the curiosity and ingenuity of persons who just wanted to achieve something, in spite of any potential financial gain.

However, the capitalist market economy seems to systematically result in ever-increasing inequality of income and wealth distribution (Piketty, 2014) and, with this, in an increasing gap between the rich and the rest of society. This effect has become an important topic of public and political discussions. The issue criticized in these discussions is that the inequality of wealth and income is becoming too extreme and increases beyond any reasonable measure. For instance, the top 0.1% in the US today possess more than 22% of the total wealth, up from 7% in the 1970s (Saez & Zucman, 2016). Others claim that today the 62 richest people in the world own as much wealth as the bottom half of humanity – 3.6 billion people (Oxfam, 2016). Many criticize the current wealth distribution and development as unfair and economically unhealthy. The judgment of unfairness is based on two concerns. First, the concern that there is no sensible correlation anymore between harder work and smarter ideas on the one hand, and higher income and wealth on the other. Second, there is doubt that everyone actually has the same opportunities. Rather some might have significantly more opportunities than others due to wealth and privileges. Extreme inequality in income and wealth can also cause economic problems, for instance, due to too much market power of a small group or overall lack of demand in society. It is easy to see the economic issues if we compare the extreme of everyone getting and having the same (that is, no inequality at all) with another extreme: one person getting and having everything, and everyone else in the society/economy getting and having nothing, or say, only the bare means for survival. It is rather obvious, that in such situations neither the economy nor society can flourish.

Assumptions underlying modern economic thought

Modern economic thought – its concepts, and results regarding the capitalist market economy – is based on some fundamental assumptions about human beings, decision-making, and economic interactions. The economic actor is understood as a self-interested rational utility-maximizer, and this drives her actions and interactions with others. However, one might doubt that this is an accurate or complete description of the human being and economic actor. There is a long tradition of criticism of the economic model, and a large body of literature referring to many limitations and flaws of the conception of the economic actor. I will highlight two aspects here that are of particular relevance in the context of this book.

First, human beings are driven by many motivations beyond mere self-interest. Many philosophers assumed that there is more than one fundamental driver that motivates humans beyond mere self-interest, and this has been confirmed by empirical research, specifically by psychological research (see, e.g., Becker, 2006; van Staveren, 2001, pp. 1–24). Of course, self-interest is an important driver of human actions. Many people will very often make decisions based on the question: What is best for me? However, as discussed in Chapter 2, humans are also ethical beings, and another driver that often guides decisions and actions is the question: What is the right thing to do? Another fundamental driver is, for instance, empathy for other beings (Smith, 2000a; Rousseau, 1995), which is demonstrated by people helping others in need or rescuing animals.

Second, the rationality of the economic actor is a pretty narrow definition of rationality. Of course, it can be called 'rational' if someone considers and consistently orders all of her preferences, and then calculates the optimal use of her means to optimally satisfy her preferences (maximizes her utility) as economics assumes. However, there are other types of rationality in play when humans make decisions. In business contexts, individuals, managers, and leaders often do not do a full optimization calculation, but rather base their decisions on heuristics, practical wisdom, or principles. This has been well studied in behavioral economics and other fields (Simon, 1947; Kahneman & Tverski, 2000; Gigerenzer & Selten, 2001; Camerer et al., 2003). People also make business decisions and other decisions based on ethical considerations, which can be based on rational analysis and reasoning, as we have demonstrated throughout Chapter 2. A decision based on a utilitarian, Rawlsian, or Kantian reflection can also be called a rational decision, just as any decision based on utility maximization.

3.5.2 Fundamental ethical principles and criticism

It is one thing to criticize the capitalist market economy, arguing that it does not, or cannot, fulfill some of its promises, that it does not, or cannot, provide the benefits it claims to deliver. One would develop another, more fundamental critical perspective when questioning whether the capitalist market economy contradicts or violates crucial ethical values and principles. Criticism of modern capitalism can also be based on one such more fundamental ethical perspective.

Any economic or business practice, in order to qualify as good or positive force, needs to respect fundamental ethical principles. Minimally, they must not violate fundamental ethical principles, and ideally support them. Proponents of the capitalist market economy usually assume that capitalism supports some ethical principles (see Section 3.4) and is at least neutral to all other fundamental ethical principles and values. If it would turn out that the economy or some business practice contradicts or violates fundamental ethical principles, it is hard to see how such an economic system or business practice could continue over time. Such an economic system may not get the support of the people acting in it or being affected by it, and sufficient support is the ultimate precondition of any social system to continue and remain stable.

What are the fundamental ethical principles that the economy needs to respect? We can refer to the ethical theories discussed in Section 2.2 to derive some fundamental principles that a good economic system would need to uphold.

Utilitarianism implies that a good economy and good business practice should increase overall happiness of all affected or involved (compared to feasible alternatives). If the theory of capitalism discussed above is right, if everybody is better off by market transaction and society benefits from economic growth, innovation, and efficiency gains, there would be no conflict with the utilitarian principle: the capitalist market economy would indeed increase overall happiness. However, in practice, people have increasingly felt left behind in today's economic system and, particularly, by globalization. If the critics are right, and only a few actually win (the capitalists or, in more recent terms, the 1%), and many lose, and more harm is done overall than good (as in the recent financial crisis), then the actual capitalist market economy becomes ethically questionable from a utilitarian point of view.

Kant's categorical imperative (CI) implies that one requirement for business being a positive force in the world would be that people are not being treated as mere means but are also considered as ends in themselves. In other words, a good economy should respect the dignity of all involved. One might doubt that today's economy is fully in line with this ethical principle. Many people in today's global economy are more or the less treated as mere means. We see many instances of exploitation in global supply chains, and in many jobs people may not be respected as ends in themselves but merely seen as means to achieve business purposes.

Virtue ethics asks business to provide a context for human flourishing or, at least, not to obstruct human flourishing. A good economy should enable all actors involved or affected by economic activities to thrive. Ideally, any job should provide opportunities for developing individual potential, for developing oneself professionally and personally, and for becoming a better professional and person. This is not always the case, though, and there are many jobs and situations in which a person cannot develop any potential and, in some cases, is even burned out. Additionally, in global supply chains, people and communities often do not really benefit in a more encompassing sense by participating in the global economy. They cannot develop their communities, improve their situations, and work toward a better future for themselves and their children.

In an extended perspective, one would ideally expect that a good economy supports the overall potential for human flourishing around the world. The economy should inspire creativity and exchange among people and cultures, and respect and preserve creative forces in nature and humans. One may doubt that the current economic system is doing so. The current economy has a tendency to suppress creativity and positive exchange among cultures, as well as a tendency to destroy creative potentials of humans and nature.

3.5.3 New criticism

New criticism refers to the new characteristics and corresponding new ethical challenges of the 21st century economy. It criticizes the established capitalist market economy on the grounds that it is unable to successfully meet these new ethical challenges (see Figure 3.1).

Today's economy has evolved and changed significantly from when the concept of the capitalist market economy was first developed. It is not the same economy as that which existed during Adam Smith's time or, say, the economy of the 1960s. Today's economy is a largely global, highly complex, and dynamic system, whose overall dimensions are many times bigger than something like the 1960s' economy. Measured in terms of gross domestic product (GDP), the world economy today is more than 30 times bigger than the economy of the 1960s. The world GDP of the 1960s was less than $2 trillion. Today it is over $70 trillion (World Bank, 2016).

Every business today is part of the complex global economic system, even a small or medium-sized business. Every business is subject to global supply and demand and global competition. For instance, many small businesses operate machines or cars with gasoline, and the price of gasoline depends on global supply and demand

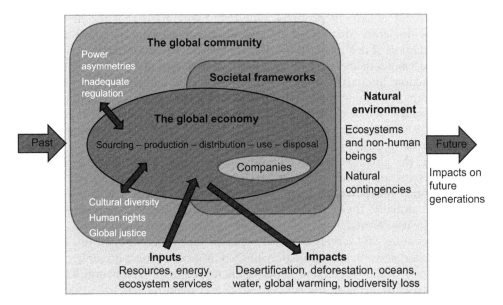

Figure 3.1 Characteristics and ethical challenges of the 21st century economy.

as well as global economic developments. Businesses can easily face new competitors from other parts of the world. Global competition and marketing have become much simpler through the global reach of the Internet. Also, the production of many consumption goods is globally outsourced today, and complex global supply chains are the norm.

Since business is becoming more and more global, one needs to consider every company as part of the global economy and also as part of a global community. Consequently, businesses face certain ethical challenges in the global context that would not be as relevant or relevant at all within a single, well-defined society. In the global context, businesses do not operate in a single and well-defined legal and regulatory system, but globally face more than a hundred different legal systems, as well as a lack of law and law enforcement in some parts of the world. This situation raises ethical questions. For instance, if there is no law or lack of law enforcement, what acts are permissible or ethically right? Likewise, what if the law is laxer than US law? Is a business then permitted to do environmental harm, or would it be acceptable to employ children or utilize slavery if some places would allow this? (See also Chapter 6.)

Another ethical issue in the global economic context involves power asymmetries. The basic idea of market capitalism is that all actors can bring in their self-interests, and these will balance out to the benefit of everyone. However, if differences in abilities and power are extreme, this mechanism does not work properly. Consider the following example of two people who meet in a desert. One person has 2 liters of water, the other person has none and is close to dying of thirst. In this situation, the first person could probably ask any price for a liter of water, and the second would pay all the money he owns. Technically, one may say that both persons are better off if they agree to exchange one liter of water for, say, $1 million: it looks like a

Pareto-improvement. However, this economic evaluation does not seem to fully fit the situation and describe it properly. One may easily argue that the first person exploited the desperate situation of the second, and that this is not at all a normal economic situation of deliberate choice and agreement. The power asymmetry in this situation undermines deliberate economic decision-making and provokes exploitation and unfair action. Similarly, we face large differences in abilities and power in the global economy, and these can easily result in abuses of power and exploitation of vulnerable groups. We face, therefore, the ethical question of what global economic interactions can be considered mutually beneficial, and what actions should be considered an abuse of power and exploitation (see Chapter 6).

Moreover, the global economy operates within a global environment that ultimately poses certain systemic constraints on the overall economic activity. The global economic system has reached a size and power that significantly impacts the environment globally (IPCC, 2014; UNEP, 2012; MEA, 2005). Economic activities depend on the use of energy and resources, many of which are limited. For instance, the world economy still largely depends on fossil fuels, such as coal, oil, and gas, which are non-renewable and ultimately limited. Many resources are only available in certain areas of the world, and sourcing them causes environmental harm. For instance, increasing demand for rubber, soya, and palm oil has led to deforestation and increasing monoculture plantations. At the same time, economic activities result in emissions and waste that also cause harm to the environment. A prominent example are CO_2 emissions that contribute to climate change. Environmental effects of economic activities encompass biodiversity loss, water scarcity, soil degradation, desertification, deforestation, and poor air and water quality, among many other effects. The impacts of today's overall global economic activities on the environment, and the expected future growth of the economy and world population, raise new and serious ethical and economic concerns. For instance, do we have a responsibility or obligation to care about nature? Does nature or non-human life have a value in itself that needs to be respected? What are the obligations of business in this context? Who has to bear the burden of environmental harm, and who benefits in a global context (environmental justice)? Environmental concerns are not merely about the wellbeing of the environment, but often come with economic concerns. Economically, environmental degradation and depletion of resources can seriously impact our and future generations' ability for economic activities as well as future economic growth.

Finally, the size and overall negative (environmental) side effects of today's economy raise serious questions about the impacts of our economic actions on future generations. The global economic system has reached a size and power that can significantly impact the ability of future generations to prosper economically and live well. This raises new ethical questions about our responsibilities and moral obligations toward future generations (even beyond the generation of our children and grandchildren). For instance, what responsibilities do we have to the future, and what responsibility does business have in particular? These are crucial ethical questions in the context of the 21st century economy.

Because of the globality, complexity, growing size, and growing environmental, global, and future impacts of the economy, the traditional question of what a good economy is needs to be reconsidered in broader terms today (see Figure 3.2). The

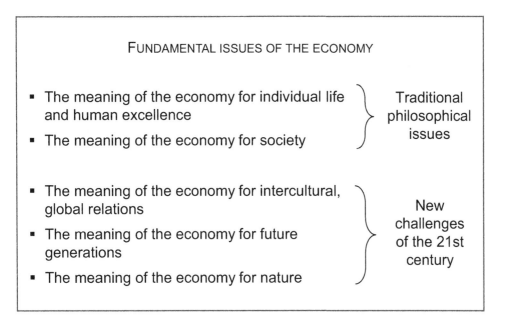

FUNDAMENTAL ISSUES OF THE ECONOMY

- The meaning of the economy for individual life and human excellence
- The meaning of the economy for society

Traditional philosophical issues

- The meaning of the economy for intercultural, global relations
- The meaning of the economy for future generations
- The meaning of the economy for nature

New challenges of the 21st century

Figure 3.2 Traditional and new ethical questions about the economy.

question is not just about a good economy for current individuals and the society anymore, as it was for Adam Smith and neoclassical economics. Rather, today we need to ask additional questions of what a good economy is for all people around the world, nature, and future generations. The traditional questions are still relevant, but we need to understand that additionally we face new ethical challenges regarding the future of the economy and business.

3.6 Shifting norms: ethics in and for the economy of the 21st century

The results of our analysis in Section 3.5.3 indicate that the criteria by which business qualifies as a positive force in the world have become more demanding. To be a positive force in the world, business needs (in some sense) to be good for individuals and society, but additionally it needs to be good for people around the world, future generations, and nature (see Figure 3.3). The capitalist market economy entailed a promise to be good for individuals and society in a certain way. However, the capitalist market economy never promised to be good for nature, and only to a limited extent to be good for future generations. The new ethical criteria are a challenge to the existing dominant model of the capitalist market economy. Many critics see substantial flaws in this type of the economy when it comes to its impact on the environment, long-term sustainability, and global impacts. Because of the new challenges of the 21st century and additional normative requirements for a future economy, we need to carefully examine how one can guarantee that the economic system fulfills these criteria and how in the future business can be a positive force in the world in a more encompassing sense.

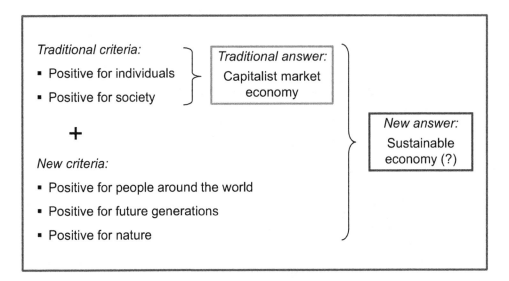

Figure 3.3 Traditional and new criteria for business being a positive force.

To realize business as a positive force in the world today and in the future will be more demanding. The economic system cannot fully guarantee that this happens simply by an invisible-hand mechanism. There are two basic ways to address new challenges and normative requirements and to cure potential negative side effects of modern business: (i) regulation and (ii) self-regulation. The more traditional approach is regulation, i.e., more laws and rules for business. This approach is neither feasible for addressing the new challenges of the economy, nor is it preferable. A global and quickly changing economic system that runs through many nations and cultures can only to a limited extent be governed by rules and regulations. We don't have (and probably don't want) a global government, and international negotiations are difficult, and can only provide basic regulatory frameworks for the global economy.

The alternative approach is self-regulation. However, the global economy has become too complex and dynamic for any traditional conceptions of market self-regulation in the sense of automatic invisible-hand processes. As discussed above, the amount of external effects, environmental impacts, long-term side effects, and power asymmetries in the global economic system limits the self-regulatory power of markets. Instead, there is a need for active internal ethical guidance of business activities. All actors in the economic system need to assume more responsibility for their own activities to guarantee that business will be a positive force in the world. Many tools that we will discuss in the remainder of this book are designed to realize such internal ethical guidance of business practice. Corporate responsibility, ethics and compliance programs, professional ethics, and other business ethics instruments are necessary from an ethical perspective to ensure that business will be a positive force in the future. From a business perspective, those instruments are at the same time crucial for future business success, as they manage risks and strategically position business toward the new challenges of the 21st century. Business ethics has indeed become a crucial instrument to navigate modern organizations through the increasingly challenging, complex, and dynamic global context of the 21st century economy.

One particular strength of the market economy is its diversity and dynamics. There is not one type or realization of a capitalist market economy or one way to do business. In practice, there is a large range of very different business models, some of which adhere more to the traditional, established market paradigm, and others which go in new ways and address the new ethical and economic challenges of the future. If the above analysis is correct, that those challenges will increasingly shape the future economy, we can expect those firms that actively recognize and address them to be more successful in the future.

Recent developments in business practice indicate that there are shifting norms in today's business world, which reflect the larger ethical challenges of the economy discussed above. For instance, corporate responsibility has become an established risk-management and strategic-management tool; we see a quickly growing number of successful and competitive social entrepreneurships, purpose-driven businesses, and sustainable businesses; and we even see changes to the legal framework for business that reflect the shifting values of business practice, such as recent legislation around benefit corporations (see Chapter 7). All these shifts indicate a normative change in the business world toward more responsibility for the environment and future generations, as well as respect for people around the world. The fact that many of the businesses that use such new approaches and broader ethical perspectives are very successful, and often outcompete other companies, indicates that there is a business case for these approaches. We will discuss normative changes in business practice in later chapters in more detail with examples ranging from small to global businesses – from small landscaping companies to benefit corporations (see Section 7.3), such as Patagonia, and global corporations, such as Nike.

Also, the diversity of the business world increasingly offers various possibilities for individuals to follow their values and interests, and there may be more and more room for realizing individual life plans in business, which would be a more expanded idea of business as a sphere of individual freedom. People should be encouraged to demand jobs and careers that help realize their individual values and life plans and should understand that they have choices and opportunities.

3.7 Two tales of the pencil

3.7.1 Tale of the pencil: the neoclassical version by Milton Friedman

The economist and Nobel prize winner Milton Friedman (1912–2006) told a basic story about a pencil to demonstrate the positive aspects of a free capitalist market economy, which we outlined in Section 3.4. He starts his story as follows: 'Look at this lead pencil. There is not a single person in the world who could make this pencil. Remarkable statement? Not at all! [. . .] Literally thousands of people cooperated to make this pencil' (Friedman, 1980). Friedman describes in detail the global division of labor that, just driven by the price mechanism of the markets, makes people work together to produce the pencil: the wood comes from some place in the US; the saw and iron ore need to be produced at other places in the world in order to be able to cut the wood; the graphite for the core of the pencil needs to be mined somewhere; the rubber at the top of the pencil comes from the rubber tree that is grown somewhere in southeast Asia; the aluminum for the cap that fixes the rubber top to the pencil needs to be extracted and produced; the glue that puts it all together needs to be sourced and added, as does the color for painting the pencil; and so on. Friedman's point here is that the market and price mechanism is the perfect system to coordinate all of these activities, and the complex global division of labor and makes people around the world cooperate in a productive, efficient, and fruitful way to create a pencil. Friedman concludes: 'That is why the operation of the free market is so essential. Not only to promote productive efficiency, but even more to foster harmony and peace among the peoples of the world' (Friedman, 1980).

Of course, Friedman's tale accurately reflects certain strengths of the capitalist market economy: efficiency, division of labor, coordination of self-interests, and so on. However, his tale does not say anything about the idealistic underlying assumptions and the limitations of the capitalist market economy, particularly in the global context. As discussed above, the market economy provides many of its positive results only if there is a proper legal framework and if all people can equally participate. Particularly in the global context, however, this is often not the case. On the global scale, we sometimes face limited or corrupt government, lack of or contradicting rules, or extreme asymmetries in power, which can result in exploitation of vulnerable groups (see Chapter 6). Also, Friedman does not discuss the question of sustainability and potential harm (external effects) to nature and future people and the resulting economic costs (see Sections 3.4 and 3.5 and Chapter 7). To demonstrate the one-sided perspective of Friedman's tale of the pencil, I will tell another version below which specifically highlights market failures and ethical issues that the traditional concept of the capitalist market economy tends to ignore.

3.7.2 An alternative tale of the pencil: considering external costs and sustainability

Consider a simple lead pencil. Literally thousands of people may have suffered and significant environmental harm may have been done in order to produce that pencil. Remarkable statement? Not at all! The black core of the pencil is made from graphite that today is predominately mined in China. The mining of graphite often results in significant environmental pollution and harm to the health of local communities. The main impacts are graphite dust released from mining and processing, which impacts air quality and crops, and the release of hydrochloric acid used in processing graphite into the environment, which is toxic. The wood for the pencil is usually cedar. Harvesting the cedar can come with typical issues of sourcing wood, such as deforestation, monocultures, overuse of pesticides, and so on. The eraser on the top of the pencil is made from synthetic or natural rubber. Natural rubber production uses natural latex from the rubber tree, which grows in tropical climates. The trees are often grown in large monocultures that have negative ecological effects, such as biodiversity loss, soil erosion, and pesticide and fertilizer accumulation in the environment and water. Increasing demand for rubber in recent years has led to significant destruction of rainforests for cultivating rubber trees (Li & Fox, 2012; Ziegler et al., 2009). The plantations have also been criticized for unethical working conditions, including safety hazards, exposing workers to pesticides and fertilizers without protection, child labor, and even slavery. Processing latex and producing rubber requires the use of chemicals, particularly sulfur. Inadequate treatment of waste water can result in significant pollution of local rivers. The eraser is typically held by an aluminum cap. The production of aluminum is well known for being extremely energy intensive. The overall assembly of the pencil is today usually not done in the US but outsourced to other countries. The usual concerns for labor conditions apply, and there is a potential for sweat shops, child labor, and further violations of international labor standards. So, overall there is a significant potential that by buying a lead pencil, one becomes involved in environmental destruction, human rights violations, and harm to people and communities involved in, or affected by, the global processes that contribute to the production of that pencil.

Both tales illustrate some aspects of today's capitalist market economy. It is important to see both perspectives together to understand the strengths and weaknesses of today's economic system and to be able to fully discuss the question of how to develop the economic system and do business for meeting today's and the future's (ethical) challenges.

References

Arrow, K. J. (1951). An extension of the basic theorems of classical welfare economics. In J. Neyman (Ed.), *Proceedings of the Second Berkeley Symposium on Mathematical Statistics and Probability* (pp. 507–532). Berkeley, CA: University of California Press.

Becker, C. (2006). The human actor in ecological economics: philosophical approach and research perspectives. *Ecological Economics*, 60, 17–23.

Becker, C. (2008). Thoreau's economic philosophy. *The European Journal of the History of Economic Thought*, 15, 211–246.

Camerer, C., Loewenstein, G., & Rabin, M. (Eds.). (2003). *Advances in Behavioral Economics*. Princeton, NJ: Princeton University Press.

Debreu, G. (1959). *Theory of Value: An Axiomatic Analysis of Economic Equilibrium*. Hoboken, NJ: Wiley-Blackwell.

Friedman, M. (1980). *Free to Choose* [Television Broadcast]. Arlington, VA: PBS.

Friedman, M. (2002). *Capitalism and Freedom*. Chicago, IL: University of Chicago Press. (Original work published 1962.)

Gigerenzer, G. & Selten, R. (2001). *Bounded Rationality: The Adaptive Toolbox*. Cambridge, MA: MIT Press.

Hayek, F. A. (2007). *The Road to Serfdom*. B. Caldwell (Ed.). Chicago, IL: University of Chicago Press. (Original work published 1944.)

Hobbes, T. (2008). *Leviathan*. Oxford: University Press. (Original work published 1651.)

IPCC [Intergovernmental Panel on Climate Change]. (2014). *Climate Change 2014. Synthesis Report*. Contribution of Working Groups I, II and III to the Fifth Assessment Report of the Intergovernmental Panel on Climate Change (Core Writing Team, R. K. Pachauri & L. A. Meyer, Eds.). Geneva: IPCC.

Kahneman, D. & Tverski, A. (2000). *Choices, Values, and Frames*. Cambridge: Cambridge University Press.

Li, Z. & Fox, J. M. (2012). Mapping rubber tree growth in mainland Southeast Asia using time-series MODIS 250 m NDVI and statistical data. *Applied Geography* 32(2), 420–432.

Marx, K. (1990). *Capital, Volume I* (B. Fowkes, Trans.) London: Penguin Books. (Original work published 1867.)

Marx, K. & Engels, F. (1998). *The Communist Manifesto*. London: Verso. (Original work published 1848.)

Mas-Colell, A., Whinston, M. D., & Green, J. R. (1995). *Microeconomic Theory*. Oxford: University Press.

MEA [Millennium Ecosystem Assessment]. (2005). *Ecosystems and Human Well-being: Synthesis*. Washington, DC: Island Press.

Oxfam. (2016). *An Economy for the 1%. How Privilege and Power in the Economy Drive Extreme Inequality and How this can be Stopped.* 210 Oxfam Briefing Paper. Oxford, UK: Oxfam GB.

Piketty, T. (2014). *Capital in the Twenty-First Century* (A. Goldhammer, Trans.). Cambridge, MA: Harvard University Press.

Rousseau, J. (1995). *Discours sur l'origine et les fondements de l'inegalite parmi les hommes. Schriften zur Kulturkritik* (K. Weigand, Ed.). Hamburg: Meiner. (Original work published 1755.)

Saez, E. & Zucman, G. (2016). Wealth inequality in the United States since 1913: evidence from capitalized income tax data. *The Quarterly Journal of Economics*, 131(2), 519–578.

Simon, H. A. (1947). *Administrative Behaviour.* New York: MacMillan.

Smith, A. (2000a). *The Theory of Moral Sentiments.* Amherst, NY: Prometheus. (Original work published 1759.)

Smith, A. (2000b). *The Wealth of Nations* (E. Cannan, Ed.). New York: The Modern Library. (Original work published 1776.)

Thoreau, H. D. (2008). *Walden, Civil Disobedience, and Other Writings* (W. Rossi, Ed.). New York: Norton.

UNEP [United Nations Environment Programme]. (2012). *Global Environment Outlook GEO-5: Environment for the Future We Want.* Malta: Progress Press.

van Staveren, I. (2001): *The Values of Economics: An Aristotelian Perspective.* London: Routledge.

World Bank. (2016). *GDP (Current US$).* World Bank. Retrieved from http://data.worldbank.org/indicator/NY.GDP.MKTP.CD.

Ziegler, A. M., Fox, J., & Xu, J. (2009). The rubber juggernaut. *Science*, 324(5930), 1024–1025.

4 Organizational ethics

Ethics of corporations, companies, and other business organizations

Organizations such as companies, corporations, or non-profit organizations play a crucial role in modern business. Most individuals are part of some organization and act not in isolation but together with others within organizational contexts. Therefore, many ethical aspects in modern business are not merely about individual ethics and decision-making but also involve ethical aspects on the organizational level and at the level of complex organizational interaction. Business organizations require internal ethical mechanisms that enable successful interactions among employees, and business organizations need to address the ethical challenges of the complex external framework in which they operate; that is, the global economic system (see Chapter 3).

Modern businesses need to manage complex internal and external relationships in order to operate successfully. Internally, organizational ethics is about establishing shared values and norms, respect and integrity, responsible professional actions, and a positive working atmosphere and ethical culture – qualities that are crucial to the success of organizations. Further, internal organizational ethics aims at minimizing all types of misconduct, such as harassment, discrimination, bribery, stealing, and insider trading: misdeeds that could significantly harm an organization. Externally, organizational ethics is about linking the business organization properly to the external framework in which it operates. This includes proper consideration of societal norms and of the diverse interests, values, expectations, and rights of various stakeholders. It also includes responsible consideration of the various societal and environmental impacts modern business activities have around the world. External organizational ethics ensures responsible and lawful actions of the organization, upholds the organization's reputation, minimizes risks and serious frictions with stakeholders that could endanger the success of the organization, and monitors and manages challenges and opportunities resulting from the environmental and sustainability aspects of the business operations. Overall, organizational ethics has become a crucial tool for the management of organizations and for ensuring long-term business success. Organizational ethics supports smooth internal interactions, minimizes internal and external frictions, and assists with navigating increasingly complex business environments, ethical challenges, and business responsibilities.

In this chapter, we discuss the various challenges of organizational ethics in detail and provide concepts and analytical tools to address them. We define basic concepts, such as responsibility and business-specific responsibilities, and analyze different elements of organizational ethics, such as corporate responsibility (CR), ethical culture, and ethics and compliance programs. This chapter specifically provides methods to determine business-specific responsibilities and develop optimal CR strategies. Overall, we aim at an encompassing perspective on the various interrelated elements of organizational ethics (Figure 4.1).

Figure 4.1 The elements of organizational ethics.

4.1 What is the moral responsibility of a business?

The next three sections, 4.1–4.3, work toward a thorough understanding of corporate responsibility (CR) and, more generally, the specific moral responsibilities of a business. To introduce this rather complex issue, we will first clarify the concept of *moral responsibility* and develop a general definition of *business-specific responsibilities*.

4.1.1 The concept of responsibility

The concept of responsibility is used in different ways and has different meanings. We speak of legal responsibilities, contractual responsibilities, personal responsibilities, responsibilities of parents, and so on. In the following we focus on responsibility as an ethical concept and define the meaning of being morally responsible.

> Definition 4.1: **Responsibility** is the ability and moral obligation to respond (in action or verbally) to normative questions concerning the rightness and wrongness of actions or states of affairs.

How can we establish that someone is responsible for something? By what reasons or criteria can we determine responsibilities? The following set of conditions typically constitutes responsibility:

1 Causality
   One crucial condition for being held responsible for some incident is that one caused it somehow. Actions have effects on others, and a person or business that

pursues an action can potentially be held responsible for the effects – that is, the consequences – of that action. If, however, there is no causal relation between the actions of a person or business and some incident, the person or business cannot be held responsible. For instance, if I cause an accident, I can be held responsible for the resulting damage, and likewise if a business causes harm or damage by its actions, it also can be held responsible. However, if an accident happens in my town that I have not caused in any way whatsoever, I cannot be held responsible.

2   Knowledge

Even if there is a causal relationship between my actions and some incident, my degree of responsibility depends on the degree of knowledge I had or could have had about the causal link. One can distinguish three typical cases: (i) I knew the consequence of my action and wanted the consequence to happen; that is, I *intended* the consequence; (ii) I didn't want the effect to occur (I didn't intend the effect), but I could have known that it would occur (potentially), because the effect of my action was reasonably foreseeable; (iii) the effect of my action was not reasonably foreseeable and I could not have known that the effect would occur.

For instance, if I crash into another person's car intentionally – that is, I foresaw the effect of my action, and strove for the effect to happen – I certainly can be held fully morally responsible and legally accountable for my action and the resulting damage. If I crash into another person's car without intending it, but rather as a result of significantly exceeding the speed limit on a busy inner-city road, I also will be held responsible for the accident, despite the fact that I had no intention to cause the damage. One can argue that I should have known that excessive speeding increases the probability of an accident. It is reasonably foreseeable that excessive speeding is dangerous and increases the likelihood of accidents. However, if I am causing damage that was not reasonably foreseeable, I am not morally responsible. Suppose, for instance, the following case. I want to visit some friends, so I drop by their house, ring the doorbell, and the house explodes as a result. There happened to be a leak in the house's gas pipe, resulting in a large accumulation of gas in the basement and on the main floor. Pressing the button to ring the bell induced a small spark in the doorbell inside the house, and this caused the gas to explode. While this scenario is very unlikely, it has in fact happened. Technically, my action (and therefore I) caused the explosion. However, I could not know or have reasonably foreseen this effect, and no one would argue that I should have known that houses can occasionally blow up by ringing doorbells, and that therefore I should have taken precautions before ringing the doorbell. No one will hold me ethically responsible.

The criterion of knowledge has a subjective and an objective aspect. What is reasonably foreseeable is to a certain extent judged objectively, referring to what we commonly expect a reasonable person to know and foresee. However, in ethical and legal judgments, subjective aspects are also considered. For instance, we understand that children or people with certain disabilities may not have the ability to fully foresee the consequences of their actions.

3   Free will

I am not responsible for actions that I was forced to do and did not do deliberately. If a person is forced at gunpoint to do something, we typically would not hold the person being forced responsible for her actions but rather the person with the gun.

4   Position and relational role

Responsibilities can also be attached to a certain role, position, or function a person has. A person can have specific responsibilities for some entity, other people, or field of activity based on her role, position, or function. For instance, parents have specific responsibilities for their children: their wellbeing, education, behavior, and so on. A leader is responsible for the area she is supposed to control. A CEO has an overarching responsibility for the company and its performance. Such role-based responsibilities often go well beyond direct personal actions and resulting effects. For instance, one can claim that a CEO is responsible for wrongdoing within the company, even if the CEO was not directly involved in the wrongdoing, and did not know about it. Here, the point is that the position of CEO carries with it substantial powers (and payment) in order to govern the entire company, and the CEO has significant possibilities to control and influence the company and the actions of its employees. If serious wrongdoing happens within the company, the CEO can be considered responsible, whether she knew about the wrongdoing or not. If she knew, she is responsible for not preventing or stopping the wrongdoing. If she didn't know, she is responsible for exactly that – for not knowing about serious wrongdoing, despite having been granted the powers and means to oversee and control the company. In other words, she is responsible for the lack of leadership.

Organizations and businesses can also have more or less well-defined societal functions or roles, which may imply specific responsibilities toward its stakeholders. For instance, a university has a function to provide research and education, and has specific responsibilities toward students, the public, donors, taxpayers, businesses, and so on. For-profit and non-profit businesses in the health care sector have specific moral responsibilities toward patients, physicians, and taxpayers, which result from their specific societal role. Such specific societal functions of organizations and businesses can result from deliberate societal design or from the unique expertise and power a business, organization, or industry has developed over time by itself.

5   Ability and power

Persons or organizations that have specific expertise, abilities, or power to act in certain situations may have more responsibility in such situations than others who lack the expertise, ability, or power. For instance, if someone is the only engineer on a team that is working on a construction project, then that person has more responsibility than all other team members to ensure that the statics of the construction is technically safe. This is a core aspect of professional ethics: specific expertise constitutes specific responsibilities (see Section 5.3). The following is another example of specific abilities and power constituting specific responsibilities. Assume there is an outbreak of a rare but very dangerous disease in some remote part of the world that is characterized by a lack of economic resources and government. Only one pharmaceutical company has unique expertise about this disease and is about to have an experimental drug ready. Even though there is no legal obligation to help fight the outbreak of the disease, and while a business is not generally obligated to assume or replace government functions, is it arguable that the specific abilities and expertise of the company imply a specific moral responsibility to help fight the outbreak of the disease.

In summary, there are different ways and typical criteria to determine moral responsibility. It makes sense to distinguish two main types of responsibility: *action-based responsibility*, which is mainly determined by criteria 1–3 of the above list, and *role-based responsibility*, which is mainly determined by criteria 4 and 5 (although, in some scenarios, the criteria may also overlap to some extent).

4.1.2 Business-specific (company-specific) responsibilities

A specific business or company usually has a well-defined competence, purpose, and mission. The business's main goals are to fulfil its purpose, provide certain goods or services, and generate profits. A business is not usually responsible for general public matters of the society (this is traditionally the task of governments) or for curing all evils in the world. However, business activities have various effects and side effects, and a business certainly is responsible for those effects according to the criteria defined above (Section 4.1.1). In addition, a business relates to a concrete set of stakeholders, and some businesses have obtained very powerful positions and functions societally and globally, and this may imply some further responsibilities with regard to the above criteria. Generally, not only individuals, but also entire organizations and businesses can be held responsible. This is in line with the current US legal framework that enables the prosecution and sentencing of both individual actors and entire organizations (see Section 4.5.2).

> Definition 4.2: **Business-specific (company-specific) responsibility** means the sum of concrete responsibilities a specific business has regarding its concrete operations, products, services, and stakeholders. This includes all ethically critical societal, environmental, global, and future effects that result from the business's activities and products.

Basically, a company is responsible for its actions and relationships, as is any individual person. However, the effects of business activities in a modern, global economy are complicated. Due to the increasing complexity of the global business world, the ethical responsibilities of a business have become a difficult subject matter. A business causes many societal, environmental, global, and long-term effects by its operations and products, and the challenge is to identify those effects, ethically evaluate them, determine to what extent the business is responsible for them, and develop feasible actions and strategies to assume responsibility and address the ethical issues identified. Furthermore, modern businesses have complex sets of stakeholders who have various characteristics, rights, and interests, and this results in specific moral obligations and responsibilities a business has toward its stakeholders.

In order to determine the responsibilities of a specific business, we need methods for analyzing its complex activities and relationships. In the following section, 4.2, we develop two methods that will enable us to determine business-specific responsibilities and responsibility strategies for a given business.

4.2 Methods for determining business-specific responsibilities

For determining the specific responsibilities of a given business, we need to identify the stakeholders and the impacts of the business, ethically evaluate those stakeholder relationships and impacts, identify the degree of responsibility the business has for them, and finally develop feasible strategies to assume responsibility. In the following, we develop two methods that can help with this task: *Ethical Life Cycle Assessment*

(ELCA)[1] and *Ethical Stakeholder Analysis* (ESA). Each method contributes to a broader understanding of how a given company is positioned within its complex business context and what responsibilities the company has in that context.

4.2.1 Determining business-specific responsibilities based on an Ethical Life Cycle Assessment (ELCA)

The ELCA is applicable to businesses that market a product. The ELCA identifies ethically critical societal, environmental, global, and long-term impacts of a business with regard to its products. To fully evaluate all such impacts, one needs to consider the entire life cycle of the product, including *sourcing* (gathering the raw materials necessary for production), *production*, *distribution*, *use*, and *disposal* of the product. Each of these stages of the product life cycle can have various positive and negative effects to people and the environment around the world. We assume that a business has many positive effects, such as providing goods and services, creating jobs, paying taxes, and contributing to fair competition that leads to efficiency, growth, and innovation, and we take those positive effects as given. However, in a complex global business world, business operations can result in many, often unintended, negative side effects for which the business needs to assume responsibility. The ELCA method helps to identify and evaluate such negative side effects, determine the degree of responsibility a company has for them, and identify optimal strategies for the company to assume responsibility and minimize negative side effects.

ELCA method

The ELCA method for determining business-specific responsibilities encompasses the following four steps:

STEP I: IDENTIFY CRUCIAL SOCIETAL, ENVIRONMENTAL, GLOBAL, AND LONG-TERM IMPACTS THAT RESULT FROM THE ENTIRE PRODUCT LIFE CYCLE

In this first step, we need to research the product life cycle and gain an overview of potentially negative impacts. For this, we divide the product life cycle into the following five stages and consider the impacts of each stage separately:

1   Sourcing (gathering of the raw materials needed to produce the product)
2   Production (the entire process of manufacturing the product)
3   Distribution (getting the product to the customers; this includes packaging, shipping, and operations of retailers)
4   Use (the entire period the product is used by a consumer or other businesses)
5   Disposal (the entire process related to discharging the product after its regular use; includes waste treatment and recycling)

STEP II: ETHICALLY EVALUATE THOSE IMPACTS – IDENTIFY CRITICAL ETHICAL ISSUES

In this step, we need to verify that the impacts identified in step I are actually 'negative.' That is, we have to establish that these pose ethical issues. For the ethical evaluation, we use the following criteria based on the methods developed in Chapter 2:

- CI principle B: all persons involved in, and affected by, the product life cycle should be treated with respect: that is, no one should be treated as a mere object; fundamental (moral) rights, such as human rights, of all persons involved in/ affected by the product life cycle should be respected; vulnerable groups should not be exploited. Any form of exploitation, abuse, or violation of human rights related to the product life cycle constitutes a serious ethical issue.
- Utilitarian principle: is overall happiness of all involved in, or affected by, the product life cycle maximized (compared to feasible alternatives)? If overall happiness is negatively impacted by the product life cycle in whatever way, this would constitute an ethical issue.
- Virtue principle B: do all involved in, or affected by, the product life cycle benefit in their personal or professional development and in the development of their communities? Is 'value' created for all? Do all have the possibility to thrive? If not, the product life cycle is ethically flawed.

To simplify the analysis of case studies, we also will use the below-defined no-harm principle, which can easily be supported and specified in different ways by the above classical ethical principles:

- No-harm principle: persons involved in, or affected by, the product life cycle should not be harmed (stricter formulation, based on Kantian ethics or virtue ethics); overall harm, including harm to the environment should be minimized (weaker version, based on utilitarianism).

In other words, for sake of simplification, we consider any substantial harm in the product life cycle as an indication of an ethically critical effect of the product.

STEP III: DETERMINE TO WHAT DEGREE THE BUSINESS CAN BE HELD RESPONSIBLE FOR THE
ISSUES IDENTIFIED IN STEPS I AND II

The fact that there exists an ethical issue in the product life cycle does not directly imply that the business is fully responsible for the issue. This is because there are many actors involved in the product life cycle beyond the business itself – suppliers, retailers, and users (customers), among others – which also might have some responsibility for a specific ethical problem occurring in the product life cycle. If the product causes some harm, there is at least some causal link to the business: the business caused the product to exist and also determined the product's specific design and characteristics. However, the product may now be owned by some person that uses it, and their way of using the product may substantially have caused the harm. Therefore, we need to determine the degree of responsibility the business has for the specific issue, as compared to other actors. To do this, we refer to three of the responsibility criteria defined in Section 4.1.1: causality, knowledge, and ability/power. We use those three criteria to determine the degree of responsibility a business has for any given issue in its product life cycle, as follows:

- To what extent did the business cause the issue?
    Some causal relationship between the business and the ethical issue is already established, as the product of the business is causing the issue. However, we need

to evaluate to what extent the business is causing the ethical issue compared to other actors in the product life cycle, such as suppliers and users. To simplify the evaluation, we will distinguish four degrees of causation: the business is not (0) a significant cause, is a minor (m) cause, is an equal (e) cause, or is the main (M) cause of the issue.

- Did the business know or could it have known that the ethical issue occurs?

  Some societal, environmental, global, or long-term side effects in the product life cycle may be well known to a business or easily foreseeable; other effects could come to the business as a complete surprise. For instance, businesses that used CFCs as refrigerants in the 1960s could not foresee that this specific cooling agent would accumulate in the atmosphere and cause a hole in the ozone layer many years later. This knowledge was not established before scientific research discovered the effect in the 1970s and 1980s. As we have argued in Section 4.1.1, the degree of knowledge matters for determining the responsibility of an actor. Thus, we need to determine in each case the degree of knowledge a business had or could have had about any ethical issue in the product life cycle. We will distinguish the following three degrees of knowledge: the business was fully aware of the issue (k), was not aware but could have known (c), or was completely surprised by the issue (s).

- How much ability, expertise, and power does the business have to address the issue?

  There are many actors besides the business involved in the product life cycle, such as governments, suppliers, and consumers, and the various actors may have more or less ability, expertise, and power to address a given issue. One needs to compare the ability/power of the business to address the issue with the ability/power of the other actors: Does the business have a small ability/power (sp), equal ability/power (ep), or the main ability/power (mp) to address and fix the issue, compared to all other actors involved?

Based on the outcome of the three criteria above, we can determine whether the business has no (nr), small (sr), equal (er), or main responsibility (mr) for an ethical issue in the product life cycle. None means that the business is not responsible at all, but the full responsibility is on some other actor. Small means that the business should take some action, but other actors have the main responsibility. Equal means that the business has a similar share of responsibility compared to other actors: the business needs to take proportionate actions and join others to share responsibility equally to address the issue. Main responsibility means that the business is the main responsible actor for the issue and has the main burden to assume responsibility and take action to address it.

For instance, if a business is the main cause of an ethical issue, knew that the issue would occur, and has the main ability and power to address the issue, we would judge that the business has the main responsibility for the issue (e.g., a flawed product design). On the other hand, if a business could not know that an issue would happen, caused it only to a small degree, and has limited power and ability to address it, we would judge that the business has only a small or even no responsibility for the issue (e.g., the case of a hammer being used to commit a crime). However, there may be more difficult cases, such as businesses that only cause an issue to a small degree, could maybe have foreseen it, but have substantially more power and ability to address it compared to all other relevant actors. Here we may judge that a business has the main responsibility to address the issue just based on the last criterion of main power and ability, which can override the first two criteria in some cases.

Consider the following example. A brewery produces beer and sells it to customers. The use of beer can have negative side effects. People can get intoxicated; pregnant women can harm their unborn children; people can get addicted; alcoholism causes severe health issues; drunk driving kills a number of people each year; underage drinking is a societal issue; and so forth. Is the brewery responsible for all this? One may think, the brewery is not responsible, but rather the consumers who abuse the product are. From this viewpoint, one may argue that the brewery has no responsibility at all. However, applying the above three criteria, we can determine that (i) there is some causal link between the business activity and those negative effects, (ii) the brewery can reasonably foresee that these effects occur – there are well-known systematic connections between the characteristic of the product, namely that it contains alcohol, and these effects, and (iii) the brewery has at least some ability and power to assume responsibility and take action to reduce these negative side effects. For instance, the brewery could use its marketing abilities and relationship with customers to foster awareness of the issue of drunk driving. The brewery could make sure that marketing does not intentionally or accidentally target underage groups. (This is not only ethically appropriate, but also in the best business interest of the brewery.) That does not mean that all the negative effects listed above are *merely* the responsibility of the brewery. These effects are, of course (and probably to a larger extent), also the responsibility of the consumers and society at large. However, the brewery has and should assume *some* responsibility, and join others to address the issue. As in many complex business cases, there is a need for *shared responsibility* of many actors involved in the issue.

STEP IV: IDENTIFY STRATEGIES FOR THE BUSINESS TO ASSUME RESPONSIBILITY AND TAKE ACTION

Finally, if we have identified the degree of responsibility a business has for certain issues in the life cycle of its product, we need to address the practical question of what concrete actions a business should undertake to assume its responsibilities and address the issues. There might be a large range of possible activities that a business could undertake. One needs to decide what good activities would be and develop an overall optimal action plan. To guide this decision, the following three criteria should be considered when evaluating possible activities for each issue:

1   Activities should effectively address the ethical issue.
2   Activities should match the degree of responsibility defined in step III.
3   Activities should be economically feasible and ideally support business success.

We will see in the example of application below that there is often a wide range of possible actions a business could undertake to address ethically critical effects in the product life cycle: redesigning the product, improving the production process, improving the supply chain, reconsidering packaging and ways of distribution, educating users, and considering recycling programs, among other actions. A good action plan effectively addresses the ethical issues identified to a degree equivalent to the business's responsibility. If the responsibility strategy is tailored carefully, it can at the same time be an instrument to foster business success, for instance by becoming more (cost-)efficient, building reputation, improving the product, reducing risks in the supply chain, developing more robust supply chains, discovering and moving into new markets, and so on. In other words, analyzing, identifying, and assuming responsibilities in the product life cycle is not just a mere cost factor for a business, but rather a strategic management move and valuable investment. It can result in a better understanding of the business operations, identification of efficiency potentials, and improvements of the product and business operations, which all ultimately support business success. An ELCA can assist with exploring and realizing the potential win-win between ethics and business (see Figure 4.2).

Example of application: ELCA of a smartphone

Case: ELCA of a smartphone to determine related business-specific responsibilities of a large, global smartphone company. We assume a hypothetical large smartphone company, such as Apple or Samsung, and analyze the product life cycle of a smartphone as it is typically set up today.

Smartphones have become important common goods that have in many ways changed individual life styles and societal interaction. By developing and marketing smartphones, a company provides value to society and contributes to economic progress. However, even though smartphones appear to be unproblematic and slick products, they have a couple of ethically critical side effects: their product life cycle causes harm to many people and the environment. To ensure that the smartphone company is a positive force for society and the world, such harmful side effects need to be identified and minimized or avoided. The following analysis identifies ethically critical impacts related to smartphones as they are typically manufactured today,

ELCA method

STEP I
IDENTIFY CRUCIAL SOCIETAL, ENVIRONMENTAL, GLOBAL, AND LONG-TERM IMPACTS OF THE PRODUCT LIFE CYCLE
Sourcing – Production – Distribution – Use – Disposal

STEP II
ETHICALLY EVALUATE THOSE IMPACTS AND IDENTIFY ETHICALLY CRITICAL ISSUES
Utilitarian principle, CI principle B, Virtue principle B
No-harm principle

STEP III
DETERMINE WHAT DEGREE OF RESPONSIBILITY THE BUSINESS HAS FOR THE ISSUES
To what extent did the business cause the issue?
Did the business know or could it have known that the issue would occur?
How much ability and power does the business have to address the issue?

STEP IV
IDENTIFY STRATEGIES FOR THE BUSINESS TO ASSUME RESPONSIBILITY AND TAKE ACTION
Activities should effectively address the ethical issues
Activities should match the degree of responsibility defined in Step III
Activities should be economically feasible and ideally support business success

Figure 4.2 The four steps of the ELCA method.

determines business-specific responsibilities, and develops an action plan to address the ethical issues. As I will argue later, addressing serious ethical issues is also in the best business interests of the smartphone company and will improve their success and competitiveness rather than impede it.

We will integrate here steps I and II of the ELCA method into one matrix to identify ethically critical impacts of the smartphone (see Table 4.1). We focus here only on certain major ethical issues in the life cycle of a smartphone. In the following, we will explain in detail the ethically critical impacts of each stage of the product life cycle that are indicated in Table 4.1.

Sourcing   The producing of smartphones requires many raw materials that need to be sourced around the world. Some materials have been identified as conflict minerals. Conflict minerals are minerals that come from areas of conflict, and their sourcing involves serious ethical issues. For many years, the Congo was the origin of many conflict minerals, such as tin, tantalum, tungsten, and gold, which are crucial for the production of smartphones (Enough, 2009; Parker & Vadheim, 2017). Warlords got those materials illegally by taking them from local communities to finance their groups and weapons. This involved killing people and other crimes, and also illegal destruction of the environment and wildlife (Enough, 2009). That these activities are serious ethical issues is easily established by all ethical theories and standards. They cause severe harm to humans and the environment, violate fundamental human rights, and disrespect the dignity of the local people, and there are certainly alternatives that are better in terms of overall happiness. The issue of conflict minerals in

Table 4.1 ELCA of a smartphone: steps I and II

	Social	*Environmental*	*Global*	*Long-term*
Sourcing	Conflict minerals		Conflict minerals	
Production	Working conditions in supplier factories	Pollution; environmental hazards; resource and energy use	Working conditions in supplier factories	Resource and energy use
Distribution		Greenhouse gas emissions from transportation; resource use and waste due to packaging		
Use	Texting while driving; potential health issues			
Disposal	E-waste	E-waste	E-waste	E-waste

smartphones is similar to other issues, such as so-called blood diamonds, which have received much public attention.

Production Smartphone production today is typically outsourced and mainly done in East Asia, particularly in China. Recent concerns about Foxconn, the main producer of Apple phones, demonstrate potential issues with working conditions, including excessive and unpaid overtime, sub-minimum wages, and health impacts (Duhigg & Barboza, 2012; Merchant, 2017). Such working conditions cause harm to the workers and are ethically problematic by standards of Kantian ethics and virtue ethics. Workers are treated as mere means, and personal flourishing is undermined. Such conditions also violate human rights and international labor standards. From a utilitarian point of view, one could argue that overall happiness can easily be increased by improving working conditions. Basic measures might only slightly increase costs but substantially improve the situation of the workers. Such improvements can also result in positive business effects, such as increased reputation, lower turnover rates, and lower liability risks.

Distribution Distribution is not a major concern in the product life cycle of a smartphone. However, packaging and transportation require resources and energy, and result in greenhouse gas emissions and waste. This is an ethical issue, as these environmental impacts harm people, future generations, and non-human life in general.

Use At a first glance, it might seem that the use of smartphones does not cause much harm. However, there is at least one serious side effect: texting while driving. Smartphone use has become a major factor in distracted driving, which causes many serious accidents. 'In 2016 alone, 3,450 people were killed. 391,000 were injured in motor vehicle crashes involving distracted drivers in 2015. During daylight hours, approximately 481,000 drivers are using cell phones while driving. That creates enormous potential for deaths and injuries on U.S. roads' (NHTSA, 2018). This certainly represents a serious ethical issue, as a significant number of people are severely harmed by the use of smartphones while driving. In addition, there has been some discussion about potential negative health effects from excessive use of smartphones. Scientific research currently does not fully support such claims, though.

Disposal A serious side effect of smartphones, and electronics in general, is e-waste. Electronic devices are used by an increasing number of people around the world and are outdated within a short period of time. People get rid of their old phones and replace them with new ones. As a result, we see an increasing stream of electronic devices being disposed. Disposal is a critical ethical issue because many electronic devices include toxic substances, such as mercury, cadmium, and lead (Grossman, 2006). In the use stage this is not an issue, but when the device is disposed of the toxic substances can leak and cause significant environmental harm. In addition, e-waste often is illegally shipped to other, mostly poor places in the world, where people make a living from extracting valuable parts, such as gold, from electronic waste. However, the extraction of valuable parts causes the toxic parts to be released into the environment. This results in serious environmental pollution and impacts the health of people in the local communities (Grossman, 2006). With this, e-waste results in serious harm to people and the environment.

We have so far identified ethically critical societal, environmental, global, and long-term impacts of smartphones. Now we need to determine to what degree the smartphone business is responsible for these issues. To do so, we will discuss some major issues in the product life cycle separately by using the three criteria defined in step III of the ELCA method:

1   To what degree did the smartphone company cause these issues?
2   Did the company know or could it have known that these issues occur?
3   How much ability, expertise, and power does the company have to address the issues?

Sourcing and the issue of conflict minerals   The smartphone company is not directly involved in the crimes and illegal activities related to the extraction of the resources. Warlords and criminals are the direct cause. However, the smartphone company causes the issue indirectly by demanding and using the conflict minerals. We may evaluate this as a minor to equal (m–e) cause. Does or could the smartphone company know about the issue? This depends on the timeline. A couple of years ago the issue was not well known and at that early point in time could have come as a surprise to a smartphone company. Today, there is plenty of research and information about the issue, and any smartphone company knows or can easily learn about the issue (k–c). Finally, who has the power, ability, and expertise to address the issue of conflict minerals? Preventing and punishing serious crimes usually is not the task of business but of governments and law enforcement. However, if there is no functional government, as in the Congo, then who should assume responsibility? A smartphone company has substantial power to establish and enforce rules for its suppliers to avoid the use of conflict minerals and get the resources from legitimate sources. Given that the smartphone company is a rather large and powerful business, it probably has more ability and power than weak or non-existing governments in some areas from which conflict minerals come. Particularly, the company has more expertise and ability than all other actors, such as US and European Union governmental agencies or consumers, to analyze and monitor its supply chain and work with its suppliers to develop mechanisms for detecting and avoiding conflict minerals. Thus, we can judge that the smartphone business has a main power to assume responsibility and address the issue (mp). Overall, we can conclude that the smartphone business has at least an equal, if not the main, responsibility for the issue of conflict minerals (er–mr).

Production and problematic working conditions   The smartphone industry today works typically with outsourced production done by a few, large suppliers, such as Foxconn, which are themselves rather powerful players. Unethical working conditions are caused by the supplier, but also result from outsourcing by the smartphone company (e). The smartphone company should know, or could easily inform itself about the working conditions at its supplier (c–k), and has equal power to address those issues (ep) because of its influence on the supplier. Overall, the smartphone company has an equal responsibility (alongside various other actors that also should assume their share of responsibility) for the working conditions at its supplier (er). Of course, the supplier needs to assume responsibility as well. In addition, local governments, which should establish and enforce proper regulations to protect workers, and even the consumers, should assume responsibility. By buying products consumers generate demand and basically drive the production of the product. Consumers have a powerful influence. If consumers stay away from problematic products, they will not be sold and produced. There have been examples where consumer boycotts made a business change its operations and address serious ethical issues. Nike, for instance, addressed ethical issues in the supply chain and substantially changed its business operations in the 1990s after serious consumer protests.

Texting while driving   As soon as the product is bought and the consumer owns it, the consumer has a main responsibility for the effects of its use. Texting while driving is a serious issue, and it is primarily the responsibility of the smartphone user to avoid this issue. However, the smartphone company should be aware of the well-known issue (k), the issue is systematically related to the functioning of smartphones – that is, it is to a small degree caused by the features of the phone (m) – and the company has some ability to act and address the issue (sp). Thus, one can argue that the company has at least a small responsibility (sr) for the issue of texting while driving. Compare the situation with (i) the abuse of alcoholic beverages and (ii) a hammer used for committing a crime. A business that produces and sells alcoholic beverages can know and foresee that there are potential dangers of abuse. The danger systematically results from the design of the product being alcoholic beverage. With this, we expect such a business to at least participate in a shared responsibility and do its part to minimize such issues, e.g., by putting warning labels on the bottles, engaging in programs for educating about the dangers of drunk driving, and so forth. However, a company that produces hammers cannot be held responsible in any way for somebody using one of the hammers to commit a crime. There is no systematic link between the design of the product and crimes. No one would ask a business producing hammers to put warning labels on the hammer or engage in educational programs about the danger of abusing hammers for criminal activities. The difference is that the causal link in the first case is systematically established by the characteristics of the product, namely containing alcohol, and it is well known that this causes a number of issues. Whereas, in the second case, the effect is somehow arbitrary, and also very rare. The issue of texting while driving seems to be more comparable to the case of alcoholic beverages than to the case of the hammer.

E-waste   Although the users discharge their phones, one can argue that main responsibility (mr) for the well-known e-waste issue (k) is with the smartphone company. The toxic effects of e-waste are originally caused by the way the smartphones have been designed and produced (m), and the smartphone company has the main expertise, ability, and power to address the resulting environmental hazards by better design (mp). Illegal shipping and other criminal activities around e-waste are only an indirect result of the lack of proactive measures a smartphone company could do to prevent the problem at the source. Key to the e-waste issue is product design, particularly non-toxic design and recyclable design, both of which are completely in the hands of the company.

STEP IV: ACTIVITIES BY WHICH THE COMPANY CAN ASSUME RESPONSIBILITY AND ADDRESS THE ISSUES IDENTIFIED

What can the company do to best assume its moral responsibilities and address the issues discussed above? What are the company's competencies, abilities, and power, and what is economically feasible? In practice, there are many ways to assume responsibility. It is a creative management task to develop optimal strategies and activities that address the issues. Ideally, the company should strive to design activities that, at the same time, sufficiently address the ethical issue, meet the company's degree of responsibility, and contribute to business success. In other words, the company ideally designs a strategy that maximizes the win-win between its moral responsibilities and its business success. In the following, we provide three examples of potential actions that result in a win-win between ethics and business success.

Addressing the issue of conflict minerals   The smartphone company could address the issue of conflict minerals by implementing, together with its suppliers, a system for monitoring and certifying all raw materials they acquire. This may include external auditing and assurance processes. In addition, the company could promote the concerted efforts and actions of the smartphone industry as a whole. The industry today is dominated by a few big players, which could work together and set up a self-commitment and common procedures to avoid conflict minerals in the industry. Such self-commitments of an industry can be powerful tools for replacing lack of regulation in the global business world. A further option would be to actively engage in the supply chain and build reliable relationships with trustworthy mining companies. The smartphone business may also engage in shared responsibility activities with other players, such as the US government or the European Union, that also have some power and ability to address the issue. For instance, in the US, the Dodd–Frank Act includes requirements for monitoring and reporting the use of conflict minerals. In practice, large companies, such as Samsung and Apple, have indeed taken several of the above-mentioned actions (Apple, 2018; Samsung, 2018).

There are obvious ethical reasons for assuming responsibility and taking some of the above-mentioned actions: no business wants people to die or get seriously hurt for their products. In addition, there also is a business case: larger ethical issues are serious business risks. No company wants its business to depend on criminals or warlords. Rather, a company would aim to secure more reliable sources for crucial resources on which its business depends. Conflict minerals also involve a reputation risk and could result in protests from consumers, similar to consumer protests related to blood diamonds. Finally, taking no action increases the risk of stricter government regulation, and the business might be better off by proactively addressing the issue by itself, using means it considers to be optimal.

Addressing the issue of texting while driving   The smartphone company could engage in various activities that raise the awareness of the dangers of texting while driving. This could include sponsoring educational programs in schools or running educational advertisements. It may also be an effective solution to join or sponsor groups that already run such activities and have experience with them. Another option would be technological solutions to texting while driving, such as more advanced voice-control options, which make texting by voice control a convenient, preferable feature of the phone. Besides ethical reasons for such activities – that is, assuming one's share of responsibility and joining efforts of others in society to address the issue – there is also an obvious business case. Reducing the issue helps avoid a situation in which society gets seriously concerned and strict regulations get imposed on the smartphone company and its products. Additionally, developing a technological solution of advanced voice control for texting offers the competitive advantage of having the better product on the market.

Addressing the issue of e-waste   Although other actors, such as consumers and governments, have some potential to address the e-waste issue, the company probably is in the best position to address the issue with regard to their own product. The key to addressing the e-waste issue is the design of electronic devices. In its design of the smartphone, the company could aim to avoid all toxic materials or reduce their use. If toxic materials do not go into the phone, they will not go into the environment later on. Another powerful tool to reduce the e-waste problem is recycling. The smartphone company could set up a program to take back their phones, possibly linked to some monetary incentives for buying a new phone. However, if the company takes the phones back, it needs to find smart ways to deal with the old phones and recycle them. The phones contain valuable materials, such as gold and rare minerals, but often the costs for extracting those materials from the phones are prohibitive. Key to economically feasible recycling is, again, design. If, at the stage of designing the phone, its potential for recycling is already considered, one may be able to regain valuable materials from old phones at reasonable costs, and reuse those materials for the production of new phones (this is a closed-loop process). For instance, the phone could be designed in a modular way or in a way that enables efficient automatic recycling. Such a design can be called sustainability design. Besides the obvious ethical advantages of sustainability design, such as less (toxic) waste, less environmental and societal harm, and less use of resources, there is also a strong business case. If a company finds economically feasible ways to regain valuable materials from their old products and use them for the production of new phones, the company gains a substantial competitive advantage in a world facing increasing scarcity of resources and energy. In addition, incentives for trading in old phones for new ones retains customers and motivates them to buy new products.

Overall, the three examples above show that moral responsibility does not have to be an economic burden for the company, and assuming responsibility and taking action does not need to harm the business. The examples illustrate ways by which the business can create a win-win between assuming its moral responsibilities and improving its business success and competitiveness.

The concept of shared responsibility

The concept of shared responsibility is important in a modern complex business world. As the above examples have illustrated, many issues in business contexts are caused by the actions of several actors together, and several parties have some ability and power to address them, such as businesses, governments, consumers, societal organizations, and United Nations organizations, among others. Societal, global, and environmental effects of production, use, and disposal of products, or global supply chain issues, are typically rather complex, and many parties are involved. It is important not to simplify, but rather carefully analyze, each case. In many cases, we can neither merely blame a single business nor can the business reject all responsibility. The crucial aspect is to properly define the share of responsibility for each case, depending on the degree of causality, knowledge, and power/abilities of all actors involved.

Exercises

1   Case: ELCA of a pencil
    Consider a business that markets pencils and is a global leader in this industry. Do an ELCA of 'a pencil.' Do some research to figure out what ethical issues can typically occur in the product life cycle of a pencil. Based on your ELCA, provide concrete recommendations for the business about how to assume responsibility and develop an action plan.

2   Case: Emerging fast food chain
    ABC Dining is an emerging fast food chain. The company provides higher-quality, healthier fast food. Its business strategy focuses on the growing market for healthier, higher-quality food. The company currently operates in four states in the US and aims at expanding nationwide in the future. Do an ECLA of the product of higher-quality healthy fast food to determine business-specific responsibilities, and recommend activities for ABC Dining to assume its responsibilities.

3   Case: ELCA of beer
    ZZZ Brewing is a medium-size, local, craft beer brewery in Colorado (semi-arid climate). Do an ELCA of beer to determine the business-specific responsibilities of this brewery, and recommend activities for the company to assume responsibility.

4.2.2 Determining business-specific responsibilities based on an Ethical Stakeholder Analysis (ESA)

Another way of identifying business-specific responsibilities of a given company is to base it on the concept of stakeholders. The term stakeholder has been promoted by Edward Freeman (Freeman & Reed, 1983; Freeman, 1984) and has become a well-established concept that is broadly used in theory and practice. Stakeholders of a given business are groups or individuals that have some interest in that business and its operations, because they are in some way involved in or affected by it. In turn, stakeholders have some degree of relevance for the business and its success. Typical stakeholder groups are employees, customers, investors, and suppliers. However, non-governmental organizations (NGOs) or consumer advocacy groups that critically monitor the operations of a given business would also count as stakeholders of the business. For instance, an environmental group that is concerned about some aspects of nature and, as a result, critically monitors the activities of a chemical company, counts as a stakeholder of that company.

> Definition 4.3: A **stakeholder** of a business is a party that has a substantiated interest in the business and its operations.

Each business has a well-defined set of stakeholders that determines the specific societal context of this business. In this stakeholder context, the business has a specific position and function. In most cases, the stakeholders of a business are not just located in one country but around the world. An Ethical Stakeholder Analysis (ESA) aims at determining business-specific responsibilities of a business by analyzing its moral relationships with all its stakeholders. An ESA does not specifically refer to impacts of a product and can also be used for analyzing business-specific responsibilities of organizations that mainly provide services, such as banks or universities. Although the impacts of products and product life cycles matter for stakeholders, we will not consider those in detail with the ESA, as these impacts can be analyzed by the ELCA method. Rather, we will develop the ESA method by referring to a role-based responsibility concept (see Section 4.1) and the concept of relational responsibility. With this, the ESA can identify business-specific responsibilities based on the moral rights of different stakeholders and the moral specifics of stakeholder relationships.

From a practical point of view, one strength of the stakeholder approach is the possibility to communicate with stakeholders and listen to their expectations, concerns, and interests. This approach has its limits, though, as some stakeholders might not be able to articulate their interests and concerns. This holds, for instance, for future generations and the environment. Other stakeholders can formulate their concerns or interests only to a limited extent, such as children or people with certain disabilities. An ESA focuses on moral obligations, responsibilities, and rights in stakeholder relationships. These can be determined in a more objective way and do not depend on the actual ability of a stakeholder to articulate them. For instance, one can argue that future people also have a right to life, liberty, and the pursuit of happiness, and we have some moral obligations not to harm the wellbeing of future generations. Or, one can argue that children have certain rights, and that we have certain moral obligations and responsibilities to protect their wellbeing. The less a stakeholder group is able to articulate its interests and concerns, the more important it is that a company recognizes and upholds the moral rights of that stakeholder group and acts responsibly toward it. For instance, any organization that has children or persons with intellectual and developmental disabilities as stakeholders has particular moral obligations to protect their rights and interests. These stakeholders are particularly vulnerable and at risk of exploitation and abuse, and so the organization has specific responsibilities toward them.

The responsibilities a business has toward its stakeholders depend on the specifics of each business and its stakeholders. The ESA helps to determine business-specific responsibilities in the stakeholder relationships of a given business. We will develop in the following the basics of an ESA method referring to the ethical methods introduced in Chapter 2.

ESA method

The ESA method for determining business-specific responsibilities encompasses the following four steps.

STEP I: IDENTIFY ALL STAKEHOLDERS OF THE BUSINESS

We first need to identify all stakeholder groups of the company. We also need to identify specific characteristics of each stakeholder relationship that are of potential ethical relevance. For instance: Who has what kind of power and ability in this relationship? Is the company significantly more powerful than the stakeholder? Does the stakeholder group significantly depend on the organization? Is the stakeholder group particularly vulnerable?

STEP II: DETERMINE SPECIFIC MORAL RIGHTS OF EACH STAKEHOLDER AND SPECIFIC MORAL
RESPONSIBILITIES THE BUSINESS HAS TO EACH STAKEHOLDER

We identify in this step moral responsibilities that result from specific characteristics of the stakeholder and the relationship with the stakeholder. For this, we refer to the ethical theories discussed in Chapter 2, specifically, the CI method B, virtue method B, and care method. We also use the concept of moral rights in this context. A *moral right* can be defined as a claim that protects fundamental interests of a person based on substantiated ethical reasoning. If a stakeholder has moral rights, the company has the obligation to respect those rights and uphold them in their interaction with the stakeholder.

- Based on Kantian ethics and the CI method B, stakeholders have the right not to be treated as mere means, but to always be respected as ends in themselves and beings endowed with reason. From this principle follows three fundamental moral rights of stakeholders, which the company has to respect. (i) The right to freedom: everyone owns him or herself (no one is owned as an object by someone else), which includes the right to privacy and self-determination; (ii) the right to being treated equally and not being discriminated against: we are all in the same way beings endowed with reason and ends in ourselves; and (iii) the right to be treated respectfully; that is, the right not to have our free will, self-determination, and self-guidance by reason infringed upon. These general moral rights need to be specified for each stakeholder, and specific moral obligations of the organization need to be determined. In many cases, specific characteristics of the stakeholder relationship, regarding power, abilities, dependencies, and vulnerability, result in specific responsibilities and obligations the organization has to uphold. For instance, what does the general right of not being treated as a mere object mean for the stakeholder group of employees? There typically exists a certain power asymmetry in the employer–employee relationship, and employees are to some extent vulnerable, as their jobs are crucial for their wellbeing. Employees having a right not to be treated as mere objects means specifically that they have a right to respectful treatment, safety, and privacy. The employer has the moral obligation to uphold these rights, for instance, by establishing policies, rules, and an organizational culture that protects them (see Section 5.1).
- Based on virtue ethics and virtue method B, stakeholders have a moral right to thrive and develop their own potential. They have the right that the organization neither impedes their possibilities to thrive, nor hinders the development of their potential, but rather supports it. For instance, people working in the supply chain are an important stakeholder group for businesses that rely on outsourced production or sourcing of raw materials. From the perspective of virtue ethics, the business has a moral obligation to manage the supply chain in a way that allows everyone working in the supply chain to develop their potential and enables local communities to progress and thrive. Another example are employees and corresponding leadership responsibilities. From a virtue ethics perspective, one can argue that leadership has a moral responsibility to provide options to employees for optimally developing their professional potential.
- From an ethics of care perspective, one can ask whether the relationships with certain stakeholders present ethically relevant qualities, such as vulnerability,

lack of power, or limited capability of the stakeholder group. If this is the case, one needs to further explore what implications these ethically relevant qualities have regarding the organization's specific responsibilities to protect the rights of the stakeholder group. In this perspective, stakeholders have a right that their vulnerability, lack of power, or lack of ability, is not ignored or abused, but rather cared for. For instance, if a business has children as stakeholder group, this would imply specific responsibilities with regard to advertising: children cannot make the same rational reflections and judgments about advertisements as adults and, as a result, are vulnerable to manipulation. Thus, a business has the moral responsibility to consider this vulnerability and either not advertise certain products to children or to design the advertisement appropriately. Another example would be a pharmaceutical company that has patients as a stakeholder group. The vulnerability of this group may imply specific ethical responsibilities that the company has toward the patients.

STEP III: DETERMINE FURTHER MORAL RESPONSIBILITIES THAT RESULT FROM THE
BUSINESS'S SPECIFIC SOCIETAL FUNCTION AND POSITION WITHIN ITS
STAKEHOLDER CONTEXT

In some cases, businesses or organizations have rather well-defined purposes or societal functions, which may imply further moral responsibilities toward the stakeholders or society in general. This is often the case for non-profit organizations, which mainly define themselves by their purpose, but it may also be the case for companies that have a well-defined societal function, such as health care, or companies that are specifically value- or purpose-driven. For instance, most universities are non-profit organizations and devoted to research and education; that is, the production and transfer of knowledge. One may say that the university, and every person working for it, has the moral responsibility to support this purpose as diligently as possible and ensure that the available financial means are optimally used for this purpose. This moral responsibility may go well beyond the immediate interests and rights of existing stakeholders of the university. For instance, a university may consider it as part of its responsibilities to foster fundamental research in various fields, even if there is no immediate stakeholder interest or short-term use, because of the potential long-term benefits the production of such fundamental knowledge has for society, the research community, and future generations.

STEP IV: DEVELOP STRATEGIES FOR THE BUSINESS TO ADEQUATELY ASSUME ITS
RESPONSIBILITIES IN STAKEHOLDER RELATIONSHIPS

Considering the previous three steps, step IV is about developing an optimal strategy for a business to ensure that the business assumes its responsibilities toward its stakeholders, respects the moral rights of all its stakeholders, and fulfills the moral responsibilities resulting from its societal function and position. The strategy can include, for instance, mechanisms for effective communication with stakeholder groups, rules and policies for interaction with stakeholders, adequate leadership style and organizational design that accommodate stakeholder rights, and implementation of ethics and compliance programs, among others. An optimal strategy should fulfill the following criteria:

ESA method

STEP I
IDENTIFY ALL STAKEHOLDERS OF THE BUSINESS

STEP II
DETERMINE SPECIFIC MORAL RIGHTS OF EACH STAKEHOLDER AND SPECIFIC MORAL RESPONSIBILITIES THE
BUSINESS HAS TO EACH STAKEHOLDER

CI principle B, virtue principle B, care method

STEP III
DETERMINE MORAL RESPONSIBILITIES THAT RESULT FROM THE BUSINESS'S SPECIFIC SOCIETAL FUNCTION AND
POSITION WITHIN ITS STAKEHOLDER CONTEXT

STEP IV
DEVELOP STRATEGIES FOR THE BUSINESS TO ADEQUATELY ASSUME ITS RESPONSIBILITIES IN THE STAKEHOLDER
RELATIONSHIPS

Strategies should effectively address the ethical aspects of all stakeholder relations
Strategies should protect the moral rights of all stakeholders and fulfill the moral responsibilities that the business
has in the stakeholder relations
Strategies should be economically feasible and ideally support business success

Figure 4.3 The four steps of the ESA method.

- The strategy should effectively address the ethical aspects of all stakeholder relations.
- The strategy should protect the moral rights of all stakeholders and fulfil the moral responsibilities of the business in its stakeholder relations.
- The strategy should be economically feasible and ideally support business success.

Figure 4.3 summarizes the ESA method.

Exercise

1 Do an ESA for a public state university to determine its responsibilities to its main stakeholder groups and society, and recommend strategies for the university to optimally fulfil its responsibilities. Assume that the university is partially sponsored by taxpayer money from the state, student tuitions, and donations from alumni and businesses. Also, the university is the largest employer in the community in which it is located.

4.3 Corporate responsibility (CR)

4.3.1 A broader perspective on the overall responsibilities of a modern business

So far, we have discussed specific responsibilities that a company has due to its concrete business operations, products, and stakeholders. In this section, we will integrate these business-specific responsibilities into an overarching concept of CR. For this, we identify some additional general responsibilities of a business and discuss concepts of CR as well as the overall responsibility of modern business.

In Section 4.2, we referred to the concept of *action-based* responsibilities of a company, and we discussed business-specific responsibilities of a company, which result from the specific effects of its products and operations on the environment and other people. We also referred to responsibilities toward stakeholders that were more *function-based* and *role-based*; that is, responsibilities that result from the specific function/role a business has for its stakeholders. In addition, one can define function-based responsibilities of a business with regard to more general and abstract functions that business has in society and with regard to the overall power the business sector has in society.

Responsibilities based on the economic function of business

Business has a general function in society that is defined particularly by business being an actor within the context of the economic system, which today means usually a capitalist market economy. We discussed the normative aspects of the economy in Chapter 3. Depending on the interpretation of the economic function of a business, one can identify different general responsibilities a business has with regard to its economic function:

1   The classical view is that, in the context of a market economy, an individual business contributes to the economy and society by striving for maximal profits through providing goods and services to other actors in the market. The (neo-) classical idea is that the business and all other economic actors focus only on their own interests (of making profits), and the market coordinates all self-interests in a way that is good for the economy and society as a whole. That is, the market will produce desired effects such as efficiency, innovation, and growth. In this perspective, the economic responsibility of a single business is to optimally fulfill its economic function by striving for profit maximization and competing with other actors for the best products and services (see, e.g., Friedman, 1970).

2   A different, more current interpretation of the economic function of business comes with the stakeholder approach (Freeman, 1984). Based on this approach, the purpose of a corporation or business is the creation of value for all its stakeholders (Freeman et al., 2007), which includes making profits for its financiers and owners. In this perspective, the economic responsibility of a business is to optimally balance various stakeholder interests and create value for all.

3   Even if a business benefits society through profit maximization and creates value for all its stakeholders, it might still not qualify as a positive force in the world. As we discussed in Chapter 3, markets largely fail to consider the wellbeing of future generations, the environment, people around the world, and aspects such as just distribution of income and wealth. In Chapter 3, we envisioned the concept of a *sustainable economy*, which would contribute to the wellbeing of individuals, society, people around the world, future generations, and the environment. The market by itself is a limited tool for establishing such a sustainable economy. Economic actors actively need to consider sustainability aspects of their activities. Thus, with regard to its function in a sustainable economy, the economic responsibilities of a business would be broader than in the more traditional perspectives of 1 and 2. They would include responsibilities for the effects of their activities on the environment, future people, and people around the world. Technically, this brings us back to the responsibilities discussed in Section 4.2, which in the context of a sustainable economy could also be considered

economic responsibilities of a business. In other words, if the economic function of a business is defined in the context of a sustainable economy, its economic responsibilities would encompass the responsibilities discussed in 1 and 2, and in Section 4.2. In current business practice, responsibilities toward sustainability have increasingly become a dominant focus of responsibility strategies and activities. Indeed, most larger corporations today issue a *sustainability report* instead of a *corporate social responsibility report* or a *corporate responsibility report* to describe the activities they undertake to assume their responsibilities as a business (KPMG, 2013).

Responsibilities based on business being a part of society in general

Besides business fulfilling a specific economic function in society, business is a part or member of society in general. Being a member of society comes with certain responsibilities. First of all, just like any member of society, businesses have to obey the laws of society. Following laws, rules, and regulations in a business context is commonly called *compliance*. Some laws and regulations may actually be specifically designed for business activities; for instance, laws regulating competition, such as the Sherman Antitrust Act. However, a business also has to follow all general laws of the society. In addition, we can expect a business to respect fundamental normative principles and values of the society, such as the principles of the constitution, and to support those principles and refrain from undermining them. Particularly, one can expect business, as a rather powerful and influential actor in society, to contribute its share in achieving fundamental societal goals and addressing crucial societal issues, even if such issues have not been caused by the business or are not directly linked to the context or economic function of business. For instance, freedom and equal opportunity are fundamental principles of the US society. However, in practice, many issues and obstacles have hindered the full realization of these principles. Various groups, like minorities or women, have been disadvantaged, and with this, the principles of equality and fairness have been undermined. Although this is not a business-specific issue, and a specific company may not have caused the issue in any way, we can ask companies to join other powerful actors, such as educational institutions and governmental agencies, to join forces and help address this issue – to assist society to actualize fundamental societal principles – just based on the fact that business is part of the society in general. This argument justifies the moral expectation for companies to implement measures of affirmative actions; that is, actions that actively aim at increasing the number of employees from underrepresented groups in a company (see also Section 4.5.1).

Philanthropy is another crucial element of more general responsibilities of business as a member of society. Philanthropy means doing something good in a general sense, and usually is about donating money or volunteering time for a good cause. Sometimes this is also called 'giving back to society,' meaning that society is the basis for any business to develop and flourish, and the business acknowledges this by supporting the society in general. Philanthropic donations do not have to do anything with the business purpose, but they could. The latter case we call *business-specific philanthropy*. For instance, a construction company could give money to some cause completely unrelated to its core business, like sponsoring classical music events. The construction company could, however, also donate to causes directly related to its business, such as donating time or money for building houses in some poor area that was hit by an earthquake.

The current term and practice of CR usually combines in various ways some of the responsibilities discussed above, and thus represents a more encompassing concept of business responsibility. CR today is a well-established ethical management instrument by which a business organization defines its policies and activities to meet its overall responsibilities to the external framework in which it operates. Over 90% of the largest corporations in the world have established CR strategies and issue CR reports (KPMG, 2013). However, CR is not restricted to large corporations. The terms *corporate responsibility* and *corporate social responsibility* (CSR) are well established, but somehow misleading, as not only corporations, but all businesses, have social and environmental responsibilities. Many small and medium-size businesses also have implemented strategies and activities to meet their societal and environmental responsibilities, although they often do not issue a formal report. We want to address CR here in a broader sense, as the societal, environmental, global, and long-term responsibilities of a business, and therefore we also sometimes speak of business responsibility in this broader sense. In the following section, we will first discuss different ways to further specify the concept of CR, and then explore the relevance of CR for business and society.

4.3.2 Defining CR

Carroll (1991) provided an influential model of corporate social responsibility, the Pyramid of Corporate Social Responsibility. It encompasses four responsibilities of a corporation: (i) the economic responsibility to be profitable, (ii) the legal responsibility to follow laws and regulations, (iii) the ethical responsibility to act 'right, just, and fair' toward stakeholders and to 'avoid harm,' and (iv) philanthropic responsibilities, which include 'to be a good corporate citizen' and 'contribute resources' to the community (Carroll, 1991, p. 40). By using the metaphor of a pyramid, the model suggests some hierarchical order of the four responsibilities: economic responsibilities come first and are on the bottom, then come legal, ethical, and philanthropic responsibilities. Carroll's classic model constitutes an important broader view of the overall responsibilities of a corporation. It has some limitations, though. Besides issues with the hierarchical order of responsibilities, the model does not specifically emphasize business-specific responsibilities or responsibilities that are crucial for contemporary business: responsibilities toward the environment, global responsibilities, and responsibilities toward future generations. The latter three responsibilities could also be called responsibility for sustainability.

I suggest the following alternative, the *Pillar Model of Corporate Responsibility*, that avoids a hierarchical structure, integrates the business-specific responsibilities we have defined in this chapter, adds the sustainability dimension, and clearly distinguishes philanthropy from core business responsibilities (see Figure 4.4).

The pillar model of CR suggests a broad understanding and definition of CR and of the overall responsibilities of a modern business. The right pillar represents all business-specific responsibilities that we defined and discussed in Section 4.2. These are the specific responsibilities that a business has with regard to the impacts of its operations, its product life cycle, and its stakeholder relations. The pillar in the center represents the responsibilities a business has due to its general economic function in

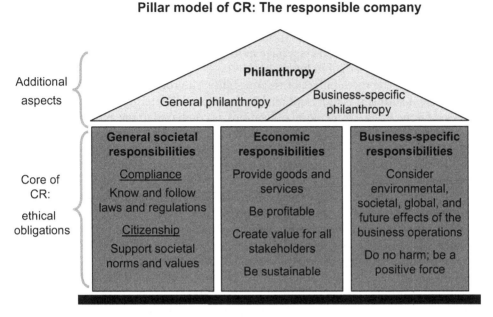

Figure 4.4 The Pillar Model of Corporate Responsibility.

society, as discussed in Section 4.3.1. The left pillar represents the general responsibilities a business has as member of society; that is, following rules and laws and being a good citizen. The roof represents philanthropy: donating or giving back to society.

The pillar model of CR essentially claims that a business needs to have all three pillars in order to be called a responsible business. The roof (philanthropy) would be an add-on but not a necessity. If any one of the pillars is lagging, we would consider a business to be irresponsible. For instance, a company that lacks compliance and violates laws or regulations is an irresponsible company. A company that lacks economic responsibilities, for instance, a company (or management) that substantially neglects competitiveness, providing the best products and services, and securing profits, can also be called irresponsible. A company that disrespects or doesn't consider the interests and rights of its stakeholders is irresponsible. Against the concept of a sustainable economy, we would also consider a general concern for sustainable business operations a responsibility and call a company that ignores aspects of sustainability irresponsible. A company that disregards the effects of its business operations and products on the environment, society, future people, and people around the world is also irresponsible.

The three fundamental pillars of responsibility are neither arbitrary nor voluntary. This is obvious with legal responsibilities and compliance. The firm cannot choose to follow the law but is required to do so. The same holds for economic responsibilities, particularly for responsibilities toward investors, shareholders, and employees. The responsibilities toward other stakeholders and for sustainability may not be as binding as legal responsibilities, but they are also not ethically arbitrary. The business-specific responsibilities constitute moral obligations of a business in as far as they address potential harm done to others or the environment. One can expect a business to consider negative side effects that its operations and products have on others, the society, and the environment. As every individual is required to consider the effects of her actions, and is morally obliged to avoid harm to others and respect others, so we can expect the same from businesses. In some cases, we can expect even more from businesses, such as when businesses have more power and abilities to assume responsibility for their actions than individuals.

In contrast to the three pillars of responsibility, the roof – that is, philanthropy – has a different status: it is more optional and not as well determined. Philanthropy is not based on the same strong moral obligations as compared to the avoidance or compensation of harm to others, or the moral obligation to respect the rights of others. Although philanthropy is ethically good and desirable, a company has no moral obligation to philanthropy: it is optional. In contrast, the three pillars constitute moral obligations for the company. Everyone and every business is obliged to follow the law, avoid harm, and respect the rights of others. This is not optional. In other words, philanthropy is a valuable ethical addition, but not a substitute for the company-specific responsibilities a business has for the impacts of its business operations and the moral rights of its stakeholders. In the worst case, philanthropy can even become a mere cover-up or whitewashing of irresponsible business practices.

Philanthropy also has no necessary or systemic link to the business purpose, operations, or products. General philanthropy can just be driven by the personal preferences or values of the owner or the employees of the business. It does not impact or change the way of doing business. Business-specific philanthropy is related to the specific business competencies, operations, or products of the company, but would also not directly impact or change the way the business operates. Whereas the roof of philanthropy does not impact or change the way a business operates (in an ethical or unethical way), the three responsibilities represented by the three pillars directly impact the way a business operates. For instance, if a company assumes responsibilities for their environmental impacts, they may change their production processes to be more efficient, change their product design to use less materials or avoid toxic materials, request that their suppliers implement more sustainable production processes, and so on.

The definition of CR suggested by the pillar model is a broad definition. In practice, most businesses use the concept of CR in a variety of ways. Often, compliance is considered as separate from CR, and economic responsibilities are assumed as self-evident. Thus, more specific concepts of CR often refer to responsibilities towards stakeholders and responsibility for sustainability, and many actual CR strategies focus on these two (and sometimes also on philanthropy). A well-known shorter definition, which refers to the older concept of CSR, and is in line with several other influential definitions, is the following definition by UNIDO (2015):

> Corporate Social Responsibility is a management concept whereby companies integrate social and environmental concerns in their business operations and interactions with their stakeholders. CSR is generally understood as being the way through which a company achieves a balance of economic, environmental and social imperatives ('Triple-Bottom-Line-Approach'), while at the same time addressing the expectations of shareholders and stakeholders.

In this book, we use the term CR as defined by the pillar model of CR. We hold that the responsibilities defined in CR do not only apply to corporations but to all types of business and organizations and, consequently, represent a broader concept of business responsibility.

4.3.3 Justification of CR: why is CR important? What are the reasons for businesses to consider and implement CR strategies?

The business case for CR

CR has become an important management tool that, if well implemented, can significantly support the success of a business. CR helps to systematically analyze and navigate the complex external framework in which a business operates. CR can help a business to identify issues, risks, and opportunities in its external framework, and can help in the development of strategies to properly address such issues, risks, and opportunities. The exact function of a CR strategy for a business depends on the company and specific design of the CR strategy. Generally, a CR strategy can provide some or all of the following potential benefits to the business.

IMPROVED STAKEHOLDER RELATIONSHIPS

Many CR strategies include a stakeholder engagement process which identifies stakeholders that are crucial to the business and interacts with them. This helps to better understand the interests and concerns of groups that are important to the business and can proactively address potential issues and conflicts. Improved stakeholder relationships are important for the success of any business or organization. It is in the best interest of a business to get along with its stakeholders. Actively managing stakeholder relations also enables a business to detect potential issues with crucial stakeholder groups early on and avoid serious conflicts, such as consumer boycotts, strikes, and lawsuits, all of which could significantly harm the business.

PROACTIVE RISK MANAGEMENT

CR can contribute to risk management. A good CR strategy scans the entire business context for existing or potential ethical issues that could become a serious threat to business success. For instance, complex supply chains and product life cycles may have unrecognized environmental and societal issues, such as the use of toxic substances or child labor. Proactively identifying or avoiding such issues reduces the risk of suddenly being confronted with them and being forced into urgent crisis management.

ATTRACTION OF HIGHLY QUALIFIED EMPLOYEES

A CR strategy can be a distinguishing factor that helps to attract and keep highly qualified employees. Employees increasingly consider ethical aspects when choosing a job, such as the values and purpose of a company, positive impacts of the company, and environmental and societal performance of the company. Highly qualified employees are crucial for the success of a business, and they usually have various other job options. It matters that a company can give credible signals to this group of employees regarding strong company values and responsible business practices. A CR strategy is a credible message of the societal and environmental responsibility and performance of a company that may resonate well with highly qualified employees.

CONTRIBUTION TO STRATEGIC MANAGEMENT

CR can be a strategic management tool. A CR strategy involves a thorough analysis of the entire business context of a company, as well as the identification of long-term risks and opportunities in the realm of societal and environmental performance. With this, a company can identify long-term environmental risks and constraints of its business – for instance, the critical dependencies on certain resources or energy – and monitor political and societal developments that may impact its business. All of these insights can be used for strategic management decisions: for strategically navigating the external framework of the business and proactively adjusting to long-term risks, constraints, and trends. For instance, Nike has used its CR as a strategic manage-ment tool to increase its sustainability performance and competitiveness. Nike has addressed two aspects that are crucial for its business: (i) societal performance regard-ing labor conditions and worker rights in the supply chain and (ii) overall efficiency of its product life cycles. Nike's CR strategy has identified various environmental aspects that are critical for its business, such as overall energy use, water and mate-rial use, waste, and carbon footprint, and has deployed innovative approaches that significantly reduce energy and resource use and shift Nike toward more sustainable and closed-loop production modes (Nike, 2017). Strategically, Nike has positioned itself with this approach for the future and aims at gaining a competitive advantage through efficiency and sustainability. Overall, more and more companies are shifting away from seeing CR primarily as a tool for reputation management or risk manage-ment, but rather consider CR as a strategic management tool.

INNOVATION AND EFFICIENCY GAINS

Detailed analyses of material and energy flows are typically part of most CR approaches. With this, the CR approach supports a better and more encompassing understanding of the energy and material use in the business operations, including supply chain and product life cycles. This enables a business to identify and realize efficiency potentials throughout the company, supply chain, and product life cycle. Efficiency gains are a business advantage, as they typically translate into cost reduc-tion and increasing competitiveness. In business practice, most companies have some focus on their environmental performance, regardless of their specific dedication to environmental or sustainability values, because of the obvious business case: there are typically significant efficiency potentials that a company can identity by a more thorough analysis of its environmental performance and immediate cost saving that can be realized. Monitoring and improvement of environmental performance is often more driven by the business case for efficiency rather than by environmental values.

IDENTIFICATION OF NEW MARKETS AND PRODUCTS

Engaging with environmental performance, efficiency, and sustainability can inspire a company to explore innovations for more efficient processes and products. CR can be a driver for sustainable innovation as the company starts actively asking whether something can be done in a more efficient or sustainable way. Efficiency and sustain-ability are driven by systemic environmental limitations, and people are increasingly seeking more efficient and sustainable solutions and products. Overall, there is a sig-nificant potential for sustainable products, new markets, and business opportunities.

For instance, a small landscaping business in the southwest of the US could develop innovative drought-resistant landscaping solutions and meet an increasing demand; companies that lead the development of the electric car or other energy-efficient cars could disrupt the entire automobile industry.

BUILDING REPUTATION

A well-designed CR strategy can increase the reputation of a company and resonate with various stakeholder groups. CR may resonate with customers who factor environmental and sustainability values into their consumption decisions and prefer to buy from a green or sustainable company. CR can resonate with current or potential employees, as discussed above. Investors are another important stakeholder group, who are probably most interested in the CR strategy of a company. CR strategies provide information about environmental and societal performance of a company and indicate how proactive a management reduces risks and strategically positions a company toward future challenges. Such information provides a crucial addition to financial data and helps investors better evaluate potentials and risks of a company. The CR report also may resonate with further stakeholder groups, such as NGOs, communities, and governments, which have specific expectations for the societal and environmental performance and responsibility of a company.

IMPROVING COMPETITIVENESS

Overall, all of the business benefits of a CR strategy discussed above have the potential to improve the competitiveness of a company, particularly in the long run.

Ethical justification of CR

In Section 4.1, we justified ethically that a business must assume to a certain degree responsibility for its activities and its relationships, subject to specific criteria. We will further elaborate the ethical justification for CR here by adding some reasons why businesses themselves need to assume responsibility, rather than hoping for market self-regulation or looking to governments to assume responsibility and take action (see also Chapter 3).

In an ideal world of neoclassical economics, we would not need CR. All individuals would bring in their interests, the market would ensure efficient results, and the government would set up rules for fair competition. The society would benefit, negative external effects would be priced in, and so on. However, in today's global and complex business world there exist various negative side effects that are not considered by the market mechanism. We face large asymmetries in power and ability, and there is no global government or global laws which could sufficiently regulate the global economy and ensure its overall efficiency. In other words, the global business world is characterized by numerous market failures and legal loopholes. In addition, we face new ethical challenges and need to consider the wellbeing of the global environment and of future generations. The market mechanism cannot guarantee by itself that we meet those new challenges. Economic actors need to assume responsibilities by themselves to guarantee the economy is a positive force, and CR is the tool for businesses to ensure that. In some way, CR is a management tool that modifies capitalism and adjusts it to the new systemic challenge and normative requirements of the 21st century economy. Ideally, CR upholds and redefines the idea of the market economy as a positive force by adjusting it to be positive for society, people around the world, the environment, and future generations (see also Chapter 3).[2]

One needs also to consider another phenomenon of the 21st century economy: the increasing number of large multi-national corporations, which have more power and abilities than many smaller nations in the world. These companies often have more abilities to address some issue in their global supply chain or product life cycle than the respective local governments that are technically supposed to address the issue. For instance, in certain West African areas, child slavery in cocoa production, which provides the raw material for the chocolate industry, persists. Local governments seem incapable of addressing and solving the issue. However, global companies that buy the cocoa from these areas, such as Nestlé, may have more power and influence to cure the issue of child slavery in their supply chain than the local governments (see Section 6.1). One can argue that in such cases power and ability imply specific responsibility, and that powerful global companies have specific moral obligations. CR can help companies identify and address such responsibilities.

What is a good CR strategy?

We know what CR is and why it is important. However, we also need to ask: What is a good CR strategy? One can expect to find CR approaches ranging from mere 'greenwashing' (i.e., deception about the environmental friendliness of a company; see Section 5.4.2) and PR to serious management tools that guide entire business operations and strategies. We want to be able to distinguish a serious well-defined CR strategy from mere greenwashing. Moreover, we would like to define and develop an *optimal* CR strategy for a given company. For this, we need to define a set of criteria for a normative judgment about CR strategies, criteria that define a *good* or *optimal* CR strategy. The following section, 4.4, provides a detailed approach for such a normative judgment. The short message is that, for a given business, a CR strategy is good if it fully assumes all business-specific responsibilities in a way that optimally serves business success. In other words, a good CR strategy is designed in a way that creates a maximal win-win between responsible business activities and business success.

4.4 Methodology for CR analysis and CR design

In the following, we develop a method to critically analyze and evaluate an existing CR strategy of a company. The method allows us to evaluate the overall quality of the CR strategy, identify ethical, economic, or formal shortcomings, and recommend improvements. With some modification, the method can also be used to develop an entirely new optimal CR strategy for a given company.

The method for CR analysis consists of three steps (see Figure 4.5). The first two steps are more descriptive and gather facts about the company and its CR strategy. To collect this information, various sources can be useful: the company's web pages, fact sheet, K-10 form (or its equivalent), and CR report, as well as existing research about the company. The third step is a normative evaluation of the quality of the CR strategy, for which we provide three sets of criteria and refer to analytical tools developed earlier in the book.

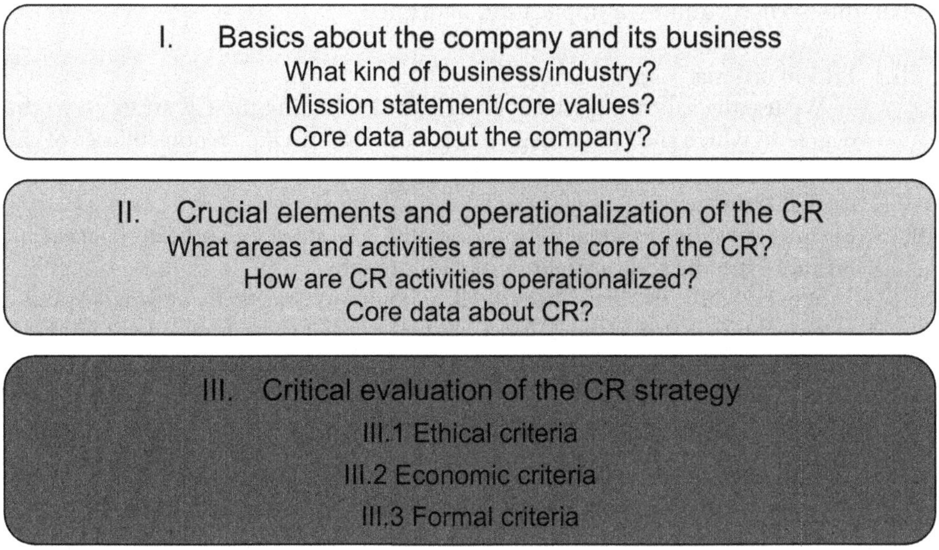

I. **Basics about the company and its business**
What kind of business/industry?
Mission statement/core values?
Core data about the company?

II. **Crucial elements and operationalization of the CR**
What areas and activities are at the core of the CR?
How are CR activities operationalized?
Core data about CR?

III. **Critical evaluation of the CR strategy**
III.1 Ethical criteria
III.2 Economic criteria
III.3 Formal criteria

Figure 4.5 Method for CR analysis.

Step I: identify basics about the company and its business

The first step identifies basic characteristics of the company and its business. We need this information because, as argued, a good CR strategy needs to be *business-specific*, that means the strategy needs to identify and address the company's business-specific responsibilities resulting from its specific operations, products, supply chains, and stakeholders (see Sections 4.1 and 4.2). Relevant information for understanding the basics of a company's business include, for instance, the industry it operates in, the product and services it offers, its locations, revenue and profits, number and type of employees, characteristics of the supply chain, and mission statement.

Step II: identify crucial elements and operationalization of the company's CR

The second step is about understanding the existing CR strategy and CR activities of the company. What are the main focuses of the CR, and what specific goals and activities does the CR emphasize? CR strategies of large companies can be rather complex, and one needs to do some analysis to identify the main focuses of a CR strategy. It is also important to look into the concrete activities and programs that the company runs under their CR, as well as how the company operates them. For instance, some companies run CR activities by themselves, whereas others seek assistance from NGOs and similar organizations for running CR activities.

Step III: critically evaluate the CR strategy

In this step, we critically evaluate the quality of the CR strategy. We want to judge whether the CR strategy is good or not. For this, we need criteria that we can apply and that allow us to support the evaluation. We will use three sets of criteria: ethical criteria, economic criteria, and formal criteria. In the following, we will develop and explain these criteria and their application in detail

III.1 Ethical criteria

We use the following ethical criteria for evaluating the CR strategy: (i) the degree to which the CR strategy meets business-specific responsibilities of the company, (ii) the effectiveness of the CR strategy, and (iii) the credibility of the CR strategy.

III.1.i Business-specific responsibilities: does the CR strategy sufficiently meet all business-specific responsibilities of the company?

We critically evaluate how well a company meets its business-specific responsibilities using the following two steps: (a) first, we determine the business-specific responsibilities of the company using an ELCA and/or ESA, and (b) then we check to what extent the existing CR strategy of the company addresses those business-specific responsibilities.

a) We need to identify the business-specific responsibilities of the company under consideration. So, we need to critically analyze the business activities and stakeholder relationships of the company to identify its specific responsibilities and moral obligations. For this, we can refer to the two methods we developed in Section 4.2: ELCA and ESA. In many cases, we do not need to apply the methods in detail and do a full analysis. It may be sufficient to identify crucial ethical issues and the main responsibilities of the company under consideration.

b) After we have identified crucial ethical impacts and moral responsibilities of the company, we need to check the existing CR strategy of the company, and verify whether it addresses those impacts and adequately assumes its business-specific responsibilities. We need to check by which activities and to what extent the business addresses its business-specific responsibilities. We need to critically evaluate whether the CR activities are sufficient to address the business-specific responsibilities. For supporting our judgment, we can use the criteria for responsibility defined in Section 4.2: causality, knowledge, and power/ability. The activities of the business to meet its business-specific responsibilities should correlate to the degree of responsibility that one can reasonably ascribe to the business when considering (i) to what extent the business causes the ethical issue, (ii) to what extent the business knows or could have known about the issue's occurrence, and (iii) how much power and ability the business has to address the issue. Also, one needs to critically evaluate whether the CR adequately considers the rights of all stakeholders and the corresponding moral obligations of the company.

III.1.ii Effectiveness: does the CR strategy effectively address ethical issues and responsibilities?

A good CR strategy needs to be effective. That means it should address and significantly reduce the ethical issues at hand and ensure robust ethical stakeholder relationships. We need to check whether the CR report of the company provides sufficient evidence for the effectiveness of the CR strategy, such as verifiable data about progress and meeting well-defined goals. One should identify and critically discuss any shortcomings with regard to effectiveness.

III.1.iii Credibility: is the CR strategy credibly maintained in all business operations?

A business usually wants to tell the best possible story about itself, including its CR activities. It is crucial to check whether the claims of the business are credible. We need to verify if the CR strategy is a serious management strategy or just PR or greenwashing. This can be done by doing some research on external perspectives on the company. What do reliable external sources, such as well-recognized NGOs, research, and governmental agencies, say about the company? Have there been recent scandals, investigations by regulatory agencies, or court verdicts that contradict the claims of the CR report? Another important aspect for credibility is external assurance for the CR report: does the company seek external assurance of its CR data by an independent trustworthy organization?

III.2 Economic criteria

III.2.i Does the CR strategy support the business success of the company?

A good CR strategy should aim at maximizing the win-win between ethics and business success. In other words, a good CR strategy is designed in a way that not only sufficiently addresses all business-specific responsibilities of the company, but at the same time supports its business success. Depending on the case, there are various ways in which a CR strategy can support business success. We can use here the list of potential business benefits from Section 4.3.3 and check whether the CR strategy actively provides some of these benefits to the company:

- Improved stakeholder relationships
- Proactive risk management
- Attraction of highly qualified employees
- Contribution to strategic management
- Innovation and efficiency gains
- Identification of new markets/products
- Building reputation
- Improving competitiveness

III.2.ii Is the CR strategy economically reasonable?

CR strategies may require substantial means. As with any investment, CR activities need economic justification. Different criteria could be used for justification. First, one may require that economic investments are at least feasible. That is, except in extreme cases, one would not require a business to maintain CR activities that could endanger its own viability. Second, from a business perspective one usually aims at an optimal investment. The optimal investment might be difficult to determine precisely with regard to CR, but, at the very least, one obviously does not want to waste money and time on CR activities that are ineffective from both an ethical and a business point of view.

III.3 Formal criteria

Formal criteria evaluate certain formal aspects of reporting CR activities and data, as well as the implementation of the CR strategy into the overall governance structure and operations of the company. Formal aspects that matter are the quality, transparency, credibility, and comparability of the CR strategy and report. Usually, formal criteria should be easy to verify by using information from the company. One should check the following aspects:

- Does the company publish a CR report?
- Does the CR report follow established reporting guidelines and business norms, such as GRI guidelines (GRI, 2018), UN Global Compact (UN, 2018), and human rights?
- Does the CR report provide measurable data and well-defined goals?
- Does the company provide external assurance for its CR data?
- Is the CR strategy integrated well into the governance structure, and does it align with other business ethics instruments?

How the formal criteria factor into the overall evaluation of the CR strategy of a company depends on the specific company. For instance, one would expect a larger corporation to publish a formal CR report and follow GRI or similar guidelines, but not expect so much from a smaller business. For small and medium-size businesses, some other forms of publishing and assurances of CR activities may also be acceptable.

The application of the above ethical, economic, and formal criteria should result in a thorough critical analysis of a company's CR strategy, and enable us to provide an evaluation of the overall quality of the CR strategy, to spot potential weaknesses and inefficiencies, and to issue recommendations for improvements.

With some modification, one can also use the above method for CR analysis for the design of a new CR strategy. For the latter purpose, one would only pursue steps I, III.1.i(a), III.1.ii, and III.3 of the method, but skip steps II and III.1.i(b). In particular, the criteria of III.1.i(a) and III.3 can serve as guidelines and requirements for designing an optimal CR strategy.

4.5 Internal ethics and culture of organizations

CR strategies focus on the overall societal and environmental responsibilities of a company, and with this specifically emphasize ethical aspects of the external context in which the company operates. This section shifts the focus to internal ethical aspects of companies and organizations. Internal ethical aspects are crucial for companies and organizations, where various people work and spend significant time together. Internal ethics is about norms and values that ensure all members of the organization act and interact in a right and good way, and that an overall atmosphere is created in which everyone feels safe, respected, and can thrive. This is desirable from an ethical point of view, but likewise crucial for the success of any organization or company. People need to do right by and trust each other in order to work successfully together toward common goals. If this is not the case, and distrust and unethical behavior, such as harassment, bullying, or stealing, corrupts an organization, proper functioning and success can be substantially undermined.

What should we ideally expect from an organization with regard to internal ethics? Based on the ethical approaches from Chapter 2, we can formulate some fundamental expectations and guidelines for internal organizational ethics. Following virtue ethics, an organization should promote personal and professional development of all its members, support development of professional and personal potential of every member/employee, and create an atmosphere in which everyone can thrive. Following Kantian ethics, an organization should ensure that everyone is treated with respect, no one is treated as mere means, and everyone is considered as ends in themselves and persons endowed with reason. This particularly implies transparent, fair, and equal treatment. From the perspective of ethics of care, an organization should care about all its employees and their wellbeing. Altogether, an organization should ideally form an internal community that is characterized by shared norms and values, which actualize in everyday actions and interactions. It may be worth noting that such an organizational ethics is very well compatible with, and actually may encourage, tough competition, challenges, and hard work.

In the following, we will spell out implications of the above general ethical guidelines for the organizational context in more detail by using the concepts of *organizational culture* and *ethical culture*.

4.5.1 Ethical culture of organizations

Any organization is characterized by a distinct culture, which is embodied in the sum of its artifacts and actions of its members. For instance, the culture encompasses the design of the organization's buildings and offices; the way employees communicate with each other, with higher level management, and with external stakeholders; the way employees and leaders dress; the design of web pages and social media presence; and so on. A crucial part of an organization's culture are values and norms. These can be explicitly defined by the mission statement, the core values of the organization, or further rules and policies. However, norms and values may also implicitly be formed and expressed by the members of the organization. In the context of internal interactions, certain expectations and norms can informally develop over time, which establish common knowledge about how things are supposed to be done, what actions are acknowledged, what behavior resonates, and so on. Often, leadership has a crucial impact. Approval and disapproval of actions and behavior by leadership sends crucial signals about what is and is not valued, as do the individual actions of leaders. Overall, the norms and values established in an organization have a crucial impact on the way all its members will act and interact with other stakeholders. We will call the entire set of formal and informal norms, values, and virtues established in an organization the *ethical culture* of the organization and consider it a fundamental subset of organizational culture.

> Definition 4.4: An **ethical culture of an organization** is the sum of explicit and implicit values, principles, and ethical reflections that underlie, and are expressed by, the interactions and actions of its members.

Of course, there exists a large diversity of different business cultures, and a large range of legitimate values and norms, which different businesses emphasize. For instance, culture and values at such companies as Google, General Electric, and Patagonia are rather different, but all three companies can be considered ethical and responsible. However, on a more fundamental level, one can distinguish companies with a strong ethical culture from companies that have a weak ethical culture or a corrupt culture, and in reality we find the entire spectrum in between. For instance, the three above-mentioned companies are more on the side of a strong ethical culture according to this spectrum (independent of their different values and culture), whereas Enron would be an example of a corrupt culture.

Underpinnings and characteristics of a strong ethical culture

How can we distinguish a strong ethical culture from a weak or corrupt culture of an organization? One can define an ethical culture as *strong* when it is grounded in, and upholds, fundamental ethical principles. In the following, we will explore principles and characteristics of a strong ethical culture in more detail. Note that there can still be a large diversity of different values emphasized and very different realizations of a strong ethical culture are possible.

KANTIAN PRINCIPLES

A strong ethical culture is grounded in the principle of respecting each member as ends in themselves and persons endowed with reason. This means that no one is treated as a mere means, that reasons are given for all matters that significantly concern a member of the organization, and that each member is empowered to participate in decisions and meaningful work. From these principles follow some specific characteristics of a strong ethical culture.

Respect and reasons

A strong ethical culture promotes and guarantees respectful behavior. Respectful behavior means that employees and leadership treat each other as ends in themselves and rational persons, and act accordingly toward all stakeholders. Respectful behavior prohibits all kind of actions that treat another person as mere means or undermines another's dignity as a free, rational person. For instance, abuse of power, harassment, or bullying, are fundamentally disrespectful. Respect further implies that reasons are established for crucial decisions that significantly impact members of the organization. Persons endowed with reason have a moral right to know why something is done to them, and the organization and leadership have the moral obligation to give reasons for such actions. A formal mechanism that establishes reasons is due process – that is, there are defined rules and procedures that determine why and how certain actions in the company are done – for instance, promotions, performance evaluations, pay raises, and termination (see also Section 5.1). Due process and well-defined policies not only provide reasons for certain actions; they also guarantee transparency, fairness, and equality, and protect against arbitrary uses of authority. Overall a strong ethical culture is characterized by transparent, reason-based decision-making. A top-down leadership approach based on mere power and not on underlying reasons would contradict the principle of respectful treatment and would reduce employees to mere objects. Also, any type of abuse of power would violate the principle of respectful treatment and be a characteristic of a corrupt culture.

Participation and open, critical discourse

From a Kantian perspective, an organization is a community of reasonable persons who should participate in decision-making and not just be mere objects of decision-making. Rational beings have thoughts, ideas, and concerns that they want to contribute to the community of which they are part. An organization/company should empower its members/employees to contribute to decision-making as far as this is feasible. The organization should empower all members to speak up, raise concerns, and make suggestions, and with this contribute to a rational, open, and transparent discourse about all matters of the organization. As a rational person, every member at every level, regardless of their positions in an organization, can bring valuable insights and thoughts that can foster a critical discourse, which recognizes various perspectives and options, and subsequently supports optimal decision-making and business success.

Responsibility

There are also certain expectations toward persons endowed with reason. In a strong ethical culture, every single member should assume responsibility for their actions and for the wellbeing of the organization, and the organization should empower every member to assume responsibility and make ethical decisions. Every member should be able to assume responsibility, make decisions, and justify them. For instance, if someone spots an issue that requires immediate attention, she should assume responsibility and address the issue, no matter what role or position she has in the organization. In a corrupt culture, employees would just ignore issues that are not in their job description and that no one told them to address. A strong ethical culture would empower people to assume responsibility by themselves and acknowledge responsible actions. It would be characterized by ethical reflection and decision-making on all levels of the organization, and by all members assuming responsibility.

VIRTUE ETHICAL PRINCIPLES

A strong ethical culture empowers all its members to develop their full professional potential and to thrive as human beings in the workplace. That would specifically mean that the culture supports the development of professional and personal virtues, and the development of the professional and personal excellence of all its members. The culture would have a holistic approach to its members: it would consider its members as human beings who strive for an overall good life, enable them to integrate their professional life with other aspects of life, and to integrate their professional identity and development with their overall personal identity and development.

A strong ethical culture is characterized by proper mechanisms of feedback and guidance, which help every member reflect on, and further develop, his own professional and personal potential. Further, every member has appropriate challenges and room for developing their own potential in an optimal way. Finally, the organization would establish mechanisms that allow for a positive integration of professional and private life, or, in other words, for an optimal work–life balance.

In contrast, a corrupt culture would merely use, or even burn out, its members/ employees, and provide no support for developing professional potential and for integrating personal and professional life.

CARE PRINCIPLES

In a strong ethical culture, everyone cares about the wellbeing of every other member of the organization, as well as of the overall welfare and success of the organization. In such a culture employees would care about their co-workers and their wellbeing.

Leaders and supervisors would care about the people who report to them; that is, not only assign and control tasks, but also assume responsibility for the wellbeing of employees. An interesting example for such a culture is New Belgium Brewery in Fort Collins, Colorado. Founded in 1991, New Belgium now is the fourth largest craft brewery in the US, with about 700 employees and over $225 million revenue (Dahl, 2016). New Belgium understands the importance of individual wellbeing in daily business. In one department, team members check in with one another every day, looking for a thumb up, thumb sideways, or thumb down. If they see a thumb down, indicating significant emotional stress, the team will do everything they can to excuse and cover for that person (K. Wallace, personal communication, June 28, 2018).[3] For instance, someone could have a rather bad day because something serious happened in her personal life. She would be better off then to not work that day and deal with the situation. This practice not only cares about the employees and their wellbeing but also makes business sense. An employee who feels very bad will likely not be able to perform well that day, and his emotional distress and lack of performance may even negatively impact the entire team (K. Wallace, personal communication, June 28, 2018). The success of New Belgium, which significantly outperforms most of its competitors, indicates that a culture of care actually improves the overall performance and success of the business.

PRINCIPLES OF FAIRNESS AND EQUALITY

In a strong ethical culture, everyone is treated fairly and equally based on well-defined, transparent, and generally acceptable rules, procedures, and principles. The principles of fairness and equality can be supported by Kantian and Rawlsian ethics. From a Kantian perspective, fair and equal treatment follows from the general principle that all persons are equally ends in themselves and have a right to be treated with respect and as beings endowed with reason. From a Rawlsian perspective, a culture of fairness needs to be grounded in principles that everyone can agree upon. The content of rules and procedures are not arbitrary in this perspective but need to be grounded in reasonable principles and be generally agreeable. For instance, rules that disadvantage some group in the organization would not be fair, as they would not receive overall agreement behind a 'veil of ignorance' (see Section 2.4).

As with many general ethical principles, fairness and equality require a lot of attention to be fully realized in business practice. Many examples show that fairness and equality are notoriously difficult to realize in certain areas. One such example is equal pay for men and women. That everyone should get paid in the same way for the same job and qualification is pretty obvious and in abstract terms generally agreed upon. However, in reality there exists a significant gender pay gap; that is, women get paid significantly less than men. Many data and much research confirm this issue as a given fact in today's society. For instance, a comparison of weekly median earnings (full time) shows that for the job of waiter/waitress women's earnings are 82% of men's earnings, for physicians/surgeons women's earnings are 80.1% of men's earnings, and for financial managers women's earnings are 65.2% of men's earnings (USDOL, 2017, pp. 16f). A strong ethical culture would pay particular attention to the full realization of fairness and equality, implement measures to address such pervasive societal issues, and ensure equal pay within its own context.

Diversity and inclusion aim at upholding equality in the context of organizations and businesses by addressing a specifically difficult issue of realizing equality within the society, or rather the lack thereof. In abstract terms equal opportunity is a fundamental and shared value. However, in reality, not everyone has equal opportunity or is treated equally. On the contrary, some groups, such as women or certain minorities have been systematically disadvantaged. This can easily be seen with some statistical data. For instance, only about 5% of all CEOs of Fortune 500 companies are women and fewer than 1% are black (Brown, 2017; Donnelly, 2018). Similarly, only about 5% of all CEOs of S&P 1500 companies are women (Desilver, 2018). As we can assume that talent and abilities are equally distributed in the population, we should expect the number of female and black CEOs to roughly mirror the share of these groups in the overall population, which would be about 50% female and 12% black CEOs. Thus, women and black people are significantly underrepresented in these top positions. This finding is not a singularity. Significant underrepresentation can also be seen in many other crucial areas. For instance, minorities are significantly underrepresented at top colleges in the US (Ashkenas et al., 2017).

These findings indicate that there exist (hidden) barriers and hindrances in society that prevent equal access and equal opportunities. There are various underlying reasons for this, and barriers can come in many shapes. For instance, various prejudices, stereotypes, and unconscious biases that can implicitly or explicitly influence hiring and promotion decisions, or institutional barriers, such as lack of equal access to excellent primary and secondary education, which early on distort equal opportunity. Underrepresentation is often rooted in a longer, complex history of discrimination. The root causes of underrepresentation are difficult societal issues that organizations and companies cannot fully cure. However, diversity and inclusion programs encompass measures of companies and organizations to actively address the issue of systematic underrepresentation within their own areas of power and control. By implementing diversity and inclusion programs, companies assume their share of responsibility to help society addressing a complex societal issue and move toward a better realization of equality.

It is worth noting here that there is not only an obvious ethics case for diversity and inclusion, but also a business case. Diversity and inclusion resonates well with various stakeholder groups, many of which mirror the diversity of the overall society. If a company or organization significantly lacks diversity, this may not resonate well with crucial stakeholders, such as customers or investors, and as a result, negatively impact business success. For instance, if a college has about 20% Hispanic students, which would roughly reflect the share of Hispanics in the US society, but only a few Hispanic faculty members, it might not resonate with those students or potential future students. Furthermore, diversity and inclusion can empower more creative thinking and innovative solutions in a company if more diverse perspectives and backgrounds are integrated into decision-making processes.

To realize diversity and inclusion, many companies and organizations run programs that actively try to increase the number of underrepresented groups. Typical measures of such diversity and inclusion programs are targeted recruiting, which would actively reach out to underrepresented groups and encourage potential candidates to apply, training programs that can, for instance, help to raise cultural awareness or address issues of unconscious biases, or mentoring programs that support the career of employees from underrepresented groups in the company/organization. Such measures are sometimes addressed with the term affirmative action. Affirmative action generally means active measures to protect and support members of societal groups that have historically been disadvantaged and discriminated against.

Defining in detail the proper set of diversity and inclusion measures can be difficult, though. Some measures can come with challenges. Consider, for instance, the following example. A company has recently decided to start a diversity and inclusion program. The program has identified significant underrepresentation of women in the company, and as a result the company aims to increase the number of female workers. When filling the next open position, and hiring a new employee, this diversity goal is considered. Consider now four scenarios: (i) among the applicants is one woman that is better qualified than all male applicants; (ii) one top female applicant is equally qualified compared to another top male applicant; (iii) one woman meets all qualifications listed in the job description and advertisement, as does another male applicant, who has some additional qualifications; (iv) some women applied, but none of them meets the qualifications defined in the job description, whereas some male applicants do. Scenario (i) is obvious. In scenario (ii) there are two equally qualified candidates, and it is ethically justifiable to hire the women based on the additional diversity goals of the company. Scenario (iii) is more difficult, but one can argue that the well-defined diversity goals of the company should factor in more than some arbitrary additional qualifications that were not defined in the job description. In scenario (iv) it might be problematic to follow the diversity goals because this could be considered unfair against the qualified male candidates.

How to develop and support a strong ethical culture

A strong ethical culture can be developed and supported in an organization by a coherent interplay of various formal and informal factors. One crucial factor is proper implementation of more technical and formal aspects of organizational design, such as (i) well-defined rules, policies, and procedures, (ii) supportive incentives and rewards, (iii) a well-implemented ethical and compliance program, and (iv) established programs promoting equality and fairness, such as the diversity and inclusion program discussed above.

A proper set of basic policies, rules, and procedures can support a strong ethical culture in various ways. Policies, rules, and procedures establish basic normative guidelines and implement due process in the company. With this, they formalize respectful, transparent, fair, and equal treatment of all employees and prevent wrongdoing, favoritism, and abuse of power. For instance, well-defined criteria and procedures for promotion guarantee transparency and fairness and prevent favoritism. Everyone in the company knows when and why someone gets promoted, which fosters a harmonious and respectful atmosphere and fair competition among the employees. In contrast, lack of criteria and rules make promotion decisions non-transparent, and allow for unfair practices, such as favoritism, that can easily poison the work atmosphere. Another example for useful basic rules is spending guidelines and second-signature requirement. Both are basic measures that help avoid wrongdoing and misuse of company funds. Proper incentives and rewards are also crucial in supporting a strong ethical culture. Employees generally observe what is rewarded and who gets promoted in an organization or company. If rewards do not reflect ethical criteria and expectations, employees might take ethics less seriously. However, if responsible actions, upholding core values, and other ethical actions are acknowledged – for instance, in annual evaluations, pay raises, and promotion decisions – this will underpin and support a strong ethical culture.

A second crucial factor for a strong ethical culture is ethical leadership and adequate leadership style. It is important that leaders on all levels act as ethical role models and exhibit ethical principles, norms, and values of the organization in their everyday actions and interactions with other members of the organization and external stakeholders. Leaders must be role models in upholding policies and procedures, supporting the core values and mission of the company, and supporting the ethical programs and the CR strategy of the company. This gives the ethical culture authenticity and credibility and sets the right tone for the entire organization and its members. Employees typically observe and orientate themselves on the behavior of their direct supervisors. If the latter act as role models of ethical behavior, it has significant positive impact on the culture of the organization. Also, a strong ethical culture can only develop if leadership empowers and acknowledges open critical discourse, and if leaders transparently base decisions on reasons, empower employees to act responsibly, and care about the wellbeing and professional development of their employees (see also Section 5.2).

Third, a strong ethical culture is promoted by proper integration of different ethical programs and activities, and ethics overall properly embedded into the governance structure of an organization. The various aspects discussed in this section need to be coherently linked to other business ethics tools, such as CR strategy and to the core values and mission of the company. It is crucial to link all ethical strategies, programs, and activities to a well-defined mission statement and to core values that are grounded in ethical principles. Ideally, the mission statement and core values function as foundational ethical principles and 'constitution' of the company, guiding all other business ethics strategies and programs as well as management decisions.

Finally, support from society and stakeholders can also help an organization or company develop and uphold a strong ethical culture. If crucial stakeholders, such as customers, investors, and employees demand, appreciate, and reward a strong ethical culture, it encourages the company to develop such a culture. A strong ethical culture is indeed often rewarded by stakeholders. An increasing number of customers prefer companies that are socially and environmentally responsible. There is also a growing amount of investment that focuses on ethically responsible companies, and employees may also be more attracted to a strong ethical culture. As a result, a strong ethical culture supports the overall success and profitability of a company, which also creates a business case for such a culture.

4.5.2 Ethics and compliance programs

Certain formal and technical measures for enabling an ethical culture of an organization are often conflated under the label *ethics and compliance program*. It is worth discussing ethics and compliance programs separately in this section, as they have become well established in practice, encompass a couple of crucial ethical measures, and establish a legal case for business ethics (in addition to the ethical case and the business case which we have emphasized in this book so far). Ethics and compliance programs promote ethical and lawful behavior within organizations and support proper and successful functioning of more complex organizations, particularly larger corporations. They minimize internal frictions and wrongdoing, professionally address internal issues and conflicts, and support professional and ethical actions and interactions of all employees.

> Definition 4.5: An **ethics and compliance program** is a formal internal mechanism that implements ethics and compliance throughout an organization.

Elements of an ethics and compliance program

An ethics and compliance program consists of several elements which work together to manage internal ethics and compliance. In the following, we discuss some typical elements of an ethics and compliance program.

CODE OF CONDUCT

As already discussed above, it is crucial for an organization to formulate the norms and values that should guide its actions. A *code of conduct* is a written standard that defines crucial normative guidelines for the professional actions of the members of the organization. Many organizations have such written standards, which can have different names, such as *code of professional conduct* or *standards of business conduct*. A code of conduct is an important element of an ethics and compliance program, as it clearly defines basic rules and expectations, and provides an internal and external message about the norms that guide the company and its employees. A typical topic of a code of conduct is, for instance, rules for accepting gifts related to professional activities. Such guidance is crucial for employees because in certain business situations a gift could easily be perceived as a bribe and have serious legal implications. A good code of conduct gives clear advice for all employees of the company when gifts are acceptable, if at all, and when they are not.

A code of conduct should reflect actual laws and regulations of the societies in which the company operates. This implies that the code must be regularly updated, as rules and laws change constantly. Secondly, a good code of conduct needs to be tailored to the specific business and practices of the company. Rules that are too general and abstract are often not very helpful in everyday business activities and concrete job situations. The code of conduct should provide specific advice and concrete examples that relate to specific job situations and typical business activities of the company. The code of conduct should also correlate with the core values of the organization, which formulate more general and abstract values, and specific policies of the organization that provide more detailed guidance.

ETHICS AND COMPLIANCE TRAINING

It is usually not enough to just formulate and publish norms and values. They need to be effectively communicated and integrated within an organization. Ethics and compliance training is a typical instrument for communicating and implementing the norms and values of the organization, specifically the guidelines of the code of conduct. A good ethics and compliance training is tailored to specific job situations and provides concrete examples and advice about how to act in various ethically or legally critical situations. The training needs to be regularly done to remind employees about the rules, and it must be regularly updated to reflect legal changes and new ethical challenges.

MECHANISMS FOR EMPLOYEES TO RAISE CONCERNS AND SPEAK UP

Essential elements of a good ethics and compliance program are mechanisms that enable and support employees to speak up and raise concerns. Typical mechanisms are, for instance, ethics hotlines or designated persons, such as ethics and compliance officers, that allow employees to safely and confidentially raise concerns. Usually companies also have some policy that prohibits any form of retaliation against employees who raise legitimate concerns. However, a strong ethical culture is also a crucial aspect. Employees need to be encouraged and empowered to identify and talk about issues and conflicts. An organization must build trust that concerns and critiques are appreciated and taken seriously. Empowering and enabling employees to speak up is crucial for the success of any company or organization because it helps to detect and solve issues and conflicts early on rather than ignoring or covering them up. The latter can easily poison the atmosphere and result in employees leaving the company, negatively impacted work performance, and, in the worst case, legal and liability issues.

MECHANISMS TO ADDRESS ISSUES

It is important to properly identify issues, but likewise it is important to professionally address them. For this, a company needs well-defined standard procedures for typical issues, as well as persons who are trained to professionally address issues. For instance, many organizations have well-defined procedures for how to react to certain rule violations. Also, professionals such as ethics and compliance officers, who are specifically trained, are often better suited to address and solve issues than immediate supervisors or higher-level management. Supervisors could easily be overwhelmed when confronted with some serious issue, such as sexual harassment.

MECHANISMS FOR PROGRAM EVALUATION

An ethics and compliance program should be critically evaluated and further developed over time. It is useful to establish mechanisms for measuring the effectiveness of the program and to increase effectiveness where necessary. For instance, the company can regularly collect data about the occurrence of certain issues, such as harassment, bullying, or stealing. The data would then indicate whether the ethics and compliance program has been effective in reducing such issues over time. The ethics and compliance program also needs to be regularly updated to reflect new issues, challenges, and regulations.

OVERSIGHT AND LEADERSHIP

All of the elements and activities described above need to be professionally managed and monitored. Larger companies often implement ethics and compliance offices, hire specialists, and establish the position of a chief compliance officer (CCO) or chief ethics and compliance officer (CECO), who leads and oversees the ethics and compliance program. Smaller businesses and organizations may want to outsource certain functions of an ethics and compliance program or integrate them into human resources. Leadership of an ethics and compliance program ideally is located at the executive level and has sufficient independence and power. Further ethics and compliance programs should be perceived as interdisciplinary tasks and delegated to an interdisciplinary team of ethics and compliance officers, who have expertise in business law, organizational ethics, and organizational psychology. Legal experts are crucial for ensuring that the ethics and compliance program properly reflects current laws and regulations that are relevant to the company and its business, and also for ensuring proper dealings with the legal aspects of more serious issues, such as stealing, sexual harassment, and so on. However, many ethical issues in an organization are below the threshold of being illegal. Yet, issues like bullying or harassment still are serious issues that need to be professionally addressed, and specialists that are trained in conflict management could help address such issues. Experts with a background in psychology or education can assist in the optimal design and delivery of the ethics and compliance training.

In conclusion, an ethics and compliance program can have different degrees of quality. A good program has all of the elements and qualities described above, is well integrated into the overall ethical approach and governance structure of an organization, and results in measurable improvements of the internal ethics of an organization.

Reasons for implementing an ethics and compliance program

There is a business case, an ethical case, and a legal case for implementing ethics and compliance programs in companies and organizations. Ethical, business, and legal reasons together have encouraged many companies and organizations to establish ethics and compliance programs and, with this, promote business ethics. From an ethical perspective, an ethics and compliance program can help promote a strong ethical culture and fosters ethical actions. From a business perspective, a well-designed ethics and compliance program (i) reduces risks for the organization that result from the wrongdoing of its members, (ii) reduces internal conflicts and increases team work and positive collaboration, (iii) establishes conflict solution mechanisms that professionally deal with and solve internal issues, and (iv) reduces potential conflict with stakeholders that result from harm done by unethical actions of the members of the organization. An ethics and compliance program, therefore, contributes in various ways to the viability and success of the organization.

In addition, there are also legal reasons for implementing an ethics and compliance program. Several legal changes since the beginning of this century, such as the Sarbanes–Oxley Act (2002), revisions of Chapter Eight of the US Sentencing Guidelines (USSG), and the Dodd–Frank Act (2010), among others, have increased the legal expectations for businesses to proactively reduce the risk of internal wrongdoing and promote an ethical culture. Some aspects of these legal frameworks go beyond classic compliance mechanisms, which provide precise rules for action and ensure the rules are followed. Rather, legal frameworks now increasingly ask businesses to assume more responsibility and establish internal mechanisms to ensure responsible actions of its employees. In other words, there is a legal push to more business ethics and ethical self-governance. The USSG are the most obvious example. The USSG strongly encourage the implementation of ethics and compliance programs and, in cases of misconduct, suggest more severe penalties for organizations that lack effective ethics and compliance programs. In the following, the reasons for an ethics and compliance program, which were outlined above, are discussed in more detail.

MINIMIZING RISKS OF EMPLOYEE MISCONDUCT

Employee misconduct can harm an entire organization in various ways. Misconduct can be directed at other members of the organization, for instance, harassment; it can contradict the interests of the organizations, for instance, cases of conflict of interest or stealing from the organization; it can harm stakeholders of the organization, such as competitors in the case of bribery. Although wrongdoing may be done intentionally some misconduct may not result from bad intentions but rather from ignorance or neglect. In complex organizational contexts employees may not be aware of doing something that could potentially harm the organization. For instance, social media use is full of pitfalls that employees may not fully observe. A well-designed ethics and compliance program helps employees better understand the various instances of potentially harmful actions and reduces overall misconduct in an organization.

MINIMIZING CONFLICTS WITH STAKEHOLDERS AND SOCIETY

An ethics and compliance program addresses internal ethics but also has implications for the relationship with external stakeholders. First of all, an ethics and compliance program minimizes internal wrongdoings that have the potential to harm external stakeholders. For instance, bribing harms competitors; accounting fraud or insider trading harms stockholders; and so on. An ethics and compliance program also reduces all kinds of internal wrongdoings that can cause conflicts with society and damage the reputation of an organization. Finally, an ethics and compliance program provides direct advice to employees regarding how to interact in an ethical and legal way with external stakeholders, such as customers and suppliers.

MINIMIZING INTERNAL FRICTIONS AND CONFLICTS

Even if we assume that all members of an organization have good intentions, there always exists the potential for internal conflicts and tensions. Issues can range from intentional misbehavior, such as bullying or harassment, to conflicts resulting from different values, to issues that are not done intentionally, but rather result from a lack of sensitivity or awareness. For instance, what is just a funny joke to one person can be rather insulting to another. A well-designed ethics and compliance program provides tools to increase or enhance awareness and respect, and reduces internal conflicts.

PROFESSIONALLY DEALING WITH ISSUES, CONCERNS, AND CONFLICTS

Preventing ethical issues is one thing, but addressing and fixing issues in a professional way when they occur is another. It is important that an organization has the ability to professionally deal with various types of internal concerns, conflicts, and issues. This minimizes the harm to the organization as a whole and ensures due process and fair treatment of all members involved or affected by an issue. An ethics and compliance office ideally has the professional tools to properly react to various ethical and legal issues. Due process and standardized procedures are crucial for effective and fair solution of issues.

Some organizations also develop crisis management strategies to quickly and effectively address severe issues and prevent potential serious crises. A crisis management strategy defines steps and responsibilities for cases in which events (wrongdoings) that have the potential to significantly harm the organization occur. For instance, if a serious case of insider trading or bribing should occur, the crisis management strategy would suggest actions that need to be taken, such as putting persons who are potentially involved on paid leave, contacting an external law firm to conduct an internal investigation, issuing a public statement about the matter and steps taken to address it, and so on. Also, the crisis management strategy would define who is in charge in different crisis scenarios and what external sources are available for assistance.

LEGAL EXPECTATIONS: THE US SENTENCING GUIDELINES (USSG)

A major incentive for establishing ethics and compliance programs comes from legal expectations. These express the interest society as a whole has in ethical business conduct. The reason for the societal interest is obvious. Recent scandals have shown that lack of ethics is not only a risk for businesses themselves but can also result in significant harm to the society. Particularly the financial crisis of 2008 has shown that damages from irresponsible business activities toward society can be very large. Thus, business ethics is a matter of public interest. This is reflected in some recent developments in the legal framework which demand more responsibility from companies and ask companies to establish internal mechanisms for promoting ethical actions and an ethical culture.

In particular, Chapter Eight of the USSG has played a crucial role this context. Chapter Eight of the USSG is about the sentencing of organizations. It provides guidelines for the punishment of organizations in cases where a member of an organization committed an offence. In such cases the individual who committed the offence certainly will be prosecuted but, at the same time, the organization will also be held accountable:

> Organizations can act only through agents and, under federal criminal law, generally are vicariously liable for offenses committed by their agents. This chapter is designed so that the sanctions imposed upon organizations and their agents, taken together, will provide just punishment, adequate deterrence, and incentives for organizations to maintain internal mechanisms for preventing, detecting, and reporting criminal conduct.
>
> (USSC, 2016, Ch. 8, Introductory comment)

The last sentence in the above quote expresses the twofold aim of the USSG: just punishment of organizations and incentives for organizations to prevent and identify internal misconduct. The USSG encourage the implementation of ethics and compliance programs to reduce internal misconduct. If, nevertheless, some misconduct happens, a well-designed ethics and compliance program would reduce the punishment for the organization: 'The two factors that mitigate the ultimate punishment of an organization are: (i) the existence of an effective compliance and ethics program; and (ii) self-reporting, cooperation, or acceptance of responsibility' (USSC, 2016, Ch. 8, Introductory comment).

The USSG also encourage organizations to actively promote an ethical culture: 'An organization shall [. . .] promote an organizational culture that encourages ethical conduct and a commitment to compliance with the law' (USSC, 2016, §8B2.1). In addition, the USSG provide concrete advice for the implementation of an ethics and compliance program into an organization's governance structure: 'The organization's governing authority shall be knowledgeable about the content and the operations of the compliance and ethics program and shall exercise reasonable oversight [. . .]' (USSC, 2016, §8B2.1). In other words, the governing authority of an organization, that is in the case of corporations the board of directors, should assume direct responsibility and oversight for the ethical aspects of the organization. Persons who lead and oversee the ethics and compliance program, such as the CCO or CECO, ideally should report directly to the board of directors and not to the CEO.

PROMOTING A STRONG ETHICAL CULTURE

An ethics and compliance program by itself is not sufficient to ensure internal ethics within an organization. However, an ethics and compliance program can contribute to, and support, an ethical culture if it is properly designed. For this, it is crucial that the ethics and compliance program builds trust and not an atmosphere of mere control. The ethical and compliance program should be grounded in ethical reasons and values and encourage ethical reflection and discourse among all members of an organization. This way, the ethics and compliance program can become a crucial element of the ethical culture of an organization.

Notes

1 The analysis of product life cycles has become more popular in recent business practice, particular for larger companies. Most companies use the method to focus on environmental impacts, such as carbon footprint or water, energy, and material use, and some companies also analyze certain societal impacts, such as health and safety issues or human rights violations. Environmental impacts are particularly easy to measure, and companies use the data to identify and realize efficiency potentials in their product life cycle. The ELCA developed in this book is designed specifically as an ethical approach, though, to identify all ethically critical impacts in the product life cycle and determine resulting ethical responsibilities.
2 One may also evaluate current CR activities of corporations more critically, as some smaller adjustment to current business practice that is not sufficient for adequately addressing social and sustainability issues of the global economic system. For specifically critical reflections on the potentials and limitations of CSR see, e.g., Kuhn and Deetz (2008) and Blowfield and Frynas (2005).
3 I am grateful to Katie Wallace, Assistant Director of Sustainability, New Belgium Brewery, for providing me this information about New Belgium's policy.

References

Apple. (2018). *Environmental Responsibility Report*. Apple. Retrieved from www.apple.com/environment.

Ashkenas, J., Park, H., & Pearce, A. (2017). Even with affirmative action, Blacks and Hispanics are more underrepresented at top colleges than 35 years ago. *The New York Times*, August 24. Retrieved from www.nytimes.com.

Blowfield, M., & Frynas, J. G. (2005). Setting new agendas: Critical perspectives on corporate social responsibility in the developing world. *International Affairs*, 81(3), 499–513.

Brown, A. (2017). *The Data on Women Leaders*. PEW [Pew Research Center]. Retrieved from www.pewsocialtrends.org/2017/03/17/the-data-on-women-leaders.

Carroll, A. B. (1991). The pyramid of corporate social responsibility: Toward the moral management of organizational stakeholders. *Business Horizons*, 34(4), 39–48.

Dahl, D. (2016). How new Belgium brewing has found sustainable success. *Forbes*, January 27. Retrieved from www.forbes.com.

Desilver, D. (2018). *Women Scarce at Top of U.S. Business – and in the Jobs that Lead There.* PEW [Pew Research Center]. Retrieved from www.pewresearch.org/fact-tank/2018/04/30/women-scarce-at-top-of-u-s-business-and-in-the-jobs-that-lead-there.

Donnelly, G. (2018). The number of Black CEOs at Fortune 500 companies is at its lowest since 2002. *Fortune*, February 18. Retrieved from http://fortune.com/2018/02/28/black-history-month-black-ceos-fortune-500.

Duhigg, C., & Barboza, D. (2012). In China, the human costs that are built into an iPad. *The New York Times*, January 26. Retrieved from www.nytimes.com

Enough [Enough Project Team]. (2009). *A Comprehensive Approach to Congo's Conflict Minerals.* Enough. Retrieved from https://enoughproject.org/files/Comprehensive-Approach.pdf.

Freeman, R. E. (1984). *Strategic Management: A Stakeholder Approach.* Boston, MA: Pitman.

Freeman, R. E., & Reed, D. L. (1983). Stockholders and stakeholders: A new perspective on corporate governance. *California Management Review*, 25(3), 88–106.

Freeman, R. E., Harrison, J. S., & Wicks, A. C. (2007). *Managing for Stakeholders.* New Haven, CT: Yale University Press.

Friedman, M. (1970). The social responsibility of business is to increase its profits. *The New York Times*, September 13. Retrieved from www.nytimes.com.

GRI. (2018). *Consolidated Set of GRI Reporting Standards.* Amsterdam: GRI. Retrieved from www.globalreporting.org/standards.

Grossman, E. (2006). *High Tech Trash: Digital Devices, Hidden Toxics, and Human Health.* Washington, DC: Island Press.

KPMG. (2013). *The KPMG Survey of Corporate Responsibility Reporting 2013.* KPMG International. Retrieved from https://home.kpmg.com/ru/en/home/insights/2013/12/the-kpmg-survey-of-corporate-responsibility-reporting-2013.html.

Kuhn, T. R., & Deetz, S. (2008). Critical theory and corporate social responsibility: Can/should we get beyond cynical reasoning? In A. Crane, D. Matten, A. McWilliams, J. Moon, & D. S. Siegel (Eds.), *The Oxford Handbook of Corporate Social Responsibility* (pp. 173–196). Oxford: Oxford University Press.

Merchant, B. (2017). *The One Device: The Secret History of the iPhone.* Boston, MA: Little, Brown & Company.

NHTSA [National Highway Traffic Safety Administration]. (2018). *Distracted Driving.* Retrieved from www.distraction.gov/stats-research-laws/facts-and-statistics.html.

Nike. (2017). *FY16/17 Sustainable Business Report.* Nike. Retrieved from http://sustainability.nike.com.

Parker, D., & Vadheim, B. (2017). Resource cursed or policy cursed? US regulation of conflict minerals and violence in the Congo. *Journal of the Association of Environmental and Resource Economists*, 4(1), 1–49.

Samsung. (2018). *Samsung Electronics Sustainability Report 2018.* Samsung. Retrieved from www.samsung.com/us/aboutsamsung/sustainability/report-and-policy.

UN [United Nations]. (2018). Global Compact. *UN Global Compact.* Retrieved from www.unglobalcompact.org.

UNIDO [United Nations Industrial Development Program]. (2015). *What is CSR?* UNIDO. Retrieved from www.unido.org/our-focus/advancing-economic-competitiveness/competitive-trade-capacities-and-corporate-responsibility/corporate-social-responsibility-market-integration/what-csr.

USDOL [U.S. Department of Labor]. (2017). *Issue Brief: Women's Earnings and the Wage Gap.* U.S. Department of Labor. Women's Bureau. Retrieved from www.dol.gov/wb/resources/Womens_Earnings_and_the_Wage_Gap_17.pdf.

USSC [United States Sentencing Commission]. (2016). *Guidelines Manual 2016.* Washington, DC: USSC. Retrieved from www.ussc.gov/sites/default/files/pdf/guidelines-manual/2016/GLMFull.pdf.

5 Individuals in the world of business
Ethical aspects of specific roles and professions

Individuals participate in various ways in the economy and business world. We all participate as consumers in the global economy; many work as employees; some are entrepreneurs, some have leadership functions; and some consider themselves members of a specific profession or work in specific fields, such as marketing, real estate, or finance. In organizations and companies, many individuals interact with each other in various different roles and positions. Whereas Chapter 4 focused on ethical aspects on the organizational level, this chapter will highlight ethical aspects on the individual level that correspond to specific jobs, roles, or functions in organizational and economic contexts. This chapter demonstrates how specific roles, positions, or functions imply specific ethical challenges and responsibilities. A leader has different responsibilities and faces different ethical challenges than her team members. Accountants, engineers, marketing experts, and computer specialists all have different professional moral responsibilities and face different types of ethical issues and challenges.

Ethical responsibilities of specific roles are not completely subjective but are to some extent defined by the characteristics of the role, professional codes, and expectations of colleagues, business partners, or the public. If one pursues a certain career, becomes a member of a profession, or accepts a specific position in an organization, one has to be aware that this comes with professional principles, responsibilities, and norms that one has to accept and uphold. In other words, in business contexts, we are not merely acting on the basis of our personal values and principles (although they certainly matter). We also have to add to them certain professional values and principles that act as important guides for our professional decisions and actions. An accountant may have and express personal values and principles at work, but she also needs to commit to the professional ethical principles of accountancy in her professional actions.

In the following, we analyze crucial examples of specific positions, roles, or functions in business contexts, and identify the specific ethical challenges, responsibilities, and rights that come with them. We start with more general and broad roles, such as being an employee or a leader, and later on discuss more specific professional roles and the concept of professional ethics.

5.1 Ethical aspects of being an employee

A large number of people participate in business contexts by being an employee. This is a rather general and broad role that encompasses all kind of employees and various contexts. However, even the general role of being an employee comes with some specific ethical aspects. An employee works for a company or organization. The employee rents out her skills and abilities in order to make a living. Most employees do not have the luxury to walk away from their employer on any given day and take another equivalent or better job. Rather, they depend on the job they have to make a living. Also, by accepting a job in a company or organization, the employee becomes subject to the power structure of that company, and a means to achieve the ends of the company. Thus, the role of being an employee is characterized by a certain degree of dependency and vulnerability, which results in specific ethical issues. In this section, we first discuss some ethical implications resulting from the dependency and vulnerability of the employee using the concept of moral rights. Secondly, we address the ethical characteristics of renting out one's skills and abilities and the resulting responsibilities of employees.

5.1.1 Moral rights of employees

Rights are fundamental claims that are grounded in ethical reasons and demand general recognition. Rights protect and guarantee crucial interests and the wellbeing of persons. Similar to the arguments in Section 4.2.2, we can infer some fundamental rights from ethical theory that hold for every person and specifically every employee:

- Based on Kantian ethics, every person has the right not to be treated as mere means but to always be respected as end in herself and being endowed with reason. From this follows further basic rights, such as (i) the right to freedom: everyone owns him or herself; no one is owned by anyone else, and this includes a right to privacy and self-determination; (ii) the right to being treated equally and not being discriminated against: we are all rational beings and ends in ourselves equally; (iii) the right to be treated respectfully, that is, to be treated as persons endowed with reason. This includes the right to not be infringed upon our free will, self-determination, and self-guidance.
- Based on virtue ethics, every person has a fundamental right to flourish and develop his or her potential toward personal excellence.
- Based on ethics of care, asymmetries in power, ability, or knowledge should not be abused but induce specific responsibilities in the context of professional relationships. Everyone has the right that his vulnerability and lack of power, ability, or knowledge is not ignored or abused, but cared for.
- The above theories imply that everyone has the right not to be harmed in person or property.

Employees have the general rights outlined above. However, these rights can be further specified for the context and characteristics of the role of the employee. We particularly need to clarify the meaning of these rights with regard to the dependency and vulnerability of employees who are subject to the power and business goals of their employers. In the following, we spell out some specific employee rights that follow from the rights outlined above.

Following Kantian ethics, employees have the right to equal, fair, and respectful treatment. This includes, for instance, the right to equal pay for equal work and the right to not be discriminated against. Respectful treatment also includes many aspects of daily interactions with colleagues and supervisors. A supervisor yelling at an employee can be considered disrespectful. Also, any form of humiliation or abuse of power can be considered disrespectful. For instance, a boss commanding an employee to do work that has no business relevance just to demonstrate her power over the employee would be disrespectful. In such cases, the employee would be treated as a mere object. From a Kantian perspective, every employee has the right to be considered as an end in himself, as a rational person, and thus, has a right not to be treated in ways exemplified above.

Respectful treatment means reason-based treatment. Employees generally have the right that reasons are given for decisions and actions that substantially affect them, their fundamental interests, and their wellbeing. Such actions are, for instance, performance reviews, pay raises, promotions, or termination of the job. Denying reasons for such actions would be disrespectful to a rational person and would treat employees as mere objects. A more formal way to establish reasons for actions that impact fundamental interests of the employee is due process. Due process establishes criteria and procedures that define how employees are evaluated, promoted, or terminated. Due process reflects the moral right of employees to reasons for actions that impact their fundamental interests, and also upholds their right to fair and equal treatment. It protects employees from discrimination, arbitrary treatment, or favoritism. Due process is in line with the concept of the rule of law, which is a cornerstone of the US society, and that of many other countries.

From a Kantian perspective, employees have a right to participation. Reasonable beings have thoughts, ideas, and concerns that they want to express and bring to the community they are part of. Employees have a right for developing and expressing thoughts, ideas, and concerns, and a right that these are adequately considered. Employees have the right to participate in the organization they are part of and in decisions that affect them. Making employees just follow commands and denying them any ability to bring in ideas, raise concerns, or ask questions means that the employee is treated as mere object and not respected as a person endowed with reason.

Participation can be realized in various ways in a company or organization: by encouraging and rewarding ideas and suggestions; by team-based decision-making; by mechanisms that collect and reflect on concerns and complaints; and so on. A specific form of participation is the democratic workplace, which allows employees to vote about certain matters of the company. In a democratic society, this is an interesting concept of participation, as it expands democracy into the workplace. In the US, democratic workplace models can be found particularly in employee-owned companies. Some of these companies are actually very successful and significantly outcompete their competitors. The business case here is that employee ownership and democratic participation can significantly increase the motivation, commitment, and engagement of all employees, which, in turn, enhances the success of the company. Democratic elements can also be found in certain corporate governance models. In the US, the traditional model of corporate governance emphasizes exclusively shareholder interests. The board of directors, which has the ultimate oversights and power over a corporation, is supposed and legally required to uphold the financial interests of the shareholders. However, some European countries have established different models of corporate governance that include a democratic element regarding the employees and their interests. Germany, for instance, has a legally required type of corporate governance in which, if the corporation has more than 2000 employees, then 50% of the board of directors must be voted in by the employees (BMJV, 2017). In this corporate governance model, the board equally considers the interests of shareholders and employees.

From Kantian ethics it further follows that employees have a right to privacy. Employees have agreed to rent out some of their abilities, skills, and time to an employer, but they have not sold themselves to the employer. Employees are still ends in themselves. They own themselves and the information about themselves and are free to decide what to do and how to live outside work. Generally, the employer has certain interests in information about the employee and in directing the actions of the employee. This is legitimate as far as it is directly related to the work the employee agreed to perform for the employer. For instance, information about personal health is the property of the employee, part of his privacy, and the employer has no right to this information. However, the employer may legitimately ask for health information if it is directly related to the job and the work performance of the employee. If a job involves heavy lifting, the employer may legitimately ask the employee to reveal any health issues that would impede or prohibit the employee from doing the job. Likewise, an employer may ask an employee not to smoke at the workplace, but smoking outside of work remains the private decision of the employee.

There are, however, many grey-area situations and cases of conflicting rights and interests. For instance, an employee can consume alcohol in his free time. It is a private matter. However, if the employee consumes too much alcohol, this can easily impact his work performance. In some cases, it is difficult to completely separate private life and job. Some private activities might not impact the work performance but conflict with the professional role. Consider, for instance, a teacher who outside work regularly posts nude pictures of himself on the Internet. Although this is a private decision and done outside of work, the employer might legitimately argue that this action is not compatible with the professional role and consider firing the employee. Another example would be the investment advisor of the leading local bank, who is seen every night at the town's casino gambling away large sums of money. Is this still OK and completely a private matter, or does this behavior undermine the professional role and harm the bank?

From a virtue ethics perspective, employees have a right to meaningful work and a supportive work environment. Meaningful work would mean inspiring, challenging work that enables employees to flourish and to develop their professional and personal potential toward excellence. Virtue ethics also stresses the importance of a supportive community for individual flourishing and excellence. Thus, employees have a right to a supportive work environment: to administration, colleagues, and supervisors supporting their work and their professional development. A supportive work environment also includes adequate equipment and training that supports the employees' work and career. A company should actively care about the professional and personal development of its employees. A company would not do right by its employees if it would disregard their professional and personal development but instead just use their given skills or even burn them out. Such treatment would also be wrong from a Kantian perspective because it would be disrespectful to rational persons and consider them as mere means. From an ethics of care perspective, a supportive work environment would also include caring about difficult personal situations and emotional distress of employees. In this perspective, employees also have a right to be cared for, that such difficult situations are accommodated by the company, for instance, by providing reasonable options to take time off.

From various ethical approaches follows that employees have a right not to get harmed in person or property. This general right has some specific implications for the employee role and workplace context. The employer often might have more knowledge about certain dangers of the job than the employee. If this is the case, it is the employee's right that the employer reveals such knowledge and takes measures to protect the employee. Further implications may result from the dependency of employees. Sometimes an employee might do dangerous work and risk her health to keep a job. If the employer knows or encourages this, it would be a case of abuse. Although there is probably broad agreement about the general ethical point that employees have a right to not get harmed, this can be a difficult practical matter. The difficulty in practice is determining the adequate measures for safety and health. In many cases, 100% protection is not possible, and so it comes down to the question of the adequate safety standard and, relatedly, to the adequate investment into safety that one can require from an employer.

Employees have some fundamental rights as outlined above, and employers have an ethical obligation to respect and uphold these rights. However, traditionally, the government has been an important institution that guarantees and protects rights. Therefore, crucial employee rights are often formalized in laws and regulations and enforced by government. As discussed in Chapter 2, laws cover ethical aspects only to some extent, and different countries have chosen different approaches to protect fundamental rights of employees by law. In the following, we discuss some typical examples for how employee rights are formalized and protected in the legal framework.

One prominent example of a legal right of employees is the right to minimum wage. In the US, a federal minimum wage is guaranteed by federal law, and many states have their own laws that set the minimum wage higher than the federal minimum wage. Recently, some cities, for instance, Seattle, set the minimum wage in their city higher than the state or federal minimum wage. Many European countries have established legal rights for paternal leave. For instance, Germany grants employees the right of three years of paternal leave per child, of which one year is paid. The payment is generally 65–100% of the person's last income, with a maximum of €1800 per month (BMFSFJ, 2015). Many countries have laws that specify the rights of employees to a minimum of vacation days. In most European countries, the legally guaranteed paid vacation is at least four weeks per year. The US actually is one of few developed countries in the world that has no law requiring a minimum of vacation days for employees. Most developed countries also have extended laws and regulations to protect the safety and health of employees. In the US, the Occupational Safety and Health Act (1970) is a crucial legal framework for such protection.

These typical legal rights aim to protect fundamental moral rights of employees, particularly against the background of (i) the danger of employees being treated as mere means, (ii) work being crucial for personal flourishing, and (iii) the vulnerability of employees facing the power of employers. Laws and regulations about safety and health of employees obviously protect their right to not be harmed. Minimum wage laws can be justified by different ethical arguments. Minimum wages protect the fundamental ability of every person to support herself through her labor and exclude the price of labor from being determined by the market mechanism of supply and demand. This obviously interferes strongly with free market mechanisms. However, many societies have a broad agreement that this interference is justified by the ethical reasons of protecting the fundamental right of every person to flourish, allow everyone to make a living through their labor, and protect employees from becoming a mere object of the market. In other words, labor is not considered an ordinary economic commodity, but rather a specific good that is fundamental to everyone's wellbeing, flourishing, and development. If the price of labor floated as a free market price, the price could, in principle, go down to a few cents in a bad economy; that is, if the supply of labor was significantly higher than the demand. This might specifically hurt vulnerable groups in the workforce and take away their ability to support themselves through their labor. More far-reaching legal rights in some countries, such as the right to minimum vacation days or paternal leave, result from a different view of what is crucial for the wellbeing and flourishing of employees and, thus, needs to be protected by law.

5.1.2 Responsibilities of employees

Employees have moral rights, but also moral responsibilities toward their employer and their coworkers. Employees can ask to be treated with respect and fairness, but one can likewise ask employees to be respectful and fair to their employer and coworkers. In the following, a couple of relevant moral responsibilities of employees are discussed.

As an employee rents out her skills and abilities to an employer, the employee has a responsibility to be truthful about her skills and abilities and has a responsibility for proper performance. It would violate basic principles of honesty and truthfulness if the employee misrepresents her abilities and skills to the employer, and such misrepresentation can harm the employer. It is also the responsibility of the employee to perform well, which means to do the job as agreed upon. Promising a certain level of performance that the employee then does not deliver is dishonest and harmful to the employer.

An employee has a responsibility to professionalism. If the employee has specialized professional skills, for instance, is an engineer, accountant, physician, or lawyer, she is responsible for performing work according to current professional standards. A specialized professional usually knows more than the employer and any other person in the company about the area of his work. No one other than the professional can fully control and verify that the work has been done by professional standards and, further, the professional has a specific ethical responsibility to ensure the quality of her work and adhere to the principles and state of the art of the profession (see Section 5.3).

As the employee has the right to not be harmed by the employer and the job, the employer has the right to not be harmed by the employee. Although an employee has no specific power over the employer, the employee could harm the employer in various ways. For instance, harm could be done by stealing goods or time from the company, misusing company resources for private purposes, negatively talking about the company in public, and so on. In particular, employee theft causes significant damage to companies. There is small and big theft. Some employees might take some office supply home and use it for private purposes. They might not even perceive their action as theft and not consider the harm as significant. However, everyone should be aware that this is still stealing, and that damages add up. Also, this is a slippery slope, and lack of discipline and respect for the company's property easily leads to more substantial abuse or stealing of the company's resources.

An employee has agreed to contribute to the company his skills, abilities, and work. Although this is limited to some well-defined job and performance, one may say that the employee has some responsibility to be committed to, and supportive of, the overall success of the company or organization. This commitment includes, for instance, that the employee spots issues and potential risks that could endanger the success of the company and either fixes or reports them; that the employee actively engages in deliberations and decision-making processes in the company; and that the employee respects, cares about, and supports his colleagues, and actively contributes to his team and to building a positive work environment.

One can also refer to the concept of loyalty to address some of the responsibilities described above. One may argue that an employee has the responsibility to be loyal to the employer, at least to a certain degree. Loyalty to the employer could include not harming the company, supporting the success of the company, and committing to the core values and mission of the company, as well as representing them when working with other stakeholders. Loyalty is limited, though. It should not include giving up any employee rights, having to go beyond the performance agreed upon, doing or supporting unethical or illegal activities, covering up wrongdoing in the company or by supervisors, and so on. Later we will argue that in extreme cases an employee may even have the moral duty to override the loyalty to the company and blow the whistle on significant wrongdoings within the company (see Section 5.5).

5.2 Ethical aspects of leadership

Leadership matters for all businesses and organizations, and there are various positions and levels of leadership. One can define leadership as an organizational function by which one person, the leader, makes others, the followers, pursue a well-defined end. Good leadership is crucial for the success and viability of organizations, and leadership is a crucial element of organizational ethics. Leadership significantly influences the ethical culture of an organization, shapes formal and informal ethical aspects, and impacts the behavior and development of all members. A crucial characteristic of the leadership function is power. Leadership roles come with a certain amount of power and control over others, which results in ethical challenges of how to properly justify and use this power. In this section, we discuss the ethical dimension of leadership by focusing on two crucial normative questions: first, what defines great leadership?, and second, what are the ethical foundations of leadership?

5.2.1 What defines great leadership?

The question 'What is great leadership?' is an evaluative question and requires criteria that define *great* (see, e.g., Ciulla, 1995). By what criteria do we judge a leader to be a great leader? By what criteria can we distinguish a great leader from a worse leader? For considering these questions, it is useful to look for examples of leaders whom we consider to be role models. One might think about persons like Thomas Jefferson, Franklin D. Roosevelt, Eleanor Roosevelt, Martin Luther King, Mahatma Gandhi, or Rosa Parks in the field of politics, and Bill Gates, Steve Jobs, Yvon Chouinard, or Warren Buffet in the field of business. However, assuming we agree on this list, what qualifies all these persons to be great leaders? By what criteria do we judge them to be role models? Moreover, what if someone would add Stalin, Hitler, or a mafia boss to our list of great leaders? Do we have criteria to make the point that Martin Luther King was a great role model, but Hitler and the mafia boss are not? In other words, what distinguishes Dr King from Hitler and the mafia boss?

In the following, we provide a set of criteria for defining a great leader/leadership, which enables us to distinguish Hitler and the mafia boss from real role models, such as Martin Luther King. We start with a basic definition that defines great leadership as leadership that is *effective* and *ethical* (Ciulla, 1995, p. 13). With this, we can specify the task of defining great leadership by defining effective and ethical leadership. We will first determine a set of criteria for effectiveness of leadership and then determine another set of criteria for ethical leadership. Great leadership would then be defined by both sets of criteria together (Figure 5.1).

What criteria would determine the effectiveness of leadership? When would we call a leader effective? One may say that a leader is effective if she successfully makes people follow, achieves the goals of the leadership (possible even after the time of the leadership), and does so in an efficient way. These three criteria are reasonable criteria for effective leadership, and we can require great leaders to fulfill them. However, Stalin or a mafia boss would also probably pass these criteria and count as effective leaders. If we would just refer to the criteria of effectiveness for defining great leadership, we could not distinguish Stalin or a mafia boss from Martin Luther King. We would need to consider them both equally as great leaders, which is counterintuitive.

What separates Martin Luther King from Stalin or the mafia boss, though, is that Dr King strived for ethical ends and employed ethical means, whereas Stalin or the mafia boss pursued ethically questionable ends with unethical means. All examples of great leaders listed above fulfill the characteristic that they pursued ethical ends, sought some greater good beyond mere self-interest, and strove for a positive impact on society and the world. This would also hold for great business leaders like Bill Gates, Steve Jobs, or Yvon Chouinard, who strived not only for personal benefit and

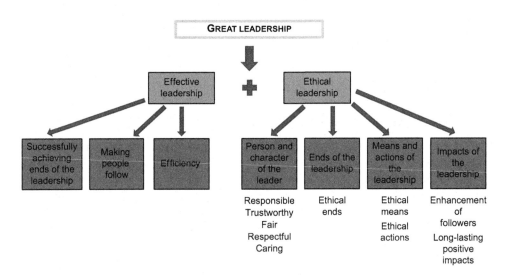

Figure 5.1 Criteria defining great leadership.

profit maximization, but also for making business a positive force in the world, and for having an overall positive impact on the world.

Great leaders also employ ethical means to make people follow. In contrast to Stalin or Hitler, who employed ethically questionable means, such as deception, manipulation, and threats, and forced people to follow, great leaders inspire people with great ideas and goals to follow them. Moreover, great leaders employ ethical means to achieve their goals, such as Martin Luther King, who advocated non-violent protest. It is a difficult question, though, whether striving for an ethical end could sometimes justify the use of unethical means. In recent history, this has been controversial with several issues. In the war against terrorism, ethically questionable means, such as torture, Guantanamo Bay detention camp, and some activities by the US National Security Agency, were justified as necessary means to win the war. However, the position that the end justifies the means is problematic. It leads to ethical contradictions. It undermines its own ethical position and principles, and, in doing so, destroys trust and credibility. Due to the loss of ethical credibility, most unethical means fire back and are actually not helpful at all to achieve ethical ends.

Positive personal character traits, including ethical character traits, are also often linked to great leaders/leadership. Being competent, visionary, and inspiring are often attributed to great leaders. In addition, one may seek certain ethical virtues in great leaders, such as responsibility, trustworthiness, credibility, care for followers, and fairness. However, many great leaders had some character flaws. No one is perfect. So, it might be too much to ask, even from a great leader and role model, to be a morally perfect person. Character strength and morality may be crucial for great leadership, though, as long as it is essential to the leadership function. Character flaws that are not crucial for the leadership function may not negatively impact and hinder great leadership.

Finally, a crucial aspect of great leadership is its overall positive impact on the followers and society. Great leaders enhance their followers and support them in becoming better persons and professionals. This is a particularly important criterion in the business world. What distinguishes the great leader or supervisor from the worse leader or supervisor is the ability of the former to recognize the potential of each follower and help him optimally develop his potential and become a better professional and person. Great leaders have positive effects beyond the leadership function and its ends. They make society and the world a better place and help followers develop their potentials and become better persons.

5.2.2 What are ethical foundations of leadership?

As discussed above, ethical characteristics are an integral part of great leadership. However, ethical leadership must ultimately be grounded in ethical principles that justify and guide it. Ethical leadership in particular must deal properly with the power attributed to it. In this section, we will explore the question of how leadership can be justified against, and grounded in, fundamental ethical principles, such as Kantian principles of respect for rational persons, virtue principles of human excellence, utilitarian principles of overall happiness, and principles of ethics of care. In the following, we outline ten principles of ethical leadership (Figure 5.2), which are deduced from ethical theory and also relate to fundamental values of modern democratic societies, such as equality, freedom, and respect for human dignity.

Principle 1	Ethical leadership is based on the fundamental values of a free and equal society of autonomous, rational persons
Principle 2	Ethical leadership serves some common good
Principle 3	Ethical leadership is respectful
Principle 4	Ethical leadership is grounded in reasonable principles rather than in oppressive or authoritarian power mechanisms
Principle 5	Ethical leadership requires only the minimum amount of power necessary to lead
Principle 6	Ethical leadership is transparent, participatory, and empowering
Principle 7	Ethical leadership is responsible
Principle 8	Ethical leadership empowers individual responsibility of followers
Principle 9	Ethical leadership promotes excellence
Principle 10	Ethical leadership cares about followers

Figure 5.2 Ten principles of ethical leadership.

Ten principles of ethical leadership

PRINCIPLE 1: ETHICAL LEADERSHIP IS BASED ON THE FUNDAMENTAL VALUES OF A FREE AND
EQUAL SOCIETY OF AUTONOMOUS, RATIONAL PERSONS

In a society of free and equal persons, it is not self-evident that one should single out someone as a leader and give her power to rule over others. In a free and equal society, the more natural decision-making model seems to be the democratic model: all people in a group or specific organization make decisions together by democratic mechanisms, such as voting. In other words, leadership requires justification and needs to be established by principles that are compatible with freedom and equality. There are, of course, obvious reasons for designating leaders, such as better achievement of well-defined ends, effectiveness and efficiency, and personal ability, experience, or knowledge. By a basic definition of leadership, leaders and their followers strive together to achieve a well-defined end. In many situations, a common end can certainly be better achieved by designating a leader and providing the leader with adequate power. Enabling a leader to make decisions for a group or organization is more effective and efficient. The larger the group or organization, the more efficiency gains can be realized by leadership. A very small group may be able to make all decisions together, but in larger organizations, joint decision-making would become very inefficient and endanger the success of an organization. Another important argument for leadership is the difference of experience, ability, and knowledge among individuals. In certain contexts, it is reasonable to ask the more experienced or skilled person to lead the other less experienced or skilled members of a group. Note, though, that in ethical matters, Kant would consider all persons as being equally competent, as do most democracies with regard to making fundamental political decisions (every person usually has one vote).

Leadership also needs to be established and controlled by acceptable mechanisms. In a society of free and equal persons, the natural mechanism to establish leadership is by agreement of all involved, or by more practicable mechanisms, such as majority vote. Also, leadership does not get absolute powers granted, but rather is subject to reasonable limitations which, in particular, implies that the leadership has to subdue itself to fundamental ethical principles, the rule of law, and due process.

PRINCIPLE 2: ETHICAL LEADERSHIP SERVES SOME COMMON GOOD

This principle follows from Kantian ethics. If leadership would not serve any common good of leaders and followers, no reasonable person would follow such leadership deliberately, which means that the leadership is either established by force or by manipulation or delusion. In all these cases leadership would be unethical. Ethical leadership must have some common good for the leader and the followers. The common good can be established indirectly and can be a rather small common ground, though. For instance, in a modern corporation, the main end of leadership is the maximization of profits for the shareholders. The board and the CEO are working for the financial interests of the shareholders and lead all members of the corporation to achieve this goal. However, there is also a basic common good of the CEO and the employees; that is, the success of the corporation, which benefits both leaders and employees. Employees perceive, for instance, their benefit consisting in a secure job, paycheck, meaningful and challenging work, a great work atmosphere, expectations of a future pay raise or promotion, and so on. If the leadership would not serve any common interest, if the employees would see no benefit at all in working for the corporation, they would not follow the leadership, but instead walk away.

In a utilitarian perspective, we could interpret Principle 2 in another way and argue that ethical leadership actually should maximize the overall happiness of all involved. This would mean that ethical leadership is leadership that creates maximum overall value for all stakeholders. Ethical leadership then must clearly define the common good for all followers and work to achieve it.

PRINCIPLE 3: ETHICAL LEADERSHIP IS RESPECTFUL: IT CONSIDERS FOLLOWERS AS REASONABLE
BEINGS AND ENDS IN THEMSELVES

This principle follows from Kant's categorical imperative. In ethical leadership, a leader never treats followers as mere means for achieving the goals of leadership, but always at the same time respects every follower as a person endowed with reason and as an end in herself.

PRINCIPLE 4: ETHICAL LEADERSHIP IS GROUNDED IN REASONABLE PRINCIPLES RATHER THAN
IN OPPRESSIVE OR AUTHORITARIAN POWER MECHANISMS

Ethical leadership legitimizes itself not by mere power but by power that is based on, and guided by, reasonable principles. That means that leadership decisions are not arbitrary but grounded in reasonable considerations and procedures. This is in line with Kantian ethics and the principle of respecting every person as a being endowed with reason. Rational beings require reasons for decisions and requests. An employee needs to understand why he is supposed to do something. In most cases, this should be obvious and not require explicit explanation. Good leadership makes reasonable decisions and has reasonable requests for employees. For instance, any request that serves the end of the leadership, or the success of the company or a given project, usually is reasonable; requests that are unrelated to the goals of the leadership, project, or company, are not reasonable. However, requests that are unethical, or illegal, are also unreasonable, even if they would serve the project or company. Part of reason-based leadership is that the leader is able and willing to provide reasons when employees are in doubt about a decision. As rational beings, employees have the right to ask why, and leaders have a responsibility to provide reasons. Denying the right to ask why or denying reasons would be disrespectful from a Kantian perspective.

Concepts of fairness and equality are also reasonable principles and belong to reason-based leadership. Leadership grounded in reasonable principles understands that everyone equally is an end in themselves and a being endowed with reason. Everyone therefore has a right to be treated equally and fairly as a rational being.

PRINCIPLE 5: ETHICAL LEADERSHIP REQUIRES ONLY THE MINIMUM AMOUNT OF POWER
NECESSARY TO LEAD

Power is not an end in itself, but a means for achieving the ends of the leadership. To avoid an unnecessary accumulation of power and potential negative side effects of power, such as abuse of power and corruption, power should always be limited in amount and time. The political system of the US, for instance, has established various limitations of power, which have over time been proven to be successful at promoting the stability and progress of the US. There are sophisticated checks and balances between the different branches of government, and there is a term limit for serving as President of the US. Generally, companies, corporations, and non-profit organizations should establish similar limitations and checks and balances. If the President of the US can serve only a maximum of eight years, it is reasonable to consider implementing similar time limits for top positions in organizations and companies, e.g., for the CEO of a corporation or the president of a university.

PRINCIPLE 6: ETHICAL LEADERSHIP IS TRANSPARENT, PARTICIPATORY, AND EMPOWERING

Ethical leadership actively includes followers in deliberations and decision-making as far as it is possible. This principle also follows from Kantian ethics and, to some extent, from virtue ethics. Respecting employees as rational persons implies considering their capacity for deliberating about means and ends of the leadership. Ethical leadership would, thus, be transparent about deliberations and decisions, and empower employees to contribute to, or participate in, decision-making as far as it is feasible. To deny any participation would result in perceiving and treating employees as mere objects, as objects that just have to follow orders and commands, but are not supposed to think by themselves and bring in their own considerations. Such a leadership approach would not only be unethical, but also impede the success of an organization. Employees that have no opportunity to participate and have little to no say in the affairs of the company or team, are probably more passive and less motivated, and their potential to contribute to the success of the team or company is not fully utilized. As everyone is a rational person, everyone has some insights and ideas to contribute. Also, people working in different jobs and levels of an organization usually recognize different issues and spot different potentials for improvement. Good leadership empowers these individual abilities and integrates different insights into the decision-making process to optimally inform leadership decisions.

PRINCIPLE 7: ETHICAL LEADERSHIP IS RESPONSIBLE: IT HAS ROLE-SPECIFIC RESPONSIBILITIES
TO FOLLOWERS, THE ORGANIZATION, THE ENDS AND MEANS OF THE LEADERSHIP, AND
STAKEHOLDERS

Leadership is a specific function that comes with role-specific responsibilities. A leader is ultimately responsible for achieving the defined ends of the leadership and for using the proper means for this purpose. Furthermore, a leader has specific responsibilities toward the followers: that their potentials are optimally integrated, that the team works well together, that their rights are respected, that they are treated respectfully, and that they can develop professional potential.

A leader also has an overarching responsibility for the defined area of the leadership. For instance, a captain is responsible for the ship, the crew, and the passengers, and was granted powers to fulfill this responsibility. The captain is responsible for the ship reaching its destination safely, for the overall condition of the ship, and for the wellbeing of crew and passengers. If anything goes wrong, the captain will be held responsible. Similarly, if anything goes wrong on a team, the team leader will have to answer to her supervisor. Or, if anything goes wrong in a corporation, the CEO will be held responsible. This does not mean that others, e.g., team members, who did something wrong, will not also be held responsible. However, it means that the leader will always be held responsible and probably be approached first. As argued in Section 4.1, it does not matter whether the captain or CEO actually was actively involved in the failure or did something wrong. The captain or CEO is responsible simply by her leadership role. She got significant powers granted to ensure that everything goes well, and if it does not, she has to assume responsibility for the failure. It also does not matter whether the leader knew about the wrongdoing or failure. If the leader knew, she is responsible for not intervening or preventing the wrongdoing or failure. If the leader did not know, she is to blame for that exactly, for not knowing, because it is part of her responsibilities to secure sufficient information about the state of affairs and activities in her area of leadership. An ethical leader assumes responsibility for the group and the area she oversees, and responds to others, such as higher-level management, stakeholders, or the public, if something goes wrong. Generally speaking, the leader has to assume responsibility and cannot completely exclude herself from responding to others, or simply blame everything on a team member.

Ethical leadership is also responsible in a fundamental sense. It must be willing and able to respond to critical questions of the followers and other stakeholders and explain decisions and actions. This is in line with treating followers and stakeholders respectfully and as rational persons. Rational persons want to understand reasons for certain decisions and withholding reasons without justification is disrespectful.

PRINCIPLE 8: ETHICAL LEADERSHIP EMPOWERS INDIVIDUAL RESPONSIBILITY OF FOLLOWERS

The fact that a leader has extended role-specific responsibilities for the area and ends of the leadership and for the followers does not mean that the followers have no responsibilities or should have no responsibilities at all. To the contrary, ethical leadership promotes shared responsibility and empowers all followers to act responsibly. Leadership should encourage and promote individual responsibility among employees so that they assume responsibility for their job and personal performance, for the team and co-workers, and are willing to take action if they spot some issue or problem. This is in line with treating followers as rational persons who have the capacity for ethical reasoning and reasonable deliberation.

PRINCIPLE 9: ETHICAL LEADERSHIP PROMOTES EXCELLENCE

Ethical leadership fosters professional and personal development, promotes the excellence of all followers, and has an overall positive impact toward stakeholders and society. This principle is an implication of virtue ethics. A great leader has the ability to read different potentials in every employee and to support every employee in the best way to optimally develop his professional and personal potential. As every person is different, potentials are different, and also the best means to support potentials are different. Good leaders have the ability to recognize the unique characteristics of each employee and help him to develop professional excellence. Doing so, ultimately, improves the excellence of the entire team and, subsequently, the excellence and success of the teamwork and its results. Great leadership enhances the skills and abilities of the followers rather than just using them, or, in the worst case, burning them out. That does not mean that ethical leadership is not challenging or demanding. However, any challenge maximizes the performance of the team and its results and promotes excellence of individual team members.

Ethical leadership promotes professional excellence, and this includes ethical attitudes and actions. One crucial aspect for this is that leaders act as role models. Employees are significantly influenced by the actions and behaviors of their supervisor. It is a crucial function of ethical leadership to consistently act in ethical ways and uphold company values, policies, and rules. This sets an example among the followers and inspires them to do the same.

In a virtue ethics perspective, individual excellence requires a supportive community. Ethical leadership thus also builds community that supports the development of each individual. This includes fostering cooperative and mutually supporting teams, and creating a fair, respectful, and caring work atmosphere in which everyone can thrive.

PRINCIPLE 10: ETHICAL LEADERSHIP CARES ABOUT FOLLOWERS

From an ethics of care perspective, ethical leadership cares about its followers. This means considering the power asymmetry as an obligation to secure the wellbeing of the followers and not just as a tool to control and command them. Ethical leaders care about the people who report to them; that is, not only assign and control tasks but also assume responsibility for their wellbeing. This includes caring about the personal and emotional wellbeing of the employees. Of course, leaders often have limited ability to actually assist with private matters and should in most cases not intervene in them. But recognition of, and empathy with, personal stress situations can be of crucial support. A leader could, for instance, release an employee from work tasks in cases of private emergencies. Caring for employees is not only an ethical principle but may benefit the success of the company as well. If leaders ignore and don't care about problems of their followers, this can easily impact the work performance and results of the respective individual and the entire team.

5.3 Professional ethics

Professionals are experts who have specialized knowledge and skills in a certain area. Classical examples of professionals are physicians, lawyers, engineers, and accountants. Professionals know more and perform better in their area of expertise than others who are not experts. Professionals are hired or consulted for specific tasks that require their expertise. The specific knowledge and asymmetry in knowledge between the professional and others who rely on their work creates specific ethical issues and challenges, as well as a need for professional ethics, which we will discuss in this section.

Specific professional expertise implies specific ethical responsibilities. If you are an expert in a certain field, others rely on and trust you. You are responsible for properly using your expertise and not abusing the fact that you know more than others in a certain field. For instance, a physician is an expert in medicine and knows more than the patient about medical matters. The patient consults the physician for his expertise and trusts that the physician provides a proper diagnosis and adequate recommendations for treatment. It would be unprofessional and unethical if the physician abuses his advantage (and the desperate situation of the patient) to trick the patient and sell him some useless drugs just for personal profit. It is part of the physician's professional ethics – that is, medical ethics – to work for the best interest of the patient, provide an objective diagnosis, and recommend state-of-the-art treatment that optimally serves the patient.

Professional ethical principles are neither arbitrary nor mere convention. They usually have to do with the specific expertise, characteristics, and public function of a profession. Professional ethics relates to the role a profession has in the society. In business contexts, professional ethics is often linked to economic principles that are relevant to a profession. For instance, the accounting profession recognizes that it has a crucial function in the economy. Reliable, objective, standardized, and comparable financial information is crucial for the proper functioning of a capitalist market economy. Many professional principles of accountancy are about ensuring the objectivity and reliability of the work of accountants and of the financial data they produce (see Section 5.3.3).

5.3.1 Professional ethics and moral self-identity

Professional ethics does not replace personal ethics. Rather it adds another layer to the ethical principles, virtues, and responsibilities of an individual. A professional has personal values, principles, and responsibilities. Besides, she may also have the specific responsibilities of an employee or a leader if she happens to be in that role. However, in addition, a professional has certain professional responsibilities and must uphold professional principles. In other words, being a professional in a certain field adds certain ethical challenges and responsibilities to the challenges and responsibilities one already has as a private person. Professional ethics and principles are more objectively defined, though, than personal values. If we become a professional, we have to adopt given professional principles and uphold them in our professional work.

More generally, it is worth noting that our moral self-identity is usually affected by the various roles we have in life and the various contexts in which we act. We develop personal values and principles as private persons. If we start a family, we have additional specific responsibilities and obligations toward our spouse and children. If we are a member of an organization or company, we are expected to uphold the core values of the company in our job and interactions with stakeholders. If we become professionals in a certain area, we are expected to uphold professional ethical principles and act professionally in our job. In other words, we are not just a private person, but we are also the spouse, the parent, the employee of some company, the member of a certain profession, a community member, and a citizen. With all these roles come specific ethical challenges, expectations, responsibilities, values, virtues, and principles, which influence and shape our personality and moral identity. At the core, though, remains our capability as ethical beings; the inner moral compass; the capacity for ethical judgment that we possess as rational beings. It is crucial that we never blindly follow organizational or professional values, or external expectation, but always critically reflect on their ethical feasibility and only adopt values and principles that we consider as ethically sound. Ideally, we will be able to build consistent layers of personal and professional ethical principles that add to each other and to our moral identity (Figure 5.3). Any serious frictions or contradictions between professional and private values are problematic, though. If we have to act at our job in a way that contradicts how we would act as private persons, this would not be optimal. It works better for someone if he chooses a profession and a company to which values and principles he can easily commit because they fit well with his personal values and principles.

5.3.2 Core principles of professional ethics

Specific professions have specific ethical challenges and responsibilities resulting from their areas of expertise. However, one can formulate some general principles of professional ethics that would hold for any profession in general and only need minor adjustments to fit distinctive characteristics of a specific profession. In the following, we define five general principles of professional ethics: competency, objectivity, responsibility, integrity, and public interest.

Competency

It is the duty of each professional to ensure their own competency when providing professional services. A professional typically must have a higher-level college degree

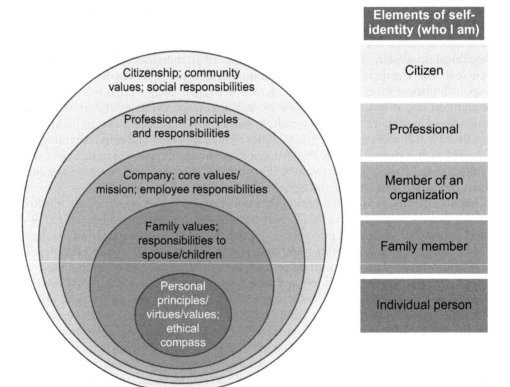

Figure 5.3 Elements of moral self-identity.

and pass some standardized tests to qualify for working in a given professional field. However, in most professions, knowledge, methods, and standards change constantly, and it is the responsibility of each professional to make sure she stays up to date with state-of-the-art methods, professional knowledge, and techniques, and to update knowledge and skills regularly. Also, most professionals further specialize during their career. A lawyer may be an expert in one area of law, but not very knowledgeable in another. An accountant might specialize in taxes or forensic accounting, but not have the same high level of expertise in other areas of accounting. It is the obligation of a professional to reveal to clients or employers what relevant areas he is competent in and what areas he is not. Because of the asymmetry in knowledge, the client or employer may not be able to judge the competency of a professional and may think that the professional can work in any area of the profession. It is up to the professional to disclose her strength and limitations to the client or employer. Working in an area/job for which one is insufficiently competent is unprofessional and irresponsible.

Objectivity

Professional work and judgment should not be biased by subjective perspectives and interests. The professional has the obligation to remain unbiased and independent of specific perspectives or interests. This is best guaranteed if the professional adheres to established professional methods and norms. The professional is not supposed to experiment with individual approaches or subjective ideas, but rather is supposed to adhere to the approved methods of the profession. The professional's work also should not be biased by personal preferences or opinions but stick to an objective perspective. Also, a professional should remain independent from all influences that could impact the objectivity and quality of the professional work. The professional work should neither be impacted by any personal interests of the professional nor affected by interests or preferences of others. For instance, a physician should not subdue judgment or professional standards to the interests and influence of pharmaceutical companies. An engineer should not subdue professional standards and sign off flawed construction plans because her boss is pressuring her to do so. An accountant should not provide a positive attestation because his spouse has a substantial investment in that corporation.

Responsibility

A professional has the responsibility to use her knowledge and skills properly, and she is responsible for the results of her work. Because the professional can often better judge the quality of her work than others for whom she is working, she has a specific responsibility to uphold and guarantee the quality of the service or work done. The professional should not abuse the asymmetry in knowledge to cheat the client or customer or provide substandard work knowing that the client or customer will not recognize this. Also, the professional should not abuse the asymmetry of knowledge for personal benefits, for instance, by providing and charging unnecessary services. For instance, a physician should not sell unnecessary treatments to the patient to make additional money. This would mean treating the client or customer as a mere means for personal benefit. Professionals should also be able and willing to answer questions and explain their approach and work to others who have a vested interest in the results. In other words, professionals should be transparent and honest about their work and not use their advantage in knowledge to withhold or hide important information from relevant stakeholders.

Integrity

Integrity by definition means avoiding conflicting and contradicting actions. A professional should uphold professional integrity by making sure that all her actions are consistent with professional standards and principles. This matters particularly in grey-area situations. In situations where there is no clearly defined rule or approach, the professional must make a judgment about how to address the situation. Professional integrity means making sure that the judgment is in line with overall professional principles and not in conflict with them. Using grey-area situations to deviate from professional principles for personal benefits or others' interests would undermine professional integrity. Grey-area cases are actually quite common in professional work. Professional fields are usually complex fields where one needs to have an expert making a professional judgment of how to best proceed. For instance, in the fields of law or medicine numerous different and complex situations occur that require a professional judgment and treatment based on the extensive knowledge and experience of the professional lawyer or physician. If cases in these fields would be straightforward, one would not need experts, but could simply run a computer program instead. However, in areas like medicine, most people probably would not like a computer program diagnosing and treating them but would prefer a physician to make a professional judgment.

Public interest

A professional typically has certain responsibilities to the general public that result from the specific public function of his area of expertise. Classical professions serve some well-defined public interest and are crucial for the overall functioning and well-being of society. Engineers have a crucial function for guaranteeing technological safety; lawyers have a crucial function for the legal system; and physicians are crucial for health care. Professionals have a professional duty to protect the public interest that their profession serves. For instance, engineers have a professional duty to protect public safety in their work. An engineer is, for instance, responsible for the technological safety of construction plans and has a duty to uphold that safety against other interests or pressures. If the engineer's boss or client would demand a cheaper solution, which the engineer judges to be dangerous, the engineer would have to resist and deny her signature/approval to such a solution.

5.3.3 The example of the accounting profession

Accounting is a specific professional field in the business world that serves a crucial function for businesses and the economy in general. 'Accounting involves gathering, classifying, summarizing, and reporting financial information about an entity to interested users such as stockholders, creditors, potential investors and creditors, governments, and other stakeholders' (Armstrong, 2002, p. 145). With the specific function of accounting come specific ethical challenges and professional responsibilities.

The field of accountancy has a strong self-identity as a profession and has developed detailed professional principles. We want to demonstrate that the accounting profession (i) upholds general principles of professional ethics and (ii) specifies those principles to meet the specific ethical challenges and responsibilities of accountants.

We refer in the following to the latest version of the *Code of Professional Conduct* (AICPA, 2018) from the American Institute for Certified Public Accountants (AICPA), which is a leading professional code for the field of accountancy in the US. We will here just highlight some general aspects of accounting ethics and neither distinguish further different roles of accountants, such as public or managerial accountants, nor identify more specific responsibilities of such specific roles.[1] In the following, we use the five principles of professional ethics from Section 5.3.2 to identify how the accounting profession refers to and upholds those principles, although the AICPA code uses slightly different categories.

Competency

The AICPA code emphasizes the professional principle of competency, i.e., that the professional needs to ensure competence in her area of work: '[An accountant] is responsible for assessing his or her own competence of evaluating whether education, experience, and judgment are adequate for the responsibility to be assumed' (AICPA, 2018, 0.300.060). The code particularly highlights the professional responsibility of accountants to stay up to date with the state-of-the-art methods of the profession and ensure sufficient qualification for professional work (AICPA, 2018, 0.300.060).

Objectivity

The AICPA code is particularly detailed about the professional principle of objectivity, i.e., that the professional should adhere to professional standards and methods and not be biased in his work by his own or others' interests. The accounting profession upholds this general professional principle and specifies it in detail to meet particular ethical challenges of accountants. In accountancy, objectivity is of more relevance and more challenging than in many other professions. Accountants must remain unbiased and independent from all kind of interests and influences. Accountants produce and evaluate financial data that have significant impacts for companies, investors, stock markets, and others. There can be various situations where financial interests could impact the independence and objectivity of an accountant, and accountants can face significant pressures and influence. For instance, a boss wants to have the best numbers possible and might pressure her accountant to manipulate the numbers. In the past, such situations have led to major accounting scandals, such as in Enron, HealthSouth, or Tyco, with large harm to these companies and their stakeholders. Another example of impact on independence and objectivity would be the situation of a family member owning significant stock of the very company the accountant is auditing. The fact that the results of the audit impact the financial interests of the family member could influence the judgment of the accountant.

In all such cases, the accountant is supposed to remain unbiased in his professional work and judgment. The AICPA code highlights objectivity and independence as important professional principles, particularly for public accountants (AICPA, 2018, 0.300.050). The code specifically considers the mere appearance of being biased as an issue that should be avoided. For instance, if a family member owns stock in the company the accountant is supposed to audit, the issue is not whether this actually impacts his judgment. The issue is that it may appear to others that the accountant is biased. Thus, objectivity is a particularly important and difficult challenge for the accounting profession, and much of the AICPA code deals with specifying the professional dealings with various issues and situations that may impact objectivity and independence.

Responsibility

The AICPA code defines the professional principle of responsibility in more general terms. The code emphasizes that accountants have a professional responsibility to 'exercise sensitive professional and moral judgments in all their activities' (AICPA, 2018, 0.300.020). The code recognizes that accountants have a crucial societal and economic function and an overall professional responsibility to various stakeholders, such as investors, clients, and the public. Also, as with any code of ethics or professional conduct, professional ethics is not limited to following rules and the law but goes beyond mere compliance and requires individual ethical judgments. Members of the accounting profession are asked to assume professional responsibility beyond existing laws and rules (AICPA, 2018, 0.300.020).

Integrity

The AICPA code upholds the professional principle of integrity, i.e., avoiding contradicting and conflicting actions, particularly in grey-area situations: 'In the absence of specific rules, standards or guidance, or in the face of conflicting opinions, [an accountant] should test decision and deeds by asking: "Am I doing what a person of integrity would do?" . . . Integrity requires [an accountant] to observe both the form and the spirit of technical and ethical standards; circumvention of those standards constitutes subordination of judgment' (AICPA, 2018, 0.300.040). This definition of integrity in the AICPA code is in line with the general professional principle of integrity defined in Section 5.3.2.

Public interest

It is a crucial part of professional ethics in general to understand which public interest the profession serves and to uphold and protect that public interest. The accounting profession recognizes this general professional principle. It clearly specifies that the public interest which the accounting profession serves and has to protect is 'the orderly functioning of commerce' (AICPA, 2018, 0.300.030). In other words, accountants are crucial for the proper functioning of the capitalist market economy. Reliable, objective, standardized, and comparable financial information is crucial for all market participants to make optimal decisions and for upholding fair competition. Particularly, investors can only make optimal investment decisions if they have objective, reliable, and comparable financial information that they can trust. Biased, unreliable financial information would lead to sub-optimal or wrong investment decisions and availability of investment capital, and inefficient financial markets, and it could easily undermine the very foundations of the capitalist market economy. The accounting profession has a crucial function for the efficiency and stability of the capital market economy. This is the public interest that accountants have to serve and protect by upholding and working according to professional principles.

5.4 Ethical challenges of working in specific business functions: the example of marketing ethics

Many employees specialize and work in specific business functions, such as marketing, finance, human resources, or IT. Each of these functions comes with specific ethical challenges and responsibilities that the specialist, who works in one of those functions, has to consider. We use the field of marketing and the role of being a marketing specialist as examples for the specific ethical challenges and ethical responsibilities of a certain business function.

Marketing is a crucial function for business and the economy in general. Marketing links a business to existing and potential markets and customers. Different areas of marketing, such as advertising, market research, pricing, and sales, contribute to linking business with customers and can increase information for both. For instance, advertising promotes the products of a business and makes people aware of the product and its features. This is a flow of information from the business to the customers, which ideally has positive effects for the customers and the business. Customers learn about available products and their characteristics, which enables them to make better informed purchasing decisions, and the business might sell more of its products. Market research establishes a flow of information in the other direction: from (potential) customers to business. Market research is a crucial part of marketing by which businesses study preferences and willingness to pay. For instance, a company wants to know what people like and do not like about their existing products and what would be perceived as improvements of the product. Companies want to understand preferences of people and analyze whether new product ideas resonate with customers, what people are willing to pay for new products or features, whether there is a (new) market they could enter, and so on. With this, marketing delivers information about customers, preferences, and markets to the business, which is crucial for optimal (strategic) management decisions and optimal satisfaction of consumer preferences.

From an ethical perspective, it is also important to recognize new technology-driven marketing possibilities. In recent years, social media, the Internet, and the collection and analysis of large amounts of data have led to new ways of marketing. For instance, tracking and analyzing online behavior of customers led to a better understanding of their preferences and potential wants, and enabled more specifically targeted advertisement. Similarly, retailers collect large amounts of data from their customers and analyze them with sophisticated computer programs to better understand and target their customers' preferences. Big data analysis, the Internet, and social media offer new possibilities to marketing, but also come with new ethical questions and challenges regarding their proper use and topics of privacy, manipulation, and transparency.

5.4.1 Normative guidelines for marketing

How can we identify specific ethical aspects of marketing and define marketing ethics? What are relevant normative criteria for marketing? We will identify normative criteria that enable us to distinguish good from bad marketing by referring to the economic and ethical specifics of the field of marketing. We refer to the inherent ethics of the capitalist market economy (see Chapter 3) to identify normative criteria following from the specific (economic) function of marketing, and we refer to general ethical principles (see Chapter 2) and discuss the application of those principles to the specifics of marketing activities.

We can define normative criteria for good and responsible marketing by recognizing the economic function of marketing in a free market economy and its underlying normative ideals of perfect markets, efficiency, and fair competition. Marketing has an important economic function in a free market economy. Marketing ideally enhances the level of information of customers and businesses, and by doing so marketing enhances potential for optimal decision-making. Sufficient information is crucial for economic actors and for markets to be efficient. Only if economic actors know all their options and have full information about prices can they make optimal decisions, and only then are markets efficient. Thus, a crucial normative economic criterion for good marketing is that it should contribute to properly informing all economic actors. In contrast, bad marketing would misinform economic actors, for instance, by making false or deceptive claims about the characteristics of a product or its price. Such misinformation would result in sub-optimal decision-making and inefficiency. Of course, false and deceptive claims can also be considered lies and thus ethically wrong. However, from an economic viewpoint, the crucial concern is not an ethical one, but simply the economic concern that false and deceptive claims cause sub-optimal decision-making and inefficiency.

Proper marketing must also follow fundamental ethical principles that we have defined in Chapter 2. Basically, marketing practices need to (i) respect the dignity of all persons involved as rational beings and ends in themselves, (ii) not undermine but support individual potentials for personal development and excellence, (iii) increase rather than decrease overall happiness, and (iv) care for all people involved or affected. For marketing, these general ethical principles have specific implications. In the following, we will identify some typical ethical challenges in marketing and provide some examples.

5.4.2 Ethical challenges in marketing

Advertising

The main ethical challenges in advertising are truthfulness, manipulation, and proper targeting. Obviously, truthfulness is a large topic in advertising. Companies aim at telling the best possible stories about their products and often stretch claims about their products. This may be acceptable to some extent. However, when claims become factually wrong or deceptive it is no longer ethically and economically acceptable. Factually wrong claims are simply lies and some ethical approaches, such as Kantian ethics and virtue ethics, consider lying generally as ethically wrong. Lying in marketing is also economically wrong, as discussed above, and harms the customers. As a result of the false claims, customers will make wrong decisions and buy products they would not have bought otherwise.

In advertising, one can find specific types of wrong or deceptive claims. A type of deceptive claim that has become a larger issue in recent years, is greenwashing. *Greenwashing* means making false or deceptive claims about the environmental friendliness of a product or company. The motivation for greenwashing is short-term profits. Green products and markets have been a fast-growing segment in recent years, and customers who have a preference for green products are often willing to pay a higher price for them. Some companies try to benefit from green markets without having green products but by merely claiming that their products are green. In many cases, though, greenwashing is revealed sooner or later and fires back on the company. In the long run, a company might lose more from greenwashing than it gains. A clear-cut example for greenwashing is the way Volkswagen (VW) was marketing their diesel cars in the US. One of VW's main marketing slogans was 'Clean Diesel,' implying that VW's diesel cars are environmentally friendly (Smith & Parloff, 2016; FTC, 2016). VW even provided numbers about low emissions of its cars to back up that claim. However, it turned out that the numbers and the claim were false, and that the cars actually had emissions well above the legally allowed limits in the US (Hotten, 2015; Smith & Parloff, 2016; FTC, 2016). VW even went so far as to manipulate the engines of their diesel cars with sophisticated software to hide the unlawful emissions from US agencies that were testing the cars (FTC, 2016; Gates et al., 2017). This was a rather extreme case of greenwashing that lured customers to buy a seemingly environmentally friendly car that actually did not meet legal emission standards.

In the US and other countries certain deceptive marketing practices are not only considered ethically questionable but forbidden by law to protect customers and efficient markets. For instance, making factually false claims about a product, such as VW made about the emissions of their diesel cars, is illegal in many countries. The US authorities actually sued VW for its greenwashing (FTC, 2016). There are, of course, larger grey areas and there is a spectrum that ranges from telling the full truth about a product to stretching the story to making false claims. In many cases, it may be OK to tell the best possible story about a product and to be silent about its limitations. Ultimately, it is the responsibility of the marketing specialist to make sure that marketing and advertisement stays in the acceptable range. Note also that one does not even have to stretch a message or make up potentially deceptive stories to better sell a product. If the product is a great product, the best marketing strategy may be to simply tell the authentic story about the product, and make sure that all potential customers know it.

Truthful advertising has grey areas and some exaggeration is ethically acceptable, particularly if everyone can recognize the exaggeration as such. It depends on the specific case whether this is OK or not. An interesting case is the slogan 'Red Bull gives you wings,' which Red Bull had used for many years to market its energy drinks (Rothman, 2014). Obviously, the literal slogan makes a false claim: nobody would ever grow wings from drinking Red Bull. No one would take that slogan literally, though. The slogan cannot be considered a lie based on a literal interpretation, because it neither aims nor actually does deceive someone with regard to its claim of growing wings. Using common sense, everyone recognizes this as metaphor. What the metaphor wants to tell us is that we get a lot of energy and power from drinking the drink. However, Red Bull actually was sued for its slogan. It was not the literal but the metaphorical meaning that was at the center of concern, though. In the lawsuit, the claim was not that someone actually believed that he would grow wings, but rather that someone believed the metaphor, that is, that he would get a lot of energy. The lawsuit argued that the amount of energy one can get from such an energy drink is actually rather small and comparable to a cup of coffee. The customer felt tricked by the slogan because it seemed to exaggerate how much energy one actually gets from the drink (Rothman, 2014; Bucher, 2014). So, the metaphor itself was considered deceptive. Red Bull ultimately settled the lawsuit, changed its slogan slightly, and offered coupons for free drinks to its customers (Bucher, 2014). The settlement probably was a good business decision. It might have been more damaging and costly for Red Bull to fight the lawsuit and get negative publicity when discussing in court (with expertise statements) whether the effects of their drinks are actually the same as the effects of a cup of coffee.

Another ethical issue in advertising is manipulation. Manipulation means treating people as mere objects by making them do something they would not do through autonomous deliberation. Manipulation is generally ethically problematic because it is disrespectful to rational beings and undermines their autonomy, freedom, and right to deliberate decision-making. Manipulation in advertisement and marketing can come in many shapes. For instance, one might manipulate customers by putting certain products in an exposed place, such as candy at the cash register at children's eye level, by product placement in TV shows, or by promoting certain beauty and health ideals in connection with specific products. Nothing like this generally is illegal and might to some extent be ethically acceptable. However, if such marketing practices significantly undermine the autonomy and free decision-making of the customers, it becomes manipulative and ethically problematic. In a Kantian perspective, such manipulative marketing strategies treat people as mere objects and not as rational beings and ends in themselves. Also, some patterns of manipulation in advertisement, such as the promotion of specific beauty ideals, have been harmful to the development of young people. For instance, anorexia has been linked to increased exposure to promotion of thin body ideals in media and advertisement (Stice et al., 1994; Hogan & Strasburger, 2008).

Manipulation is particularly an issue with regard to vulnerable groups, such as children or patients. Children are vulnerable to manipulation because they lack the ability to recognize manipulative marketing strategies. For instance, some companies sell food together with toys. Children then want the toys that come with the food and may not be able to reflect on whether they actually like the food or if it is healthy. Manipulative promotion of unhealthy food to children has been linked to the serious and increasing social issue of child obesity. In the US, some companies have voluntarily restricted their advertisement and do not advertise to younger children to avoid manipulation and assume their social responsibility, although critics consider the companies' steps insufficient (McQuaid, 2015). Advertising prescription medicine to patients is also problematic because patients may desperately seek a cure and lack the expertise and objectivity to critically evaluate the benefits and risks of the medicine. In the US, such direct-to-consumer advertisement of prescriptive drugs is controversial but legally allowed, whereas in most countries in the world it is illegal (WHO, 2009; Mackey & Liang, 2015). From an ethics of care perspective, advertising to vulnerable groups should be done only in a restrictive way, without abusing asymmetries in power, ability, and knowledge for manipulative purposes.

A related challenge of advertisement is proper targeting. Proper targeting means ensuring that advertising only addresses and reaches the proper audience. For instance, certain products, such as alcohol or tobacco, should generally not be advertised to younger people because they are not considered as fully capable of handling the risks of these products. In current marketing practice, proper targeting has become tricky, though. The use of new ways of marketing through social media and other venues makes it harder to ensure that advertisement does not reach certain non-target groups, such as children.

Pricing

Pricing is part of marketing, and ideally pricing should be transparent and fair. The principle of transparency follows from economic and ethical principles. Economically, transparency is crucial for economic agents to be able to make optimal decisions and for markets to be efficient. Disguising and confusing the actual prices of products undermines optimal decision-making. For instance, if companies offer similar food products in various weights and volumes, it becomes difficult for costumers to compare prices and make optimal decisions. Ethically, transparency is in line with respecting the autonomy and free decision-making of rational persons. As a result, some US states and other countries actually have mandatory unit pricing rules that require grocery stores to display the price per unit, which makes prices more transparent and more easily comparable for the customers.

Price discrimination is a crucial issue in pricing which can affect fairness. From an ethical perspective all people are equal, and in line with the principle of equality customers should be treated equally when it comes to pricing. However, some unequal treatment in pricing is ethically (and economically) acceptable if it is based on ethically acceptable and transparent reasons. For instance, senior discounts or discounts for veterans are acceptable because they are based on acceptable reasons, such as respect for the elderly and veterans, or the consideration of the economic situation of older persons. Also, price discounts for purchasing larger quantities are acceptable because of obvious economic reasons. However, charging women or certain minorities more is ethically unacceptable and actually illegal in some US states and other countries because such price discrimination would be based on unethical discrimination by gender, race, or religion.

Pricing that undermines competition is unacceptable for economic reasons. For instance, a large company could afford to sell a product for a couple of months with losses, just for the purpose of driving a much smaller competitor out of the market. Such predatory pricing would undermine fair competition and market efficiency. Under competition laws, predatory pricing is considered illegal in the US and other countries, if the pricing actually destroys competition and leads to monopoly power for the company that does the predatory pricing.

Market research

Market research is an important and useful tool for businesses to generate information about preferences and concerns of customers. Both businesses and customers ideally profit from market research that leads to new and better products which optimally satisfy preferences and demands. However, market research needs to adhere to ethical principles and must be based on transparency and respect. There is some risk that market research considers people as mere means to generate information and pulls information from people without their knowledge and consent. Transparency and respect in market research mean fully informing people about the purpose, method, range, and potential risks of the research, to ask for consent, to not treat people as mere means, and to care about not harming people in any way by the research.

Sale

Sales practices can come with ethical issues similar to advertising and market research. Proper sales practices need to adhere to the principles of respect, transparency, and fairness. A sales person considers the interests of his company and his own interests and has no specific duties to protect the interests of the customer. However, a sales person should adhere to basic ethical principles in interacting with customers. It is OK if the sales person tries to persuade the customer to buy a product as long as this is done in a respectful, fair, and transparent way. That is, the sales person should give accurate information about the characteristics and price of the product, and not use pressure or any manipulative or deceptive sales tactics to get a customer to buy a product. In this perspective, some common sales practices are questionable. For instance, it is questionable to first name a high, unrealistic price, just to suggest to the customer that a lower price offered later on is a very good deal. Or, it is questionable to put pressure on the customer to buy a product immediately by claiming that a special price can only be offered right now.

Database marketing/big data analysis

In recent years, new technological possibilities have created new ways of marketing. For instance, big data analysis enables identification of preferences and potential demand more precisely, and enables better tailoring of marketing messages to individual customers. However, the new possibilities also come with specific ethical challenges. We illustrate such new marketing tools and their challenges with a case related to Target's marketing presented by Duhigg (2012). In this case, Target got into trouble with a customer because it sent advertisements for baby products to his teenage daughter. The father complained to Target about the baby product ads, which he considered inappropriate to send to his daughter, and asked Target for an explanation (Duhigg, 2012, p. 196). The advertisement was sent based on an automated computer program analyzing customers' shopping decisions at Target stores. The computer program in question was running sophisticated analyses of large amounts of customers' data that Target collected at its cash registers. The program was to identify shopping patterns that allow conclusions about customers' preferences (Duhigg, 2012, pp. 187 ff). One set of patterns enabled the program to identify whether a customer might be pregnant and become a parent. Pregnant women statistically show some typical changes in their shopping behavior, for instance, they start buying large amounts of vitamin pills or buy larger amounts of lotion (Duhigg, 2012, p. 194). In doing some research, Target identified a set of products and typical changes in shopping behavior that, taken together, would indicate that a woman is pregnant. The computer program now ran all customers' data against the defined pattern to identify all customers who were potentially pregnant. This information was then used for marketing purposes to send those customers baby product advertisements and coupons early, before the baby is even born (Duhigg, 2012, p. 195).

From a marketing perspective, this is a sophisticated and effective marketing tool that increases the business's information about customer preferences and boosts its sales. Customers also seem to benefit, as they get specific and targeted information about products they are actually interested in. According to economic criteria, then, utilizing big data analysis for marketing can be considered positive. However, there are some ethical issues in this case. Particularly, the rights to privacy and self-determination seem to be undermined here. That someone is pregnant is private information, and it is up to every person to decide to whom and at what point in time they want to disclose their pregnancy. In the Target case, it turned out that the daughter actually was pregnant but had not told her father yet (Duhigg, 2012, p. 196). The right to her decision to not tell her father was undermined by Target's ads, which indicated the pregnancy to him. Based on the principles of privacy, respect, and transparency, Target should have gotten full consent from the daughter for using her shopping data the way it did. However, most customers would not recognize how much information the company can get from shopping data, and that the company can even uncover private information, such as pregnancy and potentially other information, e.g., about certain diseases. Even if the collection and use of such data is legal, it still runs into ethical issues related to privacy, transparency, autonomy, and freedom of customers.

Marketing methods using big data collection and analysis like the one illustrated above have actually become pretty common and are broadly applied to Internet and social media use. Companies track Internet use and social media, collect information, and run analytics to determine what products to advertise to individual users. This is a crucial part of the business model of successful large companies such as Facebook, Twitter, or Google. Generally, the same ethical questions regarding privacy, self-determination, consent, and transparency apply to all those marketing practices, and more recent issues were of even larger dimensions. In 2018, Facebook was confronted with a larger scandal regarding the abuse of data from more than 50 million of its customers (Cadwalladr & Graham-Harrison, 2018).

Related to the collection of large data is also the question of data security and potentially significant harm to many people if data are stolen or misused. Companies and governments like to collect all kinds of data for various purposes. It is not always clear that they can adequately protect the data and that the data are not misused for other, potentially harmful purposes. It is almost impossible to guarantee 100% data safety. Thus, collection and storage of data should be based on a precautionary principle. That is, data collection and storage should be minimized with regard to the amount of data and time of storage necessary for the defined purpose. Also, data should only be collected and stored if overall the potential benefits are significantly larger than the potential harm (following the utilitarian principle).

5.4.3 Ethics-based marketing strategies: ethical branding

Ethics can be considered as a normative guideline for good marketing, but ethics can also underpin entire marketing strategies. An example of ethics-driven marketing is ethical branding. Ethical branding does not use artificial marketing messages that link the product arbitrarily to positive images and concepts, such as happiness, health, or friendship. Rather, ethical branding is based on real stories about how the product is based on, and contributes to, societal or environmental values. The former marketing director of New Belgium Brewery describes this approach as follows:

> For our New Belgium marketing team, the recent addition to our must-read list is *How Brands Become Icons: The Principles of Cultural Branding* (2004), by Douglas Holt, the L'Oreal Chair of Marketing at Oxford University. Dr. Holt directly pierces the widely believed immutable law of marketing that brands stay inflated when pumped full of positive abstract perceptions. Rather, Holt proves that great brands are built from tangible ground. I'm sure there are more forces at work, but as I peer at the global economy, the magnet I see pushing and pulling brands is the customer insistence for authenticity, or for brands to contribute real

social and cultural value. . . . In this era of marketing communications cacophony, here's the irony: all the noise becomes opportunity for the few brands that tell an authentic story that resonates in a social and cultural context.

(Owsley, 2005, p. 137)

Ethical branding works particularly well for the increasing number of value- or purpose-driven businesses, such as Patagonia or New Belgium Brewery. Value or purpose-driven businesses, social entrepreneurships, or sustainable businesses just need to tell their story about the values and purpose(s) that underlie their operations and products. Such authentic positive stories about ethical products may resonate much better with customers than standard marketing approaches using fictional messages. Ethical branding is also rather cost-efficient and can, with a lower budget, achieve better effects than traditional marketing.

5.5 Whistleblowing

Chapter 5 has been about specific ethical aspects related to individuals acting in organizations: ethical challenges and responsibilities related to different individual roles, positions, and professional fields. In this section, we will discuss a difficult ethical situation by which any individual acting in an organization could potentially be confronted: whistleblowing. We will first clarify the ethical characteristics of whistleblowing and then provide a decision-making method for whistleblowing situations: when is it justified to blow the whistle and when is it unjustified? We will also discuss the broader individual, societal, and organizational implications of whistleblowing and recent legal developments for protecting certain kinds of whistleblowers.

5.5.1 Whistleblowing: definition and ethical aspects

Generally, whistleblowing means telling someone about internal issues or wrongdoing in an organization. The concept is sometimes used in a broader sense, encompassing internal and external whistleblowing. Internal whistleblowing means that a member of the organization internally hints at issues in the organization, for instance by informing supervisors or the ethics and compliance office. An external whistleblower, in contrast, informs some entity outside the organization about internal issues or wrongdoing in the organization of which the whistleblower is a member. In the following, I will use the term *whistleblowing* in the sense of *external whistleblowing* because this is the more classical case of whistleblowing. Internal whistleblowing is considered in the context of this book as a specific case of speaking up within an organization.

> Definition 5.1: **(External) Whistleblowing** is the intentional act of a member of an organization calling public attention to some wrongdoing of the organization.

To illustrate whistleblowing, we consider the following basic example: you work for a chemical production plant and get internal knowledge about serious risks for the public caused by the production process. To inform the public would probably result in the shutdown of the plant. Would it be right to blow the whistle in this situation? It is obvious that this is a difficult decision because both alternatives, blowing the whistle or remaining silent, have serious implications for you, the company, and the public. The situation has an ethical dimension. We want to know what the ethically best action in this situation would be. Before we look into a systematic decision-making method for this kind of situation, we first want to clarify the type of ethical issue that generally underlies a whistleblowing situation. For this, we define the concept of an *ethical dilemma* and then identify the specific ethical dilemma of whistleblowing.

> Definition 5.2: An **ethical dilemma** is a situation in which one must choose between two conflicting ethical values, norms, or principles.

In an ethical dilemma, someone is confronted with two alternatives that are both considered by themselves to be ethically right, but one cannot have them both, and no matter which alternative one chooses, one will necessarily violate the other. An ethical dilemma differs from other ethical issues, for instance, issues in which one needs to distinguish the right from the wrong, needs to identify the only ethically right alternative among various ethically inferior alternatives, or needs to decide to do the well-defined ethically right instead of the obviously ethically wrong.

How can one solve an ethical dilemma? Basically, this is done by applying ethical decision methods that we developed in Chapter 2. These methods help make a decision about what alternative overrides the other in a certain situation. For instance, with the utilitarian method, one can consider which of the two alternatives given in the dilemma maximizes the overall happiness of all affected. Another aspect in analyzing ethical dilemmas is questioning whether there actually is a dilemma. In some cases, ethical dilemmas can be solved by simply debunking them and demonstrating that the dilemma actually does not exist. For instance, someone might claim that his company faces the dilemma of either making profits or being ethical. However, as we have discussed with various examples throughout this book, both actually may go well together: ethical business practice may ultimately be more profitable. In some cases, dilemmas are not actual dilemmas but the result of the logical fallacy of a false alternative. The fallacy of false alternatives claims that there are only two alternatives available and one must choose between them. In fact, however, there are additional alternatives available, and one actually could choose another option besides the two presented, which would solve the dilemma. For instance, one may claim that telling on a friend who has cheated on another friend or not telling on the friend is an ethical dilemma. The ethical dilemma is that one can either be loyal to the one friend or to the other, but not to both. However, an alternative might be to talk to the one friend and convince him to tell the other friend the truth.

The ethical dilemma in the whistleblowing situation

In the whistleblowing situation, there is typically the following underlying ethical dilemma: one can either tell the public about the wrongdoing in the organization that is harmful to society, or not. By telling the public, one assumes one's responsibility and moral obligation to society but violates one's loyalty to the organization. By not telling, one would be loyal to the organization, but violate one's ethical obligations toward society. The whistleblower, being a member of the organization, as well as of the society, usually has a moral obligation to both: to be loyal to the organization and to be a responsible member of society (see Figure 5.4).

> Loyalty, duty, responsibility to the organization of which one is part
>
>
>
> Duty, responsibility, moral obligations to society (humanity)

Figure 5.4 The main ethical dilemma underlying the whistleblowing situation.

5.5.2 A method for analyzing whistleblowing situations

In this section, we introduce a method for analyzing whistleblowing situations and deciding whether it is ethically right to blow the whistle. Whistleblowing situations require a difficult decision that affects many people. It is crucial that someone is certain of making the right decision and can justify the decision against others. The following method consists of a three-step analysis for deciding whether whistleblowing is justified: (1) verifying the issue, (2) exploring internal ways to fix the issue, and (3) identifying ethical reasons that back up the decision (Figure 5.5).

The first step for deciding whether whistleblowing is justified in a given case is to check the facts and clarify if there really is a serious issue or wrongdoing. Personal and even professional perceptions can be biased and should be verified. For instance, an engineer discovers a flaw in the production facility, does some calculations, and

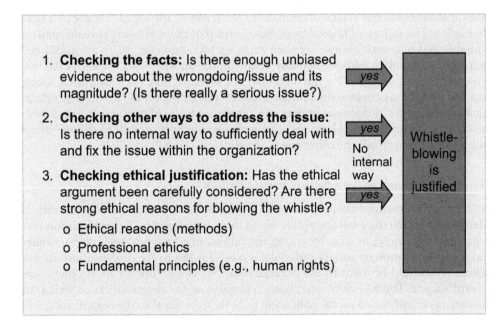

Figure 5.5 Method for analyzing whistleblowing situations.

concludes that there is a serious risk of an accident with harmful consequences to the public. However, the engineer should verify that his calculation and conclusion are correct, for instance by double-checking his calculations carefully or by asking another engineer whom he trusts to double-check his calculation and conclusion. Also, the issue at stake has to be a serious issue with the potential for significant harm. It is generally not justified to inform the public about rather small internal issues.

The second step is to check options for internally addressing and fixing the issue. All organizations have to deal with small and big issues and internal frictions. Ideally, an organization has the culture and mechanisms to properly address and solve issues internally (see Chapter 4). If a serious issue is identified in step 1, one should aim to address and fix the issue internally. This would often be preferable because an internal solution might be the most effective and least harmful solution. However, if there is no reasonable way to address and solve the issue internally, whistleblowing remains the only feasible option. Note though, that for some issues an internal path is not preferable. For instance, if the internal wrongdoing involves criminal activities, it is preferable to notify respective agencies and initiate external investigations. Keeping serious illegal wrongdoings internal can result in cover-ups or inappropriate dealings with the wrongdoing.

The third step is to consider ethical reasons for and against blowing the whistle. Even if there is a serious issue and no internal way to address the issue, whistle-blowing is not automatically justified. One needs to consider ethical reasons for and against the whistleblowing. One can refer to ethical theory, professional ethics, or fundamental ethical principles to determine whether whistleblowing is the ethically best decision. For instance, one can refer to utilitarianism and consider whether blow-ing the whistle increases or decreases overall happiness of all affected. Even if there is a serious issue that cannot be solved internally, it could be that blowing the whistle is worse in terms of overall happiness than not blowing the whistle. In a utilitarian perspective, whistleblowing can only be supported as the ethically right decision if the whistleblowing maximizes overall happiness of all affected. One can also refer to other ethical theories or to professional ethics to analyze the case. Professional ethics may sometimes require the professional to warn the public, regardless of the conse-quences in terms of overall happiness, if the public interest that the profession serves and protects is jeopardized. Another reference point is fundamental ethical principles. For instance, serious violations of constitutional principles or human rights could be reasons to blow the whistle. Only if one can support the whistleblowing with substan-tial ethical reasons is the whistleblowing justifiable. Ethical reasons are particularly important because the whistleblower needs to be able to justify the whistleblowing to himself, to his family, to co-workers, to agencies, and to the public. Whistleblowing can have far-reaching impacts on many people who may ask the whistleblower for an explanation and justification.

If all three steps of the above method support whistleblowing, it is justified. That is, for whistleblowing to be justified, there must be a serious issue, no internal way to address and solve the issue, and strong ethical reasons supporting the whistleblowing.

Whistleblowing is a measure of last resort, a final option to address serious issues when there is no other reasonable option left. Although situations where one needs to blow the whistle are rare, it is important for every person to recognize that the option of blowing the whistle exists. Each person is a rational individual and, as such, an ultimate reference point for ethics. Everyone is an ethical person with the capacity for ethical judgment. As ethical beings, we have a responsibility to critically reflect on and engage in ethical matters of the organizations and communities of which we are part. We should not deny our responsibility and shift it to others – to co-workers, supervisors, or political leaders – but recognize that every person has the same fundamental responsibilities and capacities when it comes to ethical matters. In that respect, justified whistleblowing is an expression of ethical responsibility and the moral capacity of the individual person.

5.5.3 Organizational aspects

From the perspective of the organization or company, whistleblowing of one of its members is a worst-case scenario. A justified whistleblowing case reveals some serious wrongdoing of the organization or company and can significantly impact its success. Uncovered wrongdoing that harmed the public or specific stakeholders can significantly damage the reputation of a company, lead to lawsuits, legal prosecution, fines, and liabilities, and ultimately result in financial losses. In the worst case, the entire company or organization can go down. The whistleblowing is not the cause of these damages, but only the rightful consequence of the underlying wrongdoing, which is the real cause of the trouble of the company. The trouble to the company is caused by its failure to prevent or stop the internal wrongdoing. It is, thus, in the best interest of companies and organizations to prevent whistleblowing situations, not by suppressing the very act of whistleblowing, but by ensuring early on that it never comes to the point where someone feels that she has to blow the whistle. In other words, it is in the best interest of a company or organization to have internal mechanisms in place for preventing and dealing with internal issues and wrongdoing early on. Crucial mechanisms for this are the development of a strong ethical culture and the implementation of well-designed ethics and compliance programs (see Section 4.5). An ethical culture empowers and encourages employees to speak up and raise concerns early on, and an ethics and compliance program establishes internal mechanisms to prevent and internally address issues and wrongdoings. These elements of organizational ethics are effective means to avoid the development of situations in which someone feels the moral obligation to blow the whistle.

5.5.4 Personal aspects

From the personal perspective of the whistleblower, whistleblowing is, in most cases, a very difficult decision and situation. The whistleblower has to solve a difficult ethical dilemma and decide what is the right action. If the whistleblowing is justified, the whistleblower assumes her moral obligations and responsibilities toward the public. As such, the whistleblower expresses her individuality as an ethical being and her professional responsibility. Doing the right thing is rewarding in itself and positive for the person blowing the whistle. However, blowing the whistle has historically been met with large personal risks. Many whistleblowers suffered financially, lost their job, did not find new employment, or were charged by their company. Blowing the whistle is a difficult individual decision, and the potential whistleblower often has to consider further ethical aspects and responsibilities beyond the ethical dilemma of whistleblowing, for instance, responsibilities to one's family.

In practice, employees often choose other alternatives before blowing the whistle. Many employees just walk away if they recognize internal issues or wrongdoing. Although this is a possible solution and reaction to issues in the company for which one works, it is not always the ethically best action. Walking away does not stop the wrongdoing, and if there is significant harm or violation of rights involved, the ethically better action may be to blow the whistle and stop the wrongdoing. In some cases, one may even have the ethical obligation to blow the whistle, and walking away would be irresponsible. Consider, for instance, cases where criminal activities are involved, such as bribery or sexual harassment. If one recognizes such activities in a company and just walks away, this could be considered irresponsible.

Generally, people should be empowered and rewarded for doing the right thing and acting ethically. It should not be the case that whistleblowers have to suffer for doing the right thing, or that employees are discouraged to speak up. Organizations, companies, and society should take measures to empower people for ethical action. In recent years, the US has improved the legal protection and support of whistleblowers, so that we now also see examples of whistleblowers who were rewarded and actually benefitted from blowing the whistle.

5.5.5 Societal aspects

The society has an interest in justified whistleblowing because the whistleblower typically uncovers harm to the society or to certain stakeholders. In other words, the whistleblower serves the public and helps prevent harm to the society. Thus, society should aim to empower, support, and protect whistleblowers. In the US, there has been some efforts to support whistleblowers, and several laws include whistleblower protection. The False Claims Act, which goes back to 1863, and has been revised since then several times, enables rewards to whistleblowers who uncover fraud to the government, specifically to the military and to health care programs. Under this law, a whistleblower who uncovers a fraud can get rewarded 10–30% of the recovered sum. In addition, Congress passed the Tax Relief and Health Care Act (2006) to expand whistleblower support to cases of tax fraud, which was not part of the False Claims Act. The Tax Relief and Health Care Act enables the Internal Revenue Service to reward whistleblowers who uncover serious tax fraud 15–30% of the recovered tax. The Whistleblower Protection Act, originally passed in 1989 and updated several times since then, protects federal employees, who blow the whistle against their agency, from retaliation. The Sarbanes–Oxley Act contains provisions for protecting whistleblowers who reveal corporate fraud.

Although the US has strengthened whistleblower protection by legal provisions, the protection is still limited to certain types of issues and employees. Protecting justified whistleblowing is in the best interest of society and also ethically desirable, as it empowers ethically right actions. In this perspective, laws protecting whistleblowing should be further expanded to cover all cases of justified whistleblowing and to support all whistleblowers who act in the public interest and do the ethically right action.

Note

1 See Armstrong (2002) for a broader overview of the field of accounting ethics, and Duska et al. (2011) for a detailed discussion.

References

AICPA [American Institute for Certified Public Accountants]. (2018). *Code of Professional Conduct*. AICPA. Retrieved from http://pub.aicpa.org/codeofconduct/Ethics.aspx#.

Armstrong, M. B. (2002). Ethical issues in accounting. In N. Bowie (Ed.), *The Blackwell Guide to Business Ethics* (pp. 145–164). Malden: Blackwell.

BMFSFJ [The German Federal Ministry for Family Affairs, Senior Citizens, Women and Youth]. (2015). *The ElterngeldPlus with Partnership Bonus and More Flexible Parental Leave*. BMFSFJ. Retrieved from www.bmfsfj.de/bmfsfj/meta/en/en/publications-en/the-elterngeldplus-with-partnership-bonus-and-more-flexible-parental-leave/73780.

BMJV [The German Federal Ministry of Justice and Consumer Protection]. (2017). *Mitbestimmungsgesetz [Codetermination Act] of 1976*. BMJV. Retrieved from www.gesetze-im-internet.de/mitbestg/index.html

Bucher, A. (2014). Red Bull energy drink class action settlement. *Top Class Actions*, October 6. Retrieved from https://topclassactions.com/lawsuit-settlements/closed-settlements/41577-red-bull-energy-drink-class-action-settlement.

Cadwalladr, C., & Graham-Harrison, E. (2018). Revealed: 50 million Facebook profiles harvested for Cambridge Analytica in major data breach. *The Guardian*, March 17. Retrieved from www.theguardian.com

Ciulla, J. B. (1995). Leadership Ethics: Mapping the Territory. *Business Ethics Quarterly*, 5, 5–28.

Duhigg, C. (2012). *The Power of Habit: Why We Do What We Do in Life and Business*. New York: Random House.

Duska, R., Duska, B. S., & Ragatz, J. (2011). *Accounting Ethics*. Hoboken, NJ: Wiley-Blackwell.

FTC [Federal Trade Commission]. (2016). FTC charges Volkswagen deceived consumers with its "clean diesel" campaign. *FTC*. Retrieved from www.ftc.gov/news-events/press-releases/2016/03/ftc-charges-volkswagen-deceived-consumers-its-clean-diesel.

Gates, G., Ewing, J., Russell, K., & Watkins, D. (2017). How Volkswagen's 'defeat devices' worked. *The New York Times*, March 16. Retrieved from www.nytimes.com/interactive/2015/business/international/vw-diesel-emissions-scandal-explained.html?_r=0.

Hogan, M. J., & Strasburger, V. C. (2008). Body image, eating disorders, and the media. *Adolescent Medicine*, 19, 521–546.

Hotten, R. (2015). Volkswagen: the scandal explained. *BBC News*, December 10. Retrieved from www.bbc.com/news/business-34324772.

Mackey, T. K., & Liang, B. A. (2015). It's time to shine the light on direct-to-consumer advertising. *Annals of Family Medicine*, 13, 82–85.

McQuaid, J. (2015). Despite voluntary restrictions, junk food ads aimed at kids are still a problem. *Forbes*, May 11. Retrieved from www.forbes.com.

Owsley, G. (2005). The necessity for aligning brand with corporate ethics. In S. L. True, L. Ferrell, & O. C. Ferrell (Eds.), *Fulfilling our Obligation: Perspectives on Teaching Business Ethics* (pp. 127–142). Illinois: Kennesaw State University Press.

Rothman, M. (2014). Red Bull to pay $13 million for false advertisement settlement. *Bevnet*, August 5. Retrieved from www.bevnet.com/news/2014/red-bull-to-pay-13-million-for-false-advertising-settlement.

Smith, G., & Parloff, R. (2016). Hoaxwagen: How the massive diesel fraud incinerated VW's reputation—and will hobble the company for years to come. *Fortune*, March 7. Retrieved from http://fortune.com/inside-volkswagen-emissions-scandal.

Stice, E., Schupak-Neuberg, E., Shaw, H. E., & Stein, R. I. (1994). Relation of media exposure to eating disorder symptomatology: An examination of mediating mechanisms. *Journal of Abnormal Psychology*, 103(4), 836–840.

WHO. (2009). Direct-to-consumer advertising under fire. *Bulletin of the World Health Organization*, 87, 576–577.

6 Global business ethics

The business world has become increasingly global in recent decades. Globalization has some economic and ethical advantages, but also comes with ethical challenges that we want to identify and analyze in this chapter. Globalization and global markets have the potential for many beneficial aspects. Ideally, globalization increases efficiency and productivity, enables more people around the world to participate in economic development and wealth, and brings people together to cooperate and exchange goods and services. Under ideal conditions, global production and trade benefits all countries and people. However, we currently are pretty far away from this ideal and face many challenges and issues in the global context. The main problems are (i) imperfect global markets, (ii) people becoming mere objects of the global system, (iii) significant global environmental harm and injustice, (iv) unequal distribution of income and wealth, and (v) unsustainability of the global economic system. Overcoming these economic and ethical shortcomings of the global economy is one of the main challenges of the 21st century. There will be up to 11 billion people living on earth by the end of the century, and a healthy global economy that benefits all people around the world is crucial for global stability, peace, and wellbeing. The answer to ethical and economic issues of the global economy is not to negate globalization but rather to improve it. We need to address and solve the issues of globalization and develop the global economy into a positive force for the world. This chapter critically discusses the ethical issues of globalization and ways to improve globalization by global business ethics and shared responsibility of all actors in the global economy.

In the following, we will first discuss some global business ethics cases to illustrate typical ethical issues in the global economy. We then identify the main ethical issues in global business and their underlying causes. Finally, we develop the outlines of a global business ethics and formulate basic ethical principles for global business.

6.1 Global business ethics: cases

There are many examples of ethical shortcomings in the global economy. Ethical issues can be found, for instance, in sourcing of conflict minerals (GAO, 2013; see also Chapter 4), environmentally destructive cotton production (WWF, 1999, 2018), ethically unacceptable sweat shop conditions (Rosen, 2002), child labor in cocoa production (Off, 2006; Mistrati & Romano, 2010), or the globalization of e-waste (Grossman, 2006). In this section, we discuss three exemplary cases to illustrate typical ethical issues in global business and explore underlying causes of, and potential solutions for, these issues: (i) child labor and slavery in the chocolate industry, (ii) outsourcing of production to other countries, and (iii) globalization of e-waste.

6.1.1 Case 1: child labor and slavery in the global chocolate industry

Many industries are global by necessity because some of the raw materials for these industries can only be sourced in certain countries that are different from the main markets of the final products, for instance, the US and Europe. This holds for a large range of industries and products. For instance, some rare metals that are necessary for the production of smartphones and PCs are not available in the US or Europe (see also Section 4.2); 99% of bauxite, the raw material for aluminum, is extracted outside of the US and Europe, which both have only very limited deposits of bauxite; many agricultural raw materials can only be grown in certain regions in the world that are different from the main regions of consumption: rubber trees, coffee, and cocoa plants only grow in tropical regions, but they go into products sold in other parts of the world.

In this section, we discuss the example of cocoa, which is the main raw material for the production of chocolate. Cocoa can only be grown in humid tropical climates, and 70% of the world's cocoa production comes from West Africa, mainly Ghana and the Ivory Coast, whereas the main markets for chocolate are in Europe and the US. Child labor, child trafficking, and slavery have been serious issues in cocoa production in Ghana and the Ivory Coast for many years (Off, 2006; Mistrati & Romano, 2010; Tulane University, 2015; O'Keefe, 2016). In 2013–2014 about 2.12 million children were working on cocoa farms in both countries, with 2.03 million of them under hazardous conditions (Tulane University, 2015). Among those child workers are also child slaves. For years, children have been trafficked to the Ivory Coast from neighboring countries and sold as slaves to farmers. The traffickers lure children from countries like Mali, which is one of the poorest countries in the world, and sell them then to cocoa farmers in the Ivory Coast (Mistrati & Romano, 2010). Around the year 2000, there was an estimated 12,000–15,000 child slaves working on cocoa plantations in the Ivory Coast (O'Keefe, 2016).

The ethical issues in this case are obvious. Child labor and child slavery violate international labor standards and human rights. Worldwide child labor is considered unethical because young children are vulnerable. They cannot make fully informed autonomous decisions in the same way as adults. They are vulnerable to abuse and exploitation. Also, childhood is a crucial time for developing personal potential. Children need to learn many skills in various subjects, such as math, language, sciences, history, arts, sports, and so on. If children have to work full time, their ability to go to school and develop skills is undermined. This negatively impacts their personal development, future life, and future opportunities. These arguments for child labor being unethical can be supported by ethics of care, virtue ethics, and Kantian ethics. Consequently, the Minimum Age Convention by the International Labor Organization sets the minimum age for work at 15 years (14 years in exceptions) (ILO, 1973), and the right to education is declared to be a human right (UN, 1948, article 26). Child trafficking and child slavery, which are also prevalent in cocoa production, obviously are severe violations against fundamental ethical principles and international norms. Trafficking and slavery treat children as mere objects, violate the principles of freedom and autonomy of each person, violate articles 1 and 4 of the

Universal Declaration of Human Rights (UN, 1948) and violate international labor standards (ILO, 1999).

The ethical issues in this case are pretty easy to identify. The more difficult questions in this case are: Who is responsible for these issues? and Who can take what kind of action to address and fix these issues? There are various economic players involved in this case who potentially should assume responsibility and take action: the cocoa farmers, the governments of the Ivory Coast and Ghana, the companies in the chocolate industry that produce and sell chocolate products in the US and Europe, the consumers who buy these products, and so on. Let's first have a look at the large companies in the chocolate industry, such as Hershey, Mars, and Nestlé. To what degree are these companies responsible for the issues of child labor and slavery in cocoa production? To discuss this question, we refer to the three criteria of business-specific responsibility defined in Section 4.2.1. According to these criteria we need to discuss (i) to what extent these companies cause these issues, (ii) to what extent did they know, or could they have known, about these issues, and (iii) how much power and ability do they have to address the issues, always in comparison to other players in this case.

First, there are some causal links between the large chocolate companies and the issues in cocoa production, because the companies have bought cocoa from the region for many years, and their demand for cocoa established production in its current form. Second, the issue has been well known for many years and brought to the attention of the chocolate industry. Third, the big players in the chocolate industry are multi-billion-dollar corporations which, considering their size, financial power, and influence on the supply chain, have the ability to address the issues and improve the situation. This last point is perhaps the main argument for holding the chocolate companies responsible. The leading companies in the chocolate industry are probably the most powerful of all players involved in the situation. As the main buyers of cocoa, they have the ability to influence and change their supply chain for the better if they are willing to get involved. The chocolate companies might even be more powerful than the local governments. Nestlé, for instance, has a revenue of about $90 billion, whereas the GDP of the Ivory Coast is about $40 billion. It is also reasonable from a business viewpoint to ask the chocolate companies to assume responsibility in this situation and invest money to improve the supply chain. Not only is it irresponsible to make money off of human rights violations but investing in a more ethical supply chain also reduces serious business risks of the current situation, such as loss of reputation, consumer boycotts, stricter regulations, and legal consequences. This can justify investments into ethical improvement of the supply chain to shareholders.

What actions could the large chocolate companies pursue to assume their responsibility in this case? There are various options to effect change in the supply chain. Given their market power, these companies generally have a large influence and can more easily effect change. Typical instruments for upholding human rights and environmental norms in the supply chain are (i) setting requirements for social and environmental standards, for instance, by a code for suppliers, (ii) setting up audit mechanisms to check whether these standards are met, and (iii) setting up mechanisms to educate and help the supplier firms to meet the standards. Many companies with global supply chains have such instruments in place and get involved to ensure an ethical supply chain. Actually, the large chocolate companies have started in recent years to get more involved, and they are increasing the amount of certified cocoa; that is, of cocoa that has been verified to be produced in accordance with certain ethical and environmental standards (O'Keefe, 2016). Some smaller chocolate companies have used different approaches, such as fair-trade business models, which explicitly aim to empower participation and flourishing of all partners in the supply chain. Divine Chocolate, for instance, has a specific business model in which the cocoa farmers in the supply chain in Ghana are actually co-owners of the company (Divine Chocolate, 2018). As a result, the farmers, who provide the cocoa, participate in the overall profits of the company, and they and their communities benefit and thrive from their participation in the chocolate industry (Divine Chocolate, 2018). Overall, fair-trade markets have had significant growth rates, and fair-trade companies, such as Divine Chocolate, have been very successful in recent years. More active involvement in the supply chain and ensuring fair participation and fair share might also be a smart strategic move for chocolate companies. As with many resources, cocoa production is limited overall, whereas the overall demand for chocolate is increasing. Building better and robust relationships with cocoa farmers in the supply chain can help a company secure sufficient cocoa supply in the long run.

The chocolate companies are not the only economic players in this case who have responsibilities for the situation. Primarily, one may argue, social and environmental issues and their regulation are the job of the respective government. However, in the global context, we often face local governments with limited power or limited abilities to address issues, particularly in poorer regions of the world. There are even places with no government or a corrupt government. In all such situations, global businesses might be better positioned and equipped than the local government to address issues related to their supply chains. Regarding child labor in cocoa production, the government of the Ivory Coast struggled for some years to effectively control child trafficking, child slavery, and child labor. In recent years, though, the government has been more involved in addressing these issues (O'Keefe 2016). Nevertheless, involvement of the main buyers of cocoa might be the most powerful tool to change the situation.

In addition to the governments of the sourcing countries, governments of main countries importing the cocoa or chocolate products could also take action; for instance, the US government or the European Union. These governments are quite powerful and have the ability to influence global markets and issues such as child labor and slavery. Indeed, the US Congress passed legislation in 2016 to bar imports of products to the US that have been produced by slave labor (US Code, 2017), tightening a similar but weaker provision of the 1930 Tariff Act. However, law enforcement agencies still need to be able to identify what products have been produced by slave labor, and it might be difficult to do this with a specific brand of chocolate.

Consumers are another crucial player in this case. One could argue that (i) consumers also cause the issue by their demand and consumption of unethically sourced chocolate, (ii) could know about the issue as information is increasingly available, and (iii) also have significant power to effect change. One may even argue that the ultimate power in the business world is with the consumers. Ultimately, demand determines supply and production. If consumers do not want certain products and don't buy them, those products will not be produced. In the case of chocolate, consumers have the power to effect changes by not buying chocolate with uncertain sourcing practices, but instead purchase chocolate with proven ethical sourcing. If a significant number of consumers would decide to buy ethically sourced chocolate, such as fair-trade chocolate, this would not only have a positive impact on the people who source the fair-trade cocoa, but also impact the entire chocolate market. The more consumers buying ethically sourced chocolate, the more pressure is generated on the chocolate industry to react to the consumers' preferences for ethically sourced chocolate and improve their supply chains accordingly.

The above case shows that in the global context many actors are involved who all have some responsibility and some ability/power to address and improve the situation. As with many ethical and environmental issues in the global economy, the issue of child labor and slavery in the chocolate industry is complex and can only be addressed successfully if all actors assume their fair share of responsibility and act together in a coordinated way. If every actor looks the other way or blames some other actor, such issues cannot be solved.

The issues found in the cocoa industry are not unique to it. Child labor, forced labor, and exploitation can be found in supply chains of various industries and in various places around the world; for instance, in the coffee industry, cotton production, the flower market, rubber tree plantations, or the mining of minerals and metals, among others. Proper identification of the responsibilities of all relevant economic actors and shared coordinated action are crucial to reduce these issues in the global business world.

6.1.2 Case 2: outsourcing of manufacturing jobs

One specific phenomenon of globalization, which has been extensively highlighted and debated in public discussions, is outsourcing manufacturing jobs from countries with high labor costs to countries with low labor costs. This development has shifted manufacturing jobs over the years from developed to developing countries. For instance, the fashion and textile industry employed in apparel manufacturing worldwide about 24.8 million people in 2014, up from 14.5 million in 1990 (Fashion United, 2017). In roughly the same time period, jobs in apparel manufacturing declined in the US from about 900,000 in 1990 to 150,000 in 2011 (BLS, 2012). Overall, the number of manufacturing jobs in the US declined from a maximum of nearly 20 million people in the 1970s to about 12.5 million people in 2017, whereas, in the same time, overall jobs in the US increased from fewer than 100 million to about 150 million. It should be recognized, though, that there are causes other than outsourcing that decrease manufacturing jobs; for instance, automatization.

The questions in the context of this book are whether outsourcing is an ethical issue, and, if it is, what ethical problems come with outsourcing, and how these problems can be addressed. A main issue raised in public and political discussion is the loss of jobs in developed countries. It seems to some as unethical to lay off people in the US and shift production and jobs to another country. What is the ethical argument for this perspective? In a Kantian perspective, one could argue that firing people for saving costs means to treat them as mere objects. However, outsourcing might be more positively evaluated in a utilitarian perspective. One needs to consider here that outsourcing also provides jobs to people, mostly in poorer countries, and therefore the loss and pain for the US workers is counterbalanced by job gains and happiness of other workers. Also, it should generally be easier to get another job in a developed country like the US than to find a job in a poorer, less developed country. Additionally, consumers benefit from outsourcing due to lower prices, and shareholders benefit from higher profits. If we consider all effects together outsourcing actually seems to increase the overall happiness of all parties affected and, thus, is ethical from a utilitarian point of view.

The economic perspective on outsourcing would also maintain that outsourcing produces overall benefits to all parties and that outsourcing ideally generates an economic win-win for all countries involved. Outsourcing increases division of labor and specialization and increases overall productivity and efficiency. As the job numbers of the US show, the decline in manufacturing jobs is relatively small in comparison to the overall increase of jobs in all sectors. With a rather low unemployment rate in 2018 of about 4%, or about 6 million people (BLS, 2018), the US actually seems to benefit from the large global labor force that produces many of its consumption goods at low costs. It is hardly imaginable, for instance, that the fashion industry could even find close to 25 million people in the US for manufacturing apparel, not to mention be able to manage the higher costs of US production. The minimum wage in the US is about a factor of 10 higher than the minimum wage in Indonesia or Vietnam, for instance. From an economic point of view, outsourcing is positive overall for the US, and job losses are more of a temporary problem of sectoral shifts in job availability. Ethical concerns regarding workers in the US, who lost their manufacturing jobs, could be addressed, for instance, by social support measures that help these people to find new jobs in other sectors. Such measures could be subsidizing education and job training for this group of workers.

From an ethical point of view, however, there are some further serious concerns with regard to outsourcing. A major issue is the potential risk of outsourcing environmental harm and undermining ethical standards. In other words, many companies might not only seek the advantage of lower labor costs in other countries, but also gain from lower environmental and societal standards. Outsourcing has often been related to serious human rights violations, sweat shop conditions, exploitation, and environmentally harmful production. Such issues are unethical by any ethical approach. Even the above utilitarian argument for outsourcing would no longer hold if outsourcing came with these issues. If outsourcing would be done in a way where people in developed countries lose their jobs for the sake of people in developing countries being exploited, the only groups that may benefit are the shareholders and the consumers, and overall happiness might not improve. In addition, environmental harm can negatively impact health, water supply, and food security of local communities. Significant social and environmental harm also undermines the economic argument for outsourcing. In economic terms, environmental and social harm are negative external effects. Significant external effects result in inefficiency of global markets and can turn the supposedly economic win-win of outsourcing into a win-lose (see also Chapter 3). While the outsourcing country might still win by higher profits and lower prices of consumption goods, for the developing country the economic benefits of new jobs might be overturned by high costs of social and environmental damages. If outsourcing results in sweat shop conditions and large environmental damages, the result is not only inefficient, it also deprives the developing country of the opportunity to actually develop and thrive in the global economy and burdens it with external costs instead.

In conclusion, in today's global business world outsourcing often comes with various harms and is ethically and economically problematic. Ideally, outsourcing could be economically and ethically positive. The challenge is to improve globalization and come close to the ideal of a win-win situation. In practice, this requires a shared responsibility approach and concerted efforts of various global actors. The outsourcing country would need to implement social measures to assist people who lose jobs, and in the developing countries to which the jobs are outsourced proper ethical and environmental standards need to be ensured. This requires shared responsibilities and concerted actions from the businesses themselves and the governments in developing countries, as well as stricter regulations for businesses in developed countries that do the outsourcing. Governments in the US and in Europe could hold their businesses more legally liable for ethical and environmental issues in their supply chain. For instance, in 2017, France passed the Corporate Duty of Vigilance Bill that requires large companies to carefully assess potential human rights violations and environmental harm related to all their business activities, including their supply chain. Violations can be fined €10–30 million (ECCJ, 2017).

6.1.3 Case 3: the globalization of e-waste

E-waste is a term for discarded computers, cell phones, and other electronic devices that consumers dispose of. E-waste contains a number of harmful substances, such as lead, cadmium, and mercury, and is often shipped to poor regions that lack the ability to properly deal with these substances (Grossman, 2006). The reasons for e-waste being shipped globally are twofold. First, the large amount of this type of waste overwhelms the richer countries in which it mainly originates, as consumers dispose of all kinds of electronic devices to get newer ones. Communities do not want this e-waste with its toxic components in their land-fill sites, but there is often a lack of other waste treatment options and recycling capacities to properly deal with the increasing amounts of e-waste. Secondly, e-waste does not only contain toxic components but also certain valuable materials, such as gold, silver, and platinum, among others. Criminal organizations smuggle e-waste to poor and poorly regulated places in the world, where they often exploit workers (in some cases child workers) to dismantle the devices and extract valuable materials under hazardous conditions. This results in significant harm to the health of the workers, local communities, and the local environment (Grossman, 2006). As a result, we have a situation of the globalization of e-waste. High-tech and expensive products are mainly consumed in richer parts of the world, and the waste from this consumption is dumped on, and causes harm to, poorer parts of the world. We want to discuss e-waste from an ethical perspective and to clarify what the ethical issues are in this case, who is responsible for these issues, who should take action, and what kind of action they should take to address the issues.

The ethical issues in this case are exploitation, harm to people and the environment, and environmental injustice. E-waste is smuggled to very poor areas where workers, out of desperation, will do the dangerous job for very low payment. Many workers, particularly child workers, may not even be aware of the toxicity of e-waste and of the harm that it can cause to their health. In other words, the workers are treated as mere objects and exploited, and their ability to thrive and develop their potential is undermined. Moreover, there is substantial harm done to the local communities where e-waste is shipped and deconstructed. The toxic substances are released into the air and watershed, which negatively impacts the health of the communities. This poisoning of the environment has long-term negative impacts on the ability of local communities to thrive and develop. The situation constitutes fundamental environmental injustice. The environmental harms that result from advanced electronics affect poorer regions and poorer people in the world, whereas the benefits go to richer areas and well-off people.

For identifying who has what kind of responsibility in this situation, we will again refer to the criteria of Section 4.2.1 and discuss degrees of causality, knowledge, and power related to each actor involved in the case. Regarding causality, the e-waste issue is caused by several actors together. It is caused directly by the criminal organizations which ship e-waste globally and exploit people to deconstruct the devices. The issue is also caused by governments, communities, and recyclers in richer parts of the world who cannot ensure proper handling of e-waste. Consumers technically also cause the e-waste issue by discarding their old devices. However, consumers often do their part and bring their devices to a local recycler. Finally, the e-waste issue is caused by the producers of electronic devices, not only in the sense that the producers create the products that later on become e-waste, but more specifically in the sense that the producers put the various toxic elements into the devices, which go on to cause harm to people and the environment.

Second, we need to discuss the question of who knows or can know what aspects of the issue. Now, the issues with e-waste are well known, and one could expect that all actors involved are aware of the problem. The electronic industry may have the most detailed information about the toxic aspects of e-waste, though, as they design each product and choose the materials. It is also well known that e-waste is shipped globally and causes harm around the world, but it might be difficult to get precise details of the various ways and places that are impacted.

Third, who has what power and ability to address the issue? Consumers have a limited ability to do something. The best they can do is to bring their devices to a local recycler. Communities could at least arrange for recycling places, aim to contract reliable recycling companies, and establish local codes that require e-waste to be recycled and not dumped into the regular garbage. Governments of countries with potential export of e-waste could make such export activities illegal and enforce respective laws. Both the US and the European Union actually have laws that prohibit shipping of e-waste to other countries but have had difficulties fully enforcing these laws. Governments of countries to which e-waste is shipped likewise can make this shipping illegal. However, in the global context, smugglers often choose regions in the world that have no or corrupt governments. Finally, the industry that produces/markets electronic devices probably has the largest ability to address and solve the e-waste issue. Companies, such as Samsung, Apple, HP, Toshiba, and others, are designing the products that later on become e-waste. Product design is the key to the issues, though, because only if toxic materials are put into the devices do they go on to become hazardous waste. Furthermore, product design also determines the options for recycling. If recycling would already be considered in the design and construction of devices, one could choose design that enables easy, economically feasible, automated deconstruction by robots. Such design-driven solutions to e-waste have actually been recognized by the industry recently. Several large players, like Apple and Samsung, did research into the design of their devices and were able to eliminate certain toxic materials from their designs. Newer devices are now mercury- and lead-free. Also, Apple recently started automatic recycling of its devices (Apple, 2018). Smart sustainable design and automated recycling both have the potential to solve the e-waste issue and to move the entire industry toward a closed-loop system, where valuable materials for making new devices are regained from old devices. Moreover, it would be easy for large corporations, such as Apple or Samsung, to get back their old devices using some kind of incentive program.

In the e-waste case, the industry has by far the most power and ability to address the issue. This aspect makes the industry the main responsible actor for addressing and fixing the e-waste issue. Other players, such as consumers and governments, have smaller responsibilities in this case. They must do their share of actions to address the issue, but the main burden of responsibility and action is on the industry.

The ethical issues discussed in this case are not unique and limited to e-waste. There is significant environmental injustice in the world. Many environmental harms that result from economic growth disproportionally affect poorer regions and poorer people in the world, whereas the benefits of economic growth go to richer areas and well-off people. Examples of this other than e-waste are the burdens of climate change, environmental harm from mining, and environmental degradation resulting from the sourcing of agricultural raw materials, such as palm oil, soybeans, tropical wood, or rubber.

Exercises

1   Research and critically evaluate the corporate responsibility of a large chocolate company (such as Hershey or Nestlé). Does the company address the issue of child labor and child slavery in the supply chain? By what activities? Do you think the company sufficiently assumes its business-specific responsibilities? (Use the methods and criteria of Chapter 4.)
2   Apply the ethical methods from Chapter 2 (see Table 2.3) to discuss the ethical aspects of Case 2 (outsourcing of manufacturing jobs) and Case 3 (the globalization of e-waste) in detail.

6.2 Ethical challenges of globalization and global business

Certain ethical issues are typical to the global business context, although not unique to it. In the global economy, people are often treated as mere objects and exploited by hazardous work conditions, sweat shop conditions, forced labor, child labor, and so on. Fundamental human rights and international principles are ignored and violated, such as the right to freedom and equality and the right to not have one's person or property harmed. Exploitation and violation of fundamental rights deprive people of their abilities to thrive and develop their potential, and undermine the opportunity of entire communities, regions, and countries to thrive and develop. Many places in the world also suffer significant environmental harm by global economic activities. In underdeveloped and developing countries, sourcing, production, and transportation is often done in environmentally destructive ways that cause significant harm. This holds particularly for mining crucial raw materials for industrial processes, such as gold, copper, graphite, and bauxite, and for agricultural production of crucial materials, such as cotton, palm oil, and soybeans. In many cases, environmental destruction irreversibly destroys basic ecological services, such as fresh water supply and fertile land. With this, long-term harm is done to entire regions, and their long-term potentials for development and economic growth are destroyed. Finally, social and environmental injustice is a particular issue in the global context. Environmental injustice results from environmental harm and burdens to poorer regions which are disproportionally higher than the benefits that these regions gain from the global economy. Social injustice results from the persistence of global poverty, the lack of opportunities for many regions in the world to gain from global economic development, and from unequal distribution of income and wealth in the world.

Are these ethical issues specifically global? And if so, why? Of course, all these issues can also be found within a given developed country, such as the US. However, usually these issues are much more persistent and concerning in the global context. The reason is that these ethical issues are caused by three characteristics that are specific to the global economy: (i) large asymmetries in power, capabilities, and wealth, (ii) lack of proper regulation around the world, and (iii) complexity of the global economic system.

The global context is characterized by very large asymmetries in power, capabilities, and wealth. For instance, the US has a per-capita GDP of about $60,000, whereas Burundi, one of the poorest countries in the world, has a per-capita GDP of about $300 (IMF, 2017). The median annual personal income in the US is over $30,000 (Semega et al., 2017), whereas the median annual income in Burundi is less than $150 (Phelps & Crabtree, 2013). Many countries in the world significantly lack educational opportunities and competitive systems of higher education. This causes large asymmetries in the world regarding opportunities and abilities to compete in the global economy. All these asymmetries create potential risks for abuses of power and exploitation. Very poor people who barely can make a living are often willing to work under conditions they would not accept if they were not in a desperate situation. They may endure violations of their rights, accept very low payment, and risk their health out of desperation.

Second, the global context is characterized by some lack of regulation and control. With over 190 nations in the world, there are as many different legal systems and sets of regulations, and the complexity of various different regulatory frameworks provides numerous grey areas and loopholes that can be abused for unethical practices. There are also regions and countries in the world that have limited, no, or corrupt government. Such situations create loopholes that can be exploited for unethical actions or actions that would be illegal in the perpetrator's own country. Severe human rights violations and environmental destruction often happens in regions with limited or corrupt government.

Third, the complexity of today's global economic system results in a lack of transparency, knowledge, and responsibility with regard to ethical issues in the system. For instance, the case of child labor and slavery in the chocolate industry demonstrates that ethical issues can be hidden in the complexity of supply chains, disallowing customers in other parts of the world from knowing about issues (see Section 6.1.1). Other examples are the sourcing of conflict minerals and the sourcing of cotton. Both are crucial raw materials for large industries and important consumer goods, and the sourcing of both causes major social and environmental harm. The mining of conflict minerals causes serious human rights violations and environmental destruction, and cotton is considered one of the most environmentally damaging crops due to its water- and pesticide-intensive production. Such social and environmental harm is largely unrecognized by the consumers that buy electronics and fashion products. Even the businesses in those industries often have difficulties identifying whether these raw materials have been produced ethically due to the complexity of supply chains. In the electronics industry, large players like Apple have made some progress in tracking the sources of the many materials used for their products and verifying the conditions under which those materials are sourced. In the fashion industry, companies struggle to identify the sources of the cotton that goes into their products because cotton is bought through intermediaries by various suppliers that manufacture the clothing. Such global complexities often prevent crucial actors in the global economy, such as consumers and businesses, from recognizing and understanding significant ethical issues, assuming responsibility, and addressing the issues. In the global context, serious ethical issues like human rights violations, which usually would not be accepted by consumers and businesses, can happen because they remain hidden and unrecognized in the complexity of the global economic system. This is why careful analysis of supply chains and product life cycles, using adequate analytical tools, such as Ethical Life Cycle Assessment or Ethical Stakeholder Analysis, is crucial to ensure ethical business practice, particularly in the global context (see Section 4.2).

6.3 Global business ethics: principles

We have seen that the global economy is far from perfect, and that it exhibits significant ethical and economic shortcomings. The best answer to these shortcomings is not to negate globalization, but rather to actively shape the global business world for the better. If we manage to successfully address the systemic ethical and economic issues of the global economy, then overall globalization has the potential to make the world a better place and promote the wellbeing of all people. Against the backdrop of the ethical issues and challenges of the global context, we will identify in this section basic ethical principles that can serve as normative guidelines for global business and help make global business a positive force in the world.

Is it possible to agree globally on ethical principles for business, given that there are many different nations with diverse cultures and different religions around the world? First, it is important to consider that there are already many ethical norms, principles, and values that are globally shared throughout different countries and cultures. Fundamental global norms and principles are, for instance, formulated in The Universal Declaration of Human Rights (UN, 1948), the Rio Declaration on Environment and Development (UN, 1992), and the United Nations Convention Against Corruption (UN, 2004), among others. The ethical principles in these documents have been agreed upon by almost every nation and can be considered universally accepted ethical principles, despite some differences regarding specific principles and their interpretation and application.

There are also more specific global rules and norms for business, such as the rules established by the World Trade Organization (WTO) and the International Labor Organization (ILO), which are also broadly shared among most nations. A specific function for global business is the UN Global Compact (UN, 2018). The Global Compact is a recommended ethical framework for global business which companies voluntarily can adopt. The UN Global Compact formulates ten ethical principles for global business activities that are based on the Universal Declaration of Human Rights, the Rio Declaration on Environment and Development, basic principles of the ILO, and the United Nations Convention Against Corruption.

The set of already established global normative principles can and should serve as ethical guidelines for global business. However, in the following we also want to use ethical theory to support and underpin fundamental norms and ethical principles for global business. Although the ethical theories to which we have referred in this book are mainly based on the tradition of Western philosophy, we consider them as interculturally compatible, because they provide general rational arguments and rational foundations for ethics. This is also in line with the experience that ethical arguments based on the Western tradition resonate globally. There has been broad acceptance of fundamental principles that can be deduced from ethical theory, such as human rights. Also, similar ethical approaches can be found in different cultures, for instance, virtue ethical aspects can be found in Buddhism and in Chinese philosophy, and the golden rule (see Chapter 2) can be found in various cultural and religious traditions. Therefore, we assume that basic ethical approaches and arguments are interculturally valid and use them for deducing ethical principles for the global economy. It would be a fruitful project beyond this book, though, to research to what degree these principles could be supported by non-Western philosophy, as well.

We distinguish in the following two levels of global business ethics. First, we look at a basic global business ethics, which is mainly grounded in the existing global normative frameworks described above and represents the minimum of ethical norms we can expect any business to follow. Second, we look at an advanced global business ethics, which is grounded in ethical theory and aims to make business a positive force in the world.

6.3.1 Basic global business ethics

The following reference points provide a basic ethical guideline for global business practice and a minimum of business ethics we can expect in global business.

First, business should respect fundamental rights and global norms. This includes human rights, the principles of the Rio Declaration, ILO standards, WTO rules, and the UN Convention Against Corruption, among other globally established and formalized normative principles. We can expect any business in the world, and any business that operates internationally, to not violate fundamental human rights of everyone involved in or affected by the business, to avoid harm to the environment as far as possible, and to adhere to established global norms and economic rules.

For doing business in a global context, global norms and rules are an important normative guideline for what is ethically right and wrong. Following such guidelines helps interactions with partners from different cultures. There is also a business case for following global norms, such as human rights, the Rio Declaration, or the UN Global Compact. It reduces frictions and transactions costs of interacting with international partners in different countries. Because these are broad and globally shared norms, a company can expect that they easily constitute a common ethical ground in every part of the world in which it does business. Many companies thus refer to human rights and other global norms in their codes for suppliers, corporate responsibility strategies, and other business guidelines. This reduces transaction costs because it avoids having to find a common ground of acceptable rules and principles with each business partner and for each country separately.

The second reference point for a basic global business ethics is respect for other cultures and different cultural values. The first reference point emphasized global agreements and universally shared principles. However, one also needs to consider differences between cultures and societies regarding values and norms, and the second ethical guideline for global business practice asks businesses to respect those differences. Respecting differences requires recognizing and acknowledging them. Neglect or ignorance can be disrespectful and even offensive, and any business that is substantially engaged in global business activities has the responsibility to inform itself about the specifics of other cultures and properly train its employees who are actively involved in global business interactions.

A third reference point is the ethical values and principles a business has established on its own. These are expressed in its culture, core values, ethics and compliance program, and corporate responsibility strategy, among others. Ideally, these principles have been carefully chosen and implemented for good ethical reasons and should also function as crucial guidelines in the international context. In other words, a business should adhere to its own ethical foundations and values and uphold and promote them even in difficult and challenging business contexts.

The three reference points together provide a guideline for basic global business ethics (see Figure 6.1). Universally accepted global principles, such as human rights, should provide a common ground and basic guideline for global interactions, but might not be sufficient. One could, for instance, fully comply with all human rights and still offend people from another culture by ignoring and violating their etiquette. Respect for the other culture is, thus, an additional guideline, and includes learning about and understanding the cultural differences of the regions with which one wants to do business. The values and ethical principles a business has established on its own also matter. Respecting the other culture does not imply forgoing one's business values and principles. It is not disrespectful to indicate differences in values. A business can respectfully identify differences and support its own ethical position using reasonable arguments. It would only be disrespectful if a company tries to impose values on a business partner by mere power; for instance, in a situation where the company is the more powerful economic player, and the business partner depends on business with the company. This could be considered disrespectful and cultural imperialism. On the other hand, respecting cultural differences should not mean compromising human rights and other global ethical norms. It is not disrespectful to insist on upholding human rights and other global norms, as we assume they are universally valid and agreed upon throughout all cultures.

However, there can be difficult situations and grey area cases in global contexts, which a business must carefully navigate. It can be difficult to decide what level of cultural differences must be respected, and where the border to compromising human rights or their own values and principles is. The right decision and action depends on each situation and therefore is a matter of case-by-case judgment. It is also crucial to avoid certain fallacies. For instance, businesses should not excuse ethically questionable practices by appealing to 'cultural differences.' For example, the very existence of child labor or slavery in a certain region in the world does not mean that people in that region actually value child labor and slavery and consider these issues as ethically good. Child labor and slavery just might exist due to desperation or the mere force of corrupt powers, such as warlords. It would be wrong for a business to excuse the use of child or slave labor in such a region by claiming that child and slave labor accords with the cultural values in that region. Such a claim would be factually wrong because it is not the case that the situation reflects cultural values, and it would also be ethically wrong because the business compromises basic human rights with a wrong excuse.

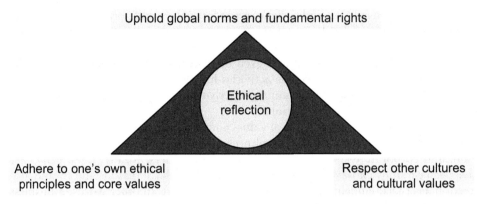

Figure 6.1 The triangle of basic global business ethics.

A business should uphold human rights and its own ethical values, while at the same time respecting cultural differences. In many cases, all of this may go well together. If not, though, the business can either try to act as a role model and promote its own values and human rights in the region, or it can decide to stay away from a region. If the business feels that it can only do business in a certain region by compromising its own values and fundamental global principles, the best ethical decision may be to just stay away.

6.3.2 Advanced global business ethics

Section 6.3.1 formulated ethical principles that at minimum we can expect businesses to follow in global contexts: respect people and their fundamental human rights, follow global norms and rules, and avoid harm to people and the environment. In short, we can expect every business in the world to do no harm. However, we could also strive for a more advanced ethical approach in global business ethics, one which aims at doing good and actively using business to be a positive force in the world. Business is a powerful force that could be used to help poorer areas improve conditions and develop themselves. Business could care about the people in the supply chain, and empower them by meaningful and fair participation. Business could set up its operations in a way that allows global partners to flourish. Business can train people in the supply chain, and provide opportunities for them. Businesses can also engage in underdeveloped markets, and provide products that meet specific regional preferences and needs.

For instance, fair-trade businesses aim at empowering people in their supply chain and care for economic, societal, and environmental conditions that allow workers and communities to flourish and develop through their participation in the supply chain. Fair-trade businesses often strengthen local communities and local cultural identities around the world and connect those communities with local markets in developed countries. By this, fair-trade businesses demonstrate that it is possible to do global business in ways that build on and strengthen local communities and values. The success of many fair-trade companies demonstrates that a win-win among different global partners is possible and a viable business model. There also is a business case for caring in this way about people in the supply chain. Empowerment and development will increase motivation, quality of work, and reliability of the supply chain.

A business could also use its knowhow to go into underdeveloped markets and use its expertise to provide specific products for local needs. Products are often designed for developed markets, which are the most profitable ones, and are not optimal for poorer, less developed regions. For instance, electric or fuel-powered pumps are not suitable for regions that have no sufficient electricity or gas supply. However, a company specializing in pumps could use its knowhow to develop a mechanical water pump, e.g., a treadmill pump, that can easily be used and maintained in poor areas with no electricity or fuel supply. In some regions, such pumps would be crucial for better water supply and could significantly improve living conditions and agricultural development. Furthermore, the company might even try to establish the production of these pumps in the region and cooperate with local partners to train employees for the production and maintenance of the pumps. The profit margins for selling mechanical pumps in such an area are probably rather small. In the long run, however, the presence in the region could be a strategic advantage. If the region develops, and the demand for more sophisticated pumps increases, the company is already well established to serve the growing market.

The social entrepreneurship movement is another example of a business model that more closely follows the concept of an advanced global business ethics. Social entrepreneurs aim at concrete positive societal or environmental impacts through their business operations. With this, they use the power of for-profit business to make a positive impact in the world. Advanced business ethics does not mean forgoing profits or being less profitable. The business model has the potential to be as profitable or even more profitable than other business models. Depending on the strategy, advanced business ethics can actually be a business advantage, as illustrated in above examples.

Overall, advanced global business ethics would be based on ethics of care and virtue ethics, strive to empower global stakeholders through business operations, and ensure that the relationship with the business enhances the stakeholder's potential to flourish and develop. In other words, advanced business ethics would actively seek to create a win-win among all global partners, so everyone actually benefits. Basically, this approach just upholds the original ideal of a free market economy in which everyone in the market benefits and is better off (see Chapter 3). Advanced global business ethics recognizes that there is no perfect, self-regulating global market, but instead large external effects, power asymmetries, and ethical issues. Consequently, advanced global business ethics asks companies to actively care about establishing a win-win in their business operations.

References

Apple. (2018). *Environmental Responsibility Report*. Apple. Retrieved from www.apple.com/environment.

BLS [Bureau of Labor Statistics]. (2012). *Spotlight on Statistics: Fashion*. BLS. Retrieved from www.bls.gov/spotlight/2012/fashion.

BLS [Bureau of Labor Statistics]. (2018). *Latest Numbers*. BLS. Retrieved from www.bls.gov.

Divine Chocolate. (2018). *About Us*. Divine. Retrieved from www.divinechocolate.com/us/about-us.

ECCJ [European Coalition for Corporate Justice]. (2017). France adopts corporate duty of vigilance law: a first historic step towards better human rights and environmental protection. *ECCJ*. Retrieved from http://corporatejustice.org/news/393-france-adopts-corporate-duty-of-vigilance-law-a-first-historic-step-towards-better-human-rights-and-environmental-protection.

Fashion United. (2017). Global fashion industry statistics – International apparel. *Fashion United*. Retrieved from https://fashionunited.com/global-fashion-industry-statistics.

GAO [United States Government Accountability Office]. (2013). *SEC Conflict Minerals Rule. Information on Responsible Sourcing and Companies Affected*. GAO-13-689, Report to Congressional Committees. Washington, DC: US Government Accountability Office.

Grossman, E. (2006). *High Tech Trash: Digital Devices, Hidden Toxics, and Human Health*. Washington, DC: Island Press.

ILO [International Labour Organization]. (1973). *Minimum Age Convention*. Geneva: ILO.

ILO [International Labour Organization]. (1999). *Worst Forms of Child Labour Convention*. Geneva: ILO.

IMF [International Monetary Fund]. (2017). World economic outlook data base. *IMF*. Retrieved from www.imf.org/external/pubs/ft/weo/2016/01/weodata/index.aspx.

Mistrati, M., & Romano, U. R. (2010). *The Dark Side of Chocolate*. [Motion picture]. Denmark: Bastard Film.

Off, C. (2006). *Bitter Chocolate: Anatomy of an Industry*. Toronto: Random House.

O'Keefe, B. (2016). Behind a Bittersweet Industry. *Fortune*, March 1. Retrieved from http://fortune.com/big-chocolate-child-labor.

Phelps, G. & Crabtree, S. (2013). Worldwide, Median Household Income About $10,000. *Gallup*, December 16. Retrieved from https://news.gallup.com/poll/166211/worldwide-median-household-income-000.aspx.

Rosen, E. I. (2002). *Making Sweatshops: The Globalization of the U.S. Apparel Industry*. Oakland, CA: University of California Press.

Semega, J. L., Fontenot, K. R., & Kollar, M. A. (2017). *Income and Poverty in the United States: 2016*. P60-259, United States Census Bureau. Retrieved from www.census.gov.

Tulane University. (2015). *2013/14 Survey Research on Child Labor in West African Cocoa Growing Areas. Final Report*. Tulane University: School of Public Health and Tropical Medicine. Retrieved from www.childlaborcocoa.org/index.php/2013-14-final-report.

UN [United Nations]. (1948). *The Universal Declaration of Human Rights*. New York: United Nations. Retrieved from www.un.org/en/documents/udhr.

UN [United Nations]. (1992). *Rio Declaration on Environment and Development*. Rio de Janeiro: United Nations. Retrieved from www.un.org/documents/ga/conf151/aconf15126-1annex1.htm.

UN [United Nations]. (2004). *United Nations Convention Against Corruption*. New York: United Nations. Retrieved from www.unodc.org/documents/brussels/UN_Convention_Against_Corruption.pdf.

UN [United Nations]. (2018). Global Compact. *UN Global Compact*. Retrieved from www.unglobalcompact.org.

US Code. (2017). *19 USC 1307: Convict-made goods; importation prohibited*. Office of the Law Revision Counsel of the US House of Representatives. Retrieved from http://uscode.house.gov/view.xhtml?req=(title:19%20section:1307%20edition:prelim).

WWF. (1999). *The impact of cotton on fresh water resources and ecosystems. A preliminary synthesis*. Background Paper. Washington, DC: WWF. Retrieved from http://wwf.panda.org/?3686/The-impact-of-cotton-on-fresh-water-resources-and-ecosystems.

WWF. (2018). *Sustainable Agriculture. Cotton*. Retrieved from www.worldwildlife.org/industries/cotton

7 Economic and ethical challenges of the 21st century

Sustainability

Colleges teach students who are going to engage in the development of business and society, seek challenges and opportunities, and shape the future of business and society. College education should, therefore, look ahead and discuss trends and future challenges and opportunities relevant to the students. Academia has always been a place in society for long-term, foundational thinking, and critical reflection on the state and future of society is a crucial responsibility of universities. One of the larger challenges of the 21st century, relevant to all areas of life, and particularly business, is sustainability. This chapter discusses the implications of sustainability for the economy and business, particularly from an ethical viewpoint.

7.1 The challenge of sustainability and ethical implications

Discussions about sustainability have emerged since the 1980s, and sustainability today is a prominent topic in many areas like politics, education, and business. The term sustainability is used in many ways and contexts. It is useful here to first clarify the concept of sustainability, the characteristics of the issues that are typically associated with the concept, and the ethical dimension of sustainability.

7.1.1 The concept of sustainability

This section highlights core aspects of sustainability and explains the meaning of the concept and the (ethical) issues it addresses.

Literally, sustainability means the ability to maintain something over time. This can refer to different things depending on the contexts in which the term is used. It can refer to the ability to maintain certain entities, such as a species, a business, or economic welfare. The term can refer to certain systems, such as ecosystems, educational systems, or economic systems. Finally, the term can also refer to the continuance of certain processes, such as economic growth, evolutionary processes, or the continuance of life on earth (Becker, 2012, p. 14).

In addition to its literal meaning, sustainability also has a normative meaning. Sustainability is rarely used in a merely descriptive way. In most instances, the term sustainability comes with a normative connotation. When people talk about sustainability they usually imply that sustainability is something positive, something we should strive for. With this, sustainability becomes the subject matter of ethics. One may wonder why sustainability is good, or why we should be sustainable, and ask for some justification. Such a justification cannot just be based on the literal meaning of sustainability. Maintaining something is not a value or norm in itself. It is not always good to maintain things. In many cases, we actually might evaluate change as better than continuance. We do not want to maintain crime, the mafia, poverty, or certain viruses and diseases, but rather we want to change things for the better (Becker, 2012).

However, sustainability does not imply that maintaining things is an end in itself. Rather, sustainability stresses that we should maintain entities, systems, or processes that we consider as fundamental for our own wellbeing and the wellbeing of people around the world, future generations, and non-human nature (WCED, 1987; Becker, 2012). This would include, for instance, crucial ecosystems, fresh water, biodiversity, fertile land, stable climate, and intact oceans, among others.

> Definition 7.1: **Sustainability** is the ability to maintain systems, processes, or entities that are essential to our future wellbeing and the wellbeing of people around the world, future generations, and nature.

Sustainability, thus, develops a broad and long-term perspective on current activities. It asks what effects our current actions have on our own future, on other people around the world, on future generations, and on non-human life.

7.1.2 The ethics of sustainability

Generally, considerations about sustainability are based on ethical assumptions regarding the relationships among contemporaries, between generations, and with nature. Sustainability (implicitly) assumes that we should care about people around the world, future people, and nature, and that we have some moral obligations and responsibilities toward other people around the world, future people, and nature. Intuitively one might agree with such assumptions, but it is not an easy task to provide explicit ethical arguments supporting them.

To some extent, here we can use the traditional ethical approaches from Chapter 2. For instance, if we follow Kant, we may say that the moral obligation to respect the dignity of every person and to never treat someone as a mere object extends to every human being, not only to people living today and in our society. We have a moral obligation to respect the dignity of people around the world as well as the dignity of future people. Similarly, one could argue that everyone has the right to not be harmed today and in the future; that everyone globally and in the future has the same right to 'life, liberty and the pursuit of happiness'; and that we have an obligation to protect the potential to flourish and live well for all people living today and in the future. Some of these arguments may even extend to nature. One could argue that we also have some obligation to minimize harm to nature and to protect the potential of nature to evolve and flourish. From an ethics of care perspective, one may add that there is some asymmetry in power and abilities between us and some other people in the world, future people, and non-human life. We can significantly impact others, future generations, and non-human nature, but they have limited or no ability to protect their own interests and wellbeing. We have the responsibility to consider this vulnerability, and care about people around the world, future people, and non-human life.

However, the ethical dimension of sustainability overall is difficult and complex and cannot fully be discussed within the frameworks of established ethical theory. Ethical questions in the sustainability context can become particularly difficult if they are about fundamental conflicts or trade-offs, for instance, between rights of contemporaries and future people, or justice toward people today, future people, and non-human beings (Becker, 2012; Becker et al., 2015; Stumpf et al., 2015).

7.1.3 The relevance of sustainability

Sustainability is an important and useful concept that puts our actions and wellbeing into a broader perspective. Sustainability emphasizes the fundamental dependence and interrelatedness of human beings. To be able to live well, humans depend on others, other generations, and nature. Sustainability particularly highlights that technology and the economy have developed in the past two centuries more against than with nature, and that this development might have come to its limits. Our technological and economic systems are about to exceed the capacities of the earth on which they ultimately depend and, with this, are about to destroy the long-term basis of life, and humans and nature's flourishing on earth (MEA, 2005; UNEP, 2012; IPCC, 2014). Sustainability stresses the fact that there are systemic environmental limits to economic activities and that exceeding those limits will have serious negative impacts on our own future, people around the world, future generations, and nature. Sustainability, thus, is in our own self-interest and also determines ethical responsibilities we have toward people around the world, future generations, and nature.

Sustainability also emphasizes that many of today's crucial environmental, economic, and ethical issues are interrelated in complex ways and that any encompassing solution requires a thorough understanding of these interrelations and underlying causes. For instance, many environmental issues, such as global warming, biodiversity loss, degradation of ecosystems, and water scarcity, are not only interrelated with each other but also driven by the same causes, such as environmental side effects of the global economy, population growth, and environmentally harmful technologies and life styles. The complexity of many sustainability issues is directly linked to the complexity of the global economic system and economic activities. The examples of global supply chains and e-waste, which we discussed in Chapter 6, illustrate that the production and consumption of our everyday goods have many negative societal and environmental impacts around the world. The production, distribution, use, and disposal of our smartphones, clothes, and food actually might harm and even kill people and substantially destroy the environment in some parts of the world, without us intending or knowing it. In other words, the current global economic system is unsustainable. It has too many harmful societal and environmental side effects and requires too much energy and too many natural resources. For achieving a sustainable future, it is not sufficient that we individually reconsider our life style or actions. Sustainability also requires changing our economic system and business operations. We can achieve a sustainable future only if we create a sustainable economy and sustainable businesses. This, however, requires concerted actions of all actors involved in the economic system: consumers, businesses, governments, and employees, among others.

7.2 Sustainable economy and sustainable business

Ideally, business is supposed to be a positive force in the world, and the economy is supposed to serve the flourishing of individuals and society. Older conceptions of the economy provided various interpretations and models of the economy being a positive force. This also holds for today's dominant model of the capitalist market economy, which is, in a certain sense, supposed to be good for individuals and societies (see Chapter 3).

However, the perspective of sustainability expands the relevant framework and normative expectations for the economy as a positive force. For a sustainable economy, not only do effects on individuals and a well-defined society matter but its effects on people around the world, future generations, and nature also matter (see also Section 3.6).

> Definition 7.2: A **sustainable economy** is an economy that serves the wellbeing of contemporaries, future generations, and nature in a systematic and well-defined way and, by this, has the ability to continue in the long run without larger frictions or crises.

It is assumed here that taking care of the wellbeing of the natural environment is a necessary precondition for the economic system to continue in the long run without serious interruptions and crises. A sustainable economy provides stability and security for people in the long run and a secure basis for us and future generations to flourish and live well. A sustainable economy is particularly crucial because we expect about 11 billion people to be alive on earth at the end of this century, up from 7.3 billion today (UN DESA, 2015). We need an economic system that can support all of those people and ensure that they can all flourish. The current economic system does not have the potential to do so, but rather would result in significant environmental destruction, global conflicts about resources and energy, and global limitations on development.

A sustainable economy cannot be designed top down by a government or another ruling entity. It can only be developed by the various actors who together form the economic system: consumers, businesses, employees, communities, non-governmental organizations, and governments, among others. Business is one crucial and powerful player in the economic system, and in the following we will focus on the potential of businesses to contribute to a sustainable economy and sustainable future. Businesses have specific abilities and power to contribute to a sustainable future, and considering sustainability is also in their self-interest. Businesses need to consider the (ethical) challenges of sustainability to sustain themselves. Sustainability is a business necessity and a business opportunity at the same time. By considering sustainability challenges, businesses can adapt to systemic environmental constraints and risks, become more efficient, discover new markets, respond to changing preferences, and so on. By doing so, businesses ensure their competitiveness and their own sustainability. They transform themselves into sustainable businesses.

> Definition 7.3: A **sustainable business** is a business that systematically considers all environmental, societal, global, and future impacts of its business operations and products and, by this, improves its competitiveness and long-term success.

7.2.1 Reasons why business should care about sustainability

There are strong ethical and economic reasons why business should care about sustainability. In the following, I list three ethical and three economic reasons.

Ethical reasons

BUSINESS GENERALLY NEEDS TO CONSIDER SOCIETAL AND GLOBAL NORMS AND VALUES

Business is part of a society or several societies and, as such, cannot ignore fundamental societal values and norms. For instance, in the US, we expect businesses to uphold fundamental constitutional principles, such as freedom and equality, and to engage in broadly shared goals, such as diversity and non-discrimination. This is a matter of being a good citizen. As sustainability increasingly becomes a broadly shared societal and global norm, one can expect business to share this norm and to do its part to realize a sustainable future for the society. There is, of course, also a related business case here: it would generally not be a good business strategy to ignore or counteract values and norms that are broadly shared in a society. This would certainly make many customers, (potential) employees, communities, and investors shy away.

ECONOMIC ACTIVITIES HAVE BEEN A MAJOR FACTOR IN CAUSING SUSTAINABILITY ISSUES

In a broader, historical perspective, the economy and business have been a major cause of many of the sustainability issues we are facing today. Economic activities have contributed to climate change, biodiversity loss, land degradation, and environmental pollution, among other issues. Although we cannot blame every business for past economic harm, we can expect any business to make sure now, and in the future, that they do not become part of the problem but part of the solution.

THE ECONOMY AND BUSINESS SHOULD IDEALLY BE A POSITIVE FORCE IN THE WORLD

Any business that is attached to the idea of being a positive force in today's world needs to consider sustainability. As argued above, the impacts of business activities to the environment, people around the world, and future generations have become significant. These impacts have reached an overall critical dimension and need to be considered actively by every company. Being a positive force in the world today requires that a business carefully considers its own environmental, global, and future impacts and aims to minimize harm and maximize benefits in this broader sustainability context.

Economic reasons

STRATEGIC MANAGEMENT

Visionary business leaders need to strategically consider systemic societal, environmental, and global constraints to their business activities to ensure competitiveness and long-term business success. The sustainability perspective enables a business to develop a broad strategic perspective on its own operations within the relevant environmental, societal, and global context. This includes an encompassing assessment of internal sustainability potentials as well as external political, societal, technological, and environmental constraints and risks. Against this background, a business is in a better position to make long-term strategic decisions and position itself for future challenges and markets. Considering sustainability in strategic management is becoming more and more relevant in business practice. For instance, Nike's strategic management is significantly based on sustainability analyses. Nike's operations and product lines are to a larger extent influenced by considerations on environmental and societal impacts, and potential future scarcities of resources and energy. Nike pursues a strategy of proactive adjustment to the sustainability aspects of their products and operations and believes that this will give them a competitive advantage in their industry (Nike, 2017). Another example is Apple, the world's most profitable company in the last few years. Apple, which has in the past been rather reluctant about social responsibility and sustainability, has recently and significantly changed its strategy in considering sustainability. Apple is now working toward an automatic recycling process for its phones. This may be the starting point of a sustainability strategy, moving toward a closed-loop model that addresses the environmental aspects of Apple's product life cycles (Apple, 2018). Current corporate responsibility strategies often focus so much on sustainability aspects of business operations and product life cycles that many companies call them sustainability strategies, and issue sustainability reports rather than traditional corporate responsibility reports.

BUSINESS OPPORTUNITIES

There are many business opportunities in the context of sustainability. Here, we will only highlight two typical business opportunities that are relevant to a broader range of companies and industries: efficiency gains and new markets. First, the most obvious one, which is already broadly recognized in business practice, is efficiency gains. Developing a sustainability perspective on business operations inspires businesses to systematically analyze their resource and energy use and enables them to identify efficiency potentials. Typical tools for a systematic efficiency analysis are, for instance, energy and material flow analysis and product life cycle assessment (see, e.g., Graedel & Allenby, 2010). If a company starts to systematically analyze material and energy use in its own operations and its supply chain, the company might recognize direct efficiency potentials, such as unnecessary waste or energy losses, which can easily be realized. In addition, the company can consider ways to redesign production, packaging, shipping methods, and product design, and explore more efficient solutions.

Businesses can realize significant efficiency gains through a sustainability approach, which ultimately can result in increased competitiveness and business success. For instance, New Belgium Brewery, the craft beer brewery located in Fort Collins, Colorado, realized large efficiency gains by various measures: these included more efficient water usage through innovative brewing technology and recycling of water used in cleaning processes, as well as less energy use through innovative processes, such as using outside cold air in the nights and winter for cooling processes. Efficiency was also increased by introducing an innovative technology for capturing methane gas from their own waste water treatment facility. The methane gas is a natural by-product of waste water treatment that usually just dissipates into the air. The company now uses captured methane as an energy source and covers about 15% of its total annual electricity needs (New Belgium, 2016). In packaging, an employee came up with a more efficient way to box beer bottles, saving a significant amount of cardboard, which translated into $720,000 annual cost savings (New Belgium, 2016). In waste management, New Belgium gives away its organic waste from the brewing process (residues from hops and barley) to farmers who use it for feeding livestock (New Belgium, 2016). The encompassing sustainability approach has made New Belgium a leader in efficiency and innovation in the industry, and one of the leading craft beer breweries in the US, outcompeting most of its competitors.

Another significant business opportunity in the context of sustainability is the identification of, and early move into, new markets. In the context of sustainability many new preferences, needs, and wants emerge that provide opportunities for businesses which recognize them and are able to come up with smart solutions to satisfy them. There have been many examples in recent years of such new markets, many of which are growing at significant rates, such as organic food, local food, green products, and fair-trade products. Preference changes in consumers are either value-driven or cost-driven. An increasing number of consumers factor in environmental or societal values when making choices and purchasing decisions, even at the cost of a higher price. This is, for instance, the case for decisions about purchasing many green or fair-trade products. However, new markets are also driven by increasing costs of energy and resources and the resulting demand for cost-efficient solutions and products. For instance, we see an increasing demand for heat pumps or solar panels in certain regions in the US, an increasing demand for better insulation solutions for existing homes, and an increasing demand for hybrid and electric cars. The various changes in needs and preferences in the sustainability context provide many great business opportunities for small and large businesses that are able to recognize and satisfy them. We will illustrate this with a few more examples in Section 7.2.2.

BUSINESS CAPABILITIES AND SOCIETAL ROLE

Business should also care about sustainability because it has the potential to help society become more sustainable. Business is a powerful societal force that can make significant contributions toward sustainable development. Other crucial societal players, such as the educational sector, the media, research universities, and legislators, can and also need to do their part. Education and media can increase competency and awareness about sustainability. Research universities can theoretically analyze sustainability issues and develop potential solutions. Legislation can set up supportive legal frameworks. Yet, business is a crucial factor for actually providing sustainable products and services to consumers and realizing sustainable solutions. It is business that ultimately will install the better insulation in a home, produce and install heat pumps or solar panels, or develop and market an innovative electric car, as Tesla has recently done. By its economic function to provide goods and services, business can substantially contribute to sustainable development and be a positive force in the society.

7.2.2 Sustainability as business opportunity and business task: examples

This section provides some further examples that illustrate to what degree sustainability has become a business opportunity in many areas, and how businesses, which recognize this opportunity, can unlock new markets and potential for profits and, at the same time, assist customers and society at large with moving toward a more sustainable life style.

Sustainable landscaping

Can a local landscaping business benefit from water scarcity? Water scarcity and sustainable water supply have become a concern in some areas of the US, particularly in the southwest. A major factor of private water consumption in the US is outdoor water use, mainly for irrigation of lawns. A green lawn has for many years been the preferred landscaping design, and many homeowners and potential buyers considered the green lawn a characteristic of a quality house. However, in many areas of the US, maintaining a green lawn requires extensive irrigation, and lawn care and irrigation systems were common business opportunities. In recent years, though, there has been significant change. People don't want to pay increasing water prices that result from water scarcity in some areas; others consider irrigation as an unnecessary waste of water; and many cities want to reduce overall water consumption to take pressure off of their increasingly scarce water supply. Although this development might at first look like a potential threat to existing lawn care and landscaping companies, the situation actually entails great business opportunities. Local landscaping companies have the expertise to explore and offer sustainable landscaping solutions that work for the specific area. A landscaping company that offers attractive drought-resistant landscaping solutions to replace existing lawns can explore a large new market and make significant profits. At the same time this local landscaper helps the people and the community change to a more sustainable life style and community, and realize water conservation of up to 50%. The landscaper has the expertise and knowhow to redesign local yards and suggest new solutions to customers who, by themselves, neither know what alternatives are possible nor can implement them alone.

Interesting details here are the word-of-mouth effect in smaller communities and the first-mover advantage. A local company might need to invest some time and money to develop its first drought-resistant front yard design (known as xeriscaping). However, because front yards are highly visible, the new design will be recognized in the neighborhood, and other homeowners may also consider this alternative solution. The landscaping business that moves first into this new market will potentially attract many other customers, and the overall business potential is significant. In some communities, one can also observe a successive change of aesthetic norms: at a certain point people start perceiving the green lawn as old-fashioned and outdated, and the xeriscaping design as the new, trendy design. In this perspective, the landscaping business actually drives part of a change in norms and preferences by which it benefits as a business and contributes to an overall value change toward sustainability.

Sustainable construction and development

Another opportunity resulting from sustainability challenges is sustainable construction and development. There are huge potentials for energy and resource savings in traditional construction. With increasing energy and water prices, and more and more people having preferences for environmentally friendly products and life styles, there is a large future market for sustainable private homes. Sustainable homes combine several aspects: use of sustainable sourced materials in construction, improved energy and water efficiency, and sustainable landscaping, among other factors. A crucial aspect of sustainable homes is the consideration of place. A sustainable home in Maine would look quite different than a sustainable home in Arizona. In Maine, insulation and sustainable ways of heating might be crucial, and one would, for instance, strive to let as much sun into the house as possible, with larger windows facing south. In Arizona, the focus needs to be more on cooling and insulation against heat, including roofing solutions that reflect solar radiation. Arizona probably also allows for the cost-efficient use of solar panels. In Maine, landscaping does not need to consider limited water supply, whereas in Arizona drought-resistant xeriscaping would be a crucial part of a sustainable private home.

Sustainable homes and development are a challenge for the construction industry because they require rethinking and changing traditional modes of construction. Specifically, planning and design need to change and consider location and sustainability issues. New approaches of integrated design need to be implemented (7group, 2018) that consider the complex interrelations between different aspects of a sustainable home. For instance, better-insulated windows are more expensive, but may result in a smaller air-conditioning unit that costs less. Input of natural light combined with bright indoor colors may result in less need of artificial light, reducing electricity use (7group, 2018). Sustainable construction requires all partners, such as engineers, electricians, plumbers, and indoor designers, to consider the use of sustainable materials, such as recycled materials, local materials, and sustainably sourced wood, and to explore new technological solutions, such as water-efficient appliances, use of natural light, solar panels, and heat pumps. Overall, sustainable construction and development are a challenge for the industry but also a significant future business opportunity, which has the potential to change the entire industry. In recent years, there has been a move in the US toward designing more sustainable buildings, with a focus on commercial and office buildings. Also, a certification process for sustainable buildings has been developed, the LEED certification, which provides a framework for evaluating to what degree a building is sustainable (USGBC, 2018). Against this backdrop, sustainable private homes have the potential to become a large future market.

Sustainable cars and sustainable transportation

Transportation is predominantly responsible for worldwide fossil fuel consumption and greenhouse gas emissions. Both the use of non-renewable fossil fuels and their contribution to climate change are serious sustainability issues. The fact that the established modes of transportation are based on fossil fuel and are not sustainable has recently begun to change the markets and, in particular, impact the automobile industry. There are growing preferences for more sustainable and efficient cars. The market potential for efficient cars has already become evident by the recent success of hybrid cars. However, against the backdrop of sustainability, this might just be the beginning of major shifts in the automobile market and automobile industry. New technologies, such as the electric car, have the potential to disrupt the entire industry and change it substantially. The actual success of Tesla demonstrates that there is a substantial market for electric cars and puts a lot of pressure on established auto makers. The well-established technology of the combustion engine may have come to its limits. For established auto makers to remain viable means they must offer more sustainable alternative engines to the costumers. The electric car may be one of several options and products for the future. Fuel cell technology might be another. In addition to markets for sustainable cars, there may also be a demand for new types of sustainable transportation, such as car sharing. With new possibilities of self-driving car technologies, rather than owning a car, more and more people might prefer to just order a car and pay for a trip when they need to go somewhere. Increasing demand for sustainable solutions may also result in new demand for public transportation, such as commuter rail systems connecting suburbs with inner cities and workplaces.

In conclusion, the above examples demonstrate that sustainability provides large business opportunities. Business is an important force for sustainable development and can help with its knowhow to provide new sustainable products and solutions. However, as for any large societal progress, sustainable development cannot be done by businesses and markets alone. Ultimately, societal progress requires a well-coordinated interplay and shared responsibilities of various societal forces: businesses, communities, customers, educational sector, legislators, and governments, among others. Many societal actors need to come together and work in the same direction, and business can only unfold its full positive power for society and societal progress if it is embedded, supported, and guided by other crucial societal forces. The following section illustrates the importance of this interplay, and particularly the need for adapting societal institutions, such as the legal framework, for enabling businesses to contribute to sustainability.

7.3 New business models and norms: the example of the benefit corporation

Classical theoretical perspectives on business have claimed that the sole purpose of business is profit maximization (Friedman, 1970), or that the main purpose of business is the creation of value for all stakeholders (Freeman et al., 2007). The sustainability perspective would theoretically claim that the purpose of business is to contribute to the wellbeing of contemporaries, future generations, and nature (Section 7.2). In business practice, however, the norms and values that underlie and drive businesses have become various and diverse. Also, one can observe some recent trends toward business models that are explicitly based on societal or environmental values.

In recent years, there has been a significant growth of new types of business that are specifically driven by ethical values: social enterprises, sustainable businesses, and purpose- or value-driven businesses. These businesses are devoted to certain societal or environmental causes and aim at well-defined positive impacts for society or the environment. Companies like Patagonia, New Belgium Brewery, and Ben & Jerry's have proven that these business models are very competitive and successful. In a certain way, these businesses represent a mix of aspects traditionally devoted to either non-profit or for-profit business models. Traditionally, non-profit organizations were devoted to specific societal or environmental causes, whereas for-profit organizations were devoted to profit-oriented businesses. However, social entrepreneurs have increasingly discovered the power of for-profit businesses for pursuing societal or environmental causes. The growing number of social enterprises, sustainable, and purpose-driven businesses use the for-profit business model to pursue a specific cause or societal or environmental purpose. The result is new types of business that are devoted to a well-defined cause while being profit oriented at the same time. This makes sense from an ethical and a business perspective. From an ethical perspective, the for-profit business model might just be a stronger and better tool to achieve certain causes. From a business perspective, value-driven and sustainable businesses have several competitive strengths and resonate well with customers, employees, communities, and investors. Social entrepreneurs and sustainable businesses serve new markets and preferences, and often adapt better to future and global systemic challenges.

However, these new types of businesses do not fit very well into established concepts and categories of business – including the legal frameworks we have built over decades based on older concepts of business and the economy. The *benefit corporation* has been a recent approach to adjust the legal framework and create a new legal form of business that fits to these new types of business and better protects them legally. Since 2010, an increasing number of states in the US have passed laws that establish the benefit corporation as a 'new type of corporate legal entity' (Clark & Vranka, 2013, p. 1). As of 2018, 34 states in the US have passed such laws (Benefit Corporation, 2018).

The basic idea behind the benefit corporation is to establish a legal type of business that allows social entrepreneurs and sustainable, purpose-driven businesses to use the advantages of the corporate business model without endangering the specific social or environmental purpose of their business. The benefit corporation allows bringing in external investors and capital for further growth while maintaining the specific purpose of the business. Generally, the benefit corporation is defined by some distinctive characteristics (Clark & Vranka, 2013; Benefit Corporation, 2017):

- A benefit corporation must have a corporate purpose of creating public benefit. The public benefit can be specified by a certain societal or environmental purpose.
- The directors of a benefit corporation have the duty to protect the interests of all core stakeholders and to uphold the purpose of the benefit corporation.
- The benefit corporation has an obligation to issue annual reports on their progress in achieving its purpose.

These characteristics clearly distinguish the benefit corporation from the traditional concept of the corporation. A traditional corporation can have any purpose as long as it is a legal one, whereas the benefit corporation is legally required to formulate a more specific purpose of creating public benefit; that is, to formulate a well-defined positive social or environmental impact of its business. Secondly, the obligations of the directors of the benefit corporation differ significantly from the traditional corporate model. In a traditional corporation, the board of directors has the sole legal obligation to serve the financial interests of the shareholders. The narrowly defined legal obligation would not be well suited for social entrepreneurs and purpose-driven businesses. In the traditional corporate model, the board of directors has no legal obligation and few possibilities to protect the purpose of the business as a value in itself, or to consider other stakeholders, such as employees. To adopt the traditional corporate model would pose some risks to the identity of a purpose-driven business, and societal entrepreneurs who are attached to the purpose or cause of their business may shy away from the option to turn their business into a traditional corporation. For instance, in a takeover situation, the board of directors might have a hard time rejecting a financially attractive offer from another, larger company, even if they could foresee the takeover endangering the purpose or cause of their company. The board is legally required to primarily act in the financial interests of the shareholders, and some shareholders might sue the board if it rejects a financially attractive offer.

In contrast, the benefit corporation defines the legal obligations of the board of directors in a way that explicitly supports the concept of purpose-driven businesses. The directors must protect not only the financial interests of shareholders, but also the interests of other core stakeholders and the well-defined purpose of the benefit corporation. This type of corporation is therefore much more attractive for social entrepreneurs who are attached to the social and environmental purpose of their business and would like to see it maintained when getting external investors and capital for growing their business.

Furthermore, benefit corporations are legally required to report on their progress in serving their purpose, which typically means reporting on their societal or environmental performance. This reporting requirement also distinguishes benefit corporations from traditional corporations, which in the US are not legally required to report on environmental and societal performance. The reporting requirement for the benefit corporation results in more transparency and credibility, which may resonate well with its main stakeholders.

The benefit corporation is an attractive legal framework for the growing number of social entrepreneurs and sustainable, purpose-driven businesses. Being a benefit corporation is a credible and well-defined feature that helps such businesses distinguish and position themselves in the marketplace. The legal form of the benefit corporation may resonate well with the growing number of customers who have preferences for green products and for buying from socially and environmentally concerned businesses. The benefit corporation also may resonate with the increasing number of employees and highly qualified college graduates who prefer to work for purpose-driven and sustainable businesses. Finally, the benefit corporation is of interest to various types of investors (Clark & Vranka, 2013; Benefit Corporation, 2018).

Traditional investors who base their decisions on return of investment and risk may be attracted by benefit corporations. They might not be so interested in the benefit purpose but may expect higher returns and lower risks from benefit corporations, due to higher transparency and competitiveness. Traditional investors might consider competitive advantages, such as better adaptations to sustainability challenges, higher efficiency, a more robust customer base, better positioning in new markets, and better motivated and qualified employees. However, the benefit corporation may particularly attract investors who base their investment decisions on personal values and ethical reasons. Similar to consumers who make buying decisions not only on price and quality but consider ethical aspects of the product, there are also small and large investors who make investment decisions not solely based on risk and expected returns, but also factor in ethical aspects. Value-based investment is a growing field. In the US, sustainable, responsible, and impact investing (SRI) represents about 18% of total assets under management, or roughly $6.5 trillion (US SIF, 2014, p. 12); 'the individuals, institutions, investment companies, money managers and financial institutions that practice SRI seek to achieve long-term competitive financial returns together with positive societal impact' (US SIF, 2014, p. 12). For these investors, the benefit corporation is of particular interest, as it serves both their financial interests and their ethical values (see also Clark & Vranka, 2013).

Some investors maximize return of investment and are also engaged in philanthropic giving. They may consider the investment in benefit corporations as an optimal way to combine investment interests and philanthropy. Investment in a benefit corporation can be more efficient than separating investment and philanthropic giving. If a traditional investment generates, for instance, significant environmental harm, and the same investor donates money to environmental causes, the two activities counteract each other. In other words, it is pretty inefficient if someone, on the one hand, destroys the environment by maximizing return of investment and, on the other, uses (part of) the money gained to restore (part of) the environment. One could get a much better overall result for the money by directly investing in an environmentally conscious business. Another example would be investing in a business that does significant societal harm in the supply chain, while at the same time donating money to help the same people who have been exploited by the business. Again, it may be much more efficient to just invest in a fair-trade company or social entrepreneurship that benefits the people in the supply chain directly through its business activities.

Overall, norms and values have become more relevant in contemporary business, and companies more explicitly address sustainability challenges. We specifically see the emergence of sustainable, value-, and purpose-driven businesses, which make environmental or societal concerns the core of their business models. The case of the benefit corporation demonstrates that changing norms and values in business can require changes to the legal framework for business. Finally, social enterprises, sustainable, value-, and purpose-driven businesses, and benefit corporations demonstrate the flexibility of capitalism. The capitalist model seems to be capable of encouraging and adopting such new types of business and, thus, may have the potential to transform over time into a sustainable economy.

References

Apple. (2018). *Environmental Responsibility Report*. Apple. Retrieved from www.apple.com/environment.

Becker, C. (2012). *Sustainability Ethics and Sustainability Research*. New York: Springer.

Becker, C., Ewringmann, D., Faber, M., Petersen, T., & Zahrnt, A. (2015). Endangering the natural basis of life is unjust: On the status and future of the sustainability discourse. *Ethics, Policy, and Environment*, 18(1), 60–67.

Benefit Corporation. (2017). *Model Benefit Corporation Legislation*. Benefit Corporation. Retrieved from http://benefitcorp.net.

Benefit Corporation. (2018). *What is a Benefit Corporation?* Benefit Corporation. Retrieved from http://benefitcorp.net.

Clark, W. H. & Vranka, L. (2013). *White Paper. The Need and the Rationale for the Benefit Corporation: Why it is the Legal Form that Best Addresses the Needs of Social Entrepreneurs*. Benefit Corporation. Retrieved from http://benefitcorp.net/node/2340.

Freeman, R. E., Harrison, J. S., & Wicks, A. C. (2007). *Managing for Stakeholders*. New Haven, CT: Yale University Press.

Friedman, M. (1970). The social responsibility of business is to increase its profits. *The New York Times*, September 13.

Graedel, T. E., & Allenby, B. R. (2010). *Industrial Ecology and Sustainable Engineering*. Upper Saddle River, NJ: Prentice Hall.

IPCC [Intergovernmental Panel on Climate Change]. (2014). *Climate Change 2014. Synthesis Report*. Contribution of Working Groups I, II and III to the Fifth Assessment Report of the Intergovernmental Panel on Climate Change [Core Writing Team, R. K. Pachauri & L. A. Meyer (Eds.)]. Geneva: IPCC.

MEA [Millennium Ecosystem Assessment]. (2005). *Ecosystems and Human Well-being: Synthesis*. Washington, DC: Island Press.

New Belgium. (2016). *Sustainability*. New Belgium Brewery. Retrieved from www.newbelgium.com/sustainability.

Nike. (2017). FY16/17 Sustainable Business Report. Nike, Inc. *Nike*. Retrieved from http://sustainability.nike.com.

7group. (2018). *Lessons Learned* (video). Retrieved from http://sevengroup.com/videos.

Stumpf, K. H., Baumgärtner, S., Becker, C., & Sievers-Glotzbach, S. (2015). The justice dimension of sustainability. A systematic and general conceptual framework. *Sustainability*, 7(6), 7438–7472.

UN DESA [United Nations, Department of Economic and Social Affairs]. (2015). *World Population Prospects: The 2015 Revision, Key Findings and Advance Tables*. Working paper no. ESA/P/WP.241. New York: United Nations. Retrieved from https://esa.un.org/unpd/wpp/publications/files/key_findings_wpp_2015.pdf.

UNEP [United Nations Environment Programme]. (2012). *Global Environment Outlook GEO-5: Environment for the Future we Want*. Malta: Progress Press.

USGBC [US Green Building Council]. (2018). *LEED is Green Building*. Retrieved from https://new.usgbc.org/leed.

US SIF [US Forum for Sustainable and Responsible Investment]. (2014). *Report on Sustainable, Responsible and Impact Investing Trends 2014: Executive Summary*. Washington, DC: US SIF. Retrieved from www.ussif.org/annualreports.

WCED [World Commission on Environment and Development]. (1987). *Our Common Future*. Oxford: Oxford University Press.

Conclusion

Business can be a force for good, but likewise it has the potential to be destructive to individuals, societies, and the environment. As a force for good, business contributes to the flourishing of individuals and societies around the world, while also respecting the natural environment and non-human life. Business can be an overall creative and positive power. It can bring forth new products and goods that improve individual lives and society. Business can provide sustainable products and solutions, like the electric car or green buildings, and business can positively interconnect people across cultures for their mutual benefit. Business can provide meaningful work and opportunities for individuals to develop their potentials and ideas, and it can promote the flourishing of societies. An ideal business world serves as catalyst for interconnecting people and stimulating fruitful commerce among various cultures around the world. However, business also can easily become a rather destructive force that harms individuals, societies, global relations, and the environment. The 2008 financial crisis and global warming are prominent examples of the harmful potential of business. Businesses can burn out employees and destroy the environment, and economic issues easily can result in global harm, tensions between nations, and even war. For both the positive and negative potentials of business there are plenty of historic examples, and throughout history societies have attempted to ensure that business and the economy serve them in a positive way.

Ethical guidance is crucial for ensuring that business and the economy are positive forces in the world. Two factors are specifically important for fostering the positive potentials of business: first, the proper design of the economic system in accordance with fundamental values and ethical principles, and, second, the ethical integrity and moral responsibility of the economic actors in the system, that is, entrepreneurs, managers, employees, customers, and regulatory agents, among others. The first aspect is a top-down approach that relies on laws and regulations on the local, national, and international scales. In the past, the focus often was on the top-down approach, based on the idea that a perfect competitive (global) market system would take care of most ethical aspects and enable a global economy that automatically is good and creates welfare for all. However, the second aspect, the ethics of the individual actors, has become more and more important, as the limitations of rules and regulations for a complex, dynamic, and global business world become obvious. Ethical awareness and responsibility among various economic actors is increasing overall. Businesses assume more responsibility, for instance, by implementing corporate responsibility strategies or engaging in their supply chains. Consumers are more ethically aware, and we see growing fields of ethical consumption, such as local, green, and fair-trade consumption. Investors increasingly focus on socially responsible investments, and there is substantial growth of social entrepreneurship and sustainable businesses.

Although laws and regulations remain an important basic ethical framework for business, they alone will not be sufficient for establishing business as a positive force in the 21st century. We will need to further develop the bottom-up approach of ethical responsibilities taken by all economic actors for their economic activities and the resulting environmental, societal, global, and long-term implications. It is the responsibility of all of us as community members and citizens to engage in the political process of promoting proper regulations and guidelines for business activities. However, even more importantly, it is the responsibility of all of us in our various roles in the economy, as consumers, employees, leaders, investors, entrepreneurs, and professionals, to assume ethical responsibilities for our business activities and their impacts, and with this to ensure that business is a positive force that contributes to a sustainable future.

Index

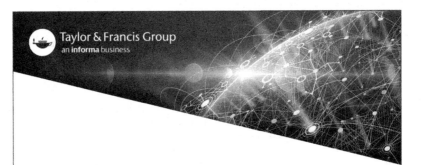

Printed in the United States
by Baker & Taylor Publisher Services